How to Buy and Sell Apartment Buildings

How to Buy and Sell Apartment Buildings

Second Edition

Eugene E. Vollucci

Stephen E. Vollucci

WILEY

John Wiley & Sons, Inc.

Published by John Wiley & Sons, Inc., Hoboken, New Jersey.
Published simultaneously in Canada.

For general information on our other products and services please contact our
Customer Care Department within the United States at (800) 762-2974, outside the
United States at (317) 572-3993 or fax (317) 572-4002.

Wiley also publishes its books in a variety of electronic formats. Some content that
appears in print may not be available in electronic books. For more information about
Wiley products, visit our web site at www.wiley.com.

Library of Congress Cataloging-in-Publication Data:

Vollucci, Eugene E., 1939–
    How to buy and sell apartment buildings / Eugene E. Vollucci, Stephen
Vollucci.—2nd ed.
       p. cm.
    Includes index.
    ISBN 0-471-65343-8 (pbk. : alk. paper)
      1. Apartment houses. 2. Real estate business. 3. Real estate investment.
  I. Vollucci, Stephen. II. Title.
    HD1390.5.V64 2004
    333.33'8—dc22

2003068780

Printed in the United States of America.

10 9 8 7 6 5 4 3 2

Contents

Preface

Over the years, we have discovered that there are three dangerous misconceptions or myths about real estate. These myths either cause people to make bad investment decisions or avoid real estate entirely. This book is devoted to dispelling these roadblocks to investing in real estate and paving the way to becoming wealthy.

One hazardous myth involves cash flow. If you think you can become wealthy in real estate with cash flow, you might as well be straightening up the deck chairs on the Titanic. It simply is not going to happen. The way you become wealthy in real estate is through appreciation.

You can become wealthier with cash flow, but only after you have obtained a certain level of wealth. If you're thinking about investing in rental property, you should have some degree of certainty what the appreciation will be. That is what this book is all about: Giving you the guidance you need to determine when and how much appreciation there will be.

The second myth is that there are no more tax benefits. When the tax reform act was passed in 1986, it eliminated many real estate tax benefits. Tax benefits happen to be the second most important reason people invest in rental real estate. The *most* important reason is to make money. But tax benefits let the government pay for part of your investment. Your return after taxes is much greater with tax benefits. Robert Bruss, the national real estate syndicated columnist, in his *2003 Realty*

Tax Tips points out the additional tax benefits of exchanging your way to tax-free wealth by the use of an Internal Revenue code 1031 tax deferred exchange. This book provides the most up-to-date strategies on not only avoiding taxes on *exchanges* but also on *outright sales.*

The third myth involves location. You've heard the term location, location, location . . . and location *is* very important. But too many investors confuse location with local. Investors tend to look at rental properties within a short driving distance of where they live. However, if there are no opportunities for appreciation in those areas, you should not be looking *locally.* You should be looking at pockets of opportunity no matter where they exist. This book not only shows you *where* to buy and sell apartment buildings, it also shows you how to determine "when" to make your purchase.

In this book, we recommend one type of property, a precise methodology, and a practical philosophy. We won't bore you with generalities. However, we do promise to teach you how to become wealthy. To that task, we're deeply committed.

It is important to note that as of the date of the printing of this book, there is significant real estate tax legislation in progress. To get the latest updates and more information, contact The Center for Real Estate Studies, at (800) 955-3135. We hope this book gives you the knowledge to invest wisely and brings you good fortune.

ACKNOWLEDGMENTS

A book doesn't happen by itself. I would like to extend my personal thanks to Mike Hamilton of John Wiley & Sons for his insight and commitment to *How to Buy and Sell Apartment Buildings;* to others at Wiley including Kimberly Vaughn, Linda Witzling, and Michelle Becker; and to Nancy Marcus Land, Brenda Hunter, and the rest of the team at Publications Development Company.

EUGENE E. VOLLUCCI
STEPHEN E. VOLLUCCI

1

An Investment Plan to Create Wealth

DISCOVER LIFE'S THREE CHRONOLOGICAL INVESTMENT PERIODS

Our investment philosophy is based on an individual's chronological time line, which consists of three periods: (1) asset accumulation, (2) wealth building, and (3) asset conservation.

The financial journey through life's time line starts at different levels, depending on whether you were born with a plastic or a silver spoon in your mouth. As you travel through your time line, your investment options change. Knowing where you are and what options are available will help you make the right choices.

How and when you make these choices is what this chapter is all about!

A Winning Financial Plan up to Age 35

The first chronological period of your life—mid-twenties to mid-thirties—should be devoted to accumulating assets and acquiring basic necessities. When you're just starting out, your assets are usually limited and the major portion of your income goes for the basic needs—food, clothing, and shelter.

This is the time to save, save, save! Amass as many investment dollars as possible. Your approach to investing during this period should be through tax-deferred plans at work or Individual Retirement Accounts (IRAs). Your degree of risk should be moderate. Investments included in this category are AAA corporate bonds, blue chip stocks, and growth-oriented no-load mutual funds.

Every effort should be made to purchase a home now. The advantages, from tax savings and equity buildup, historically outweigh the short-term benefits of lower monthly rent payments.

Be careful when sheltering yourself and your family from liability. Only pay for protection when you're purchasing life insurance. Purchase whole life insurance if it will yield a higher rate of return than other investments. After reading the chapter on asset protection, you might seriously consider reducing your liability coverage.

Remember, your main financial goal during this time is tax-deferred accumulation of capital. Don't take risks with your investments. Save as much as you can so that when you enter the next phase of the time line you'll be ready to move forward.

Investing between the Ages of 35 and 50

After earnings have increased, assets have been accumulated, and basic necessities are under control, it's time to move on. Ready or not, you must face the challenges during this aggressive investment period of your life, when you are between your mid-thirties and early fifties.

WHY IT IS MATHEMATICALLY IMPOSSIBLE TO BECOME WEALTHY EARNING 20 PERCENT PER YEAR

Aggressive investments are designed to create maximum wealth while controlling risks. The value of these investments must increase substantially for you to become wealthy. Investing $6,000 at 20 percent simply isn't going to do it. After taxes and inflation, mathematically it's impossible. Look at Table 1.1 to see the data that is summarized in Figure 1.1.

The Best Financial Plan for You

Your best financial plan is to create the maximum wealth during this aggressive investment period of your life. Build financial security

Table 1.1 Number of years to amass the purchasing power of a millionaire.

Year	Inflation Rate 3%	Inflation Rate 5%	Inflation Rate 7%	Year	Inflation Rate 3%	Inflation Rate 5%	Inflation Rate 7%
1	6,623	6,487	6,350	46	565,191	216,761	81,454
2	7,311	7,013	6,721	47	623,892	234,340	86,206
3	8,070	7,581	7,113	48	688,689	253,345	91,235
4	8,909	8,196	7,528	49	760,216	273,892	96,558
5	9,834	8,861	7,967	50	839,172	296,104	102,191
6	10,855	9,580	8,431	51	926,329	320,118	108,153
7	11,983	10,356	8,923	52	1,022,537	346,080	114,462
8	13,227	11,196	9,444	53		374,147	121,140
9	14,601	12,104	9,995	54		404,490	128,207
10	16,117	13,086	10,578	55		437,294	135,687
11	17,791	14,147	11,195	56		472,759	143,603
12	19,639	15,295	11,848	57		511,100	151,981
13	21,679	16,535	12,539	58		552,550	160,847
14	23,930	17,876	13,271	59		597,362	170,231
15	26,416	19,326	14,045	60		645,808	180,162
16	29,159	20,893	14,865	61		698,183	190,673
17	32,188	22,588	15,732	62		754,805	201,797
18	35,531	24,420	16,650	63		816,020	213,570
19	39,221	26,400	17,621	64		882,199	226,029
20	43,294	28,541	18,649	65		953,746	239,216
21	47,791	30,856	19,737	66		1,031,095	253,172
22	52,754	33,358	20,888	67			267,942
23	58,234	36,063	22,107	68			283,573
24	64,282	38,988	23,397	69			300,117
25	70,958	42,150	24,762	70			317,626
26	78,328	45,568	26,206	71			336,156
27	86,463	49,264	27,735	72			355,768
28	95,443	53,259	29,353	73			376,523
29	105,355	57,579	31,066	74			398,489
30	116,298	62,248	32,878	75			421,737
31	128,376	67,297	34,796	76			446,341
32	141,710	72,754	36,826	77			472,381
33	156,428	78,655	38,975	78			499,940
34	172,674	85,034	41,249	79			529,106
35	190,608	91,930	43,655	80			559,974
36	210,405	99,385	46,202	81			592,643
37	232,257	107,446	48,897	82			627,218
38	256,379	116,159	51,750	83			663,810
39	283,007	125,580	54,769	84			702,537
40	312,400	135,764	57,964	85			743,523
41	344,846	146,775	61,346	86			786,900
42	380,662	158,678	64,925	87			832,807
43	420,197	171,547	68,712	88			881,393
44	463,839	185,460	72,721	89			932,814
45	512,013	200,500	76,964	90			987,234
				91			1,044,829

Tax Rate: 31%, Rate of Return: 20%, Initial Investment: $6,000

Source: The Center for Real Estate Studies.

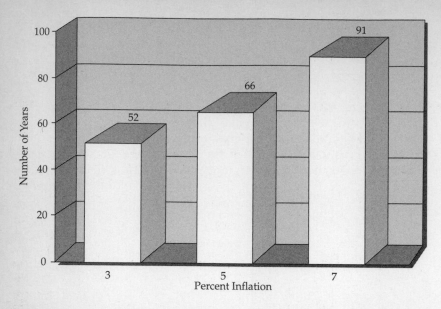

Figure 1.1   Number of years to amass the purchasing power of a millionaire. *Source:* The Center for Real Estate Studies.

yourself. Don't rely on others to do it for you. Many people who relied on major banks and insurance companies for financial security ended up short when these institutions failed. The social security system will not do much better.

You should be careful not to over diversify your assets or adopt a "hold-back" attitude. You must concentrate your assets into one or two aggressive investments rather than spreading them out. Diversification often leads to ineffectiveness.

What if you fail during this period? What is your down side? If you consider your ability to bounce back because of your age, the political clout of your generation, taxes, and inflation, the real risk is minimized. Make your aggressive investments now. As you get older, your ability to rebound declines. If you do not try at this stage in your investment time line, you probably will never do it, and more importantly, you will never know whether you could have made it.

What It Takes to Become Wealthy

Becoming wealthy requires taking "controlled" risks. If anyone tells you that they became wealthy without taking any risks, they either inherited wealth or they won the lottery.

If you're afraid to take risks, *don't do it.* Your mental health is far more important than your financial health. However, not taking financial risks becomes a risk in itself. No-risk investments have lower rates of return. Higher rates of inflation and taxes will eventually cause you to lose with these types of investments.

If risk taking makes you feel vibrant and alive, go for it! Especially during this exciting chronological period of your life.

Your ability to take risks depends on your financial and emotional capabilities. Financial capabilities are based on age, occupation, number of dependents, health, investment knowledge, and net worth. Emotional capabilities refer to whether or not you can sleep after you've invested the $6,000. The quiz in Figure 1.2 tests your tolerance for taking risks.

		(Circle One)
1.	I prefer working on a commission basis.	Yes No
2.	I have my car checked according to the maintenance schedule.	Yes No
3.	I would invest in gold.	Yes No
4.	I make my own decisions.	Yes No
5.	I want to be self-employed.	Yes No
6.	I like going to Las Vegas, Nevada.	Yes No
7.	I would bet on a horse if I got a tip from someone I know.	Yes No
8.	I prefer working for the government.	Yes No
9.	I would invest in a venture capital firm.	Yes No
10.	I prefer investing in certificates of deposit.	Yes No
11.	I like surprises.	Yes No
12.	I make daily decisions that affect other people.	Yes No
13.	I own a sports car.	Yes No
14.	I would rather play than watch sports.	Yes No
15.	I have enough in the bank to carry me through 12 months.	Yes No
16.	I have my attorney help me with my financial decisions.	Yes No
17.	I own a vacation condominium.	Yes No
18.	I like to go to different restaurants.	Yes No
19.	I enjoy traveling.	Yes No
20.	The challenge is the most important thing.	Yes No
21.	I prefer investments that produce income rather than appreciation.	Yes No
22.	I prefer to read.	Yes No
23.	I would have been a Western pioneer.	Yes No
24.	I exercise daily.	Yes No
25.	I purchase investments with borrowed money.	Yes No

SCORE: If you answered yes to 1, 3, 4, 5, 6, 7, 9, 11, 12, 13, 14, 17, 18, 19, 20, 23, 24, 25, you have a very high tolerance for risk. If you answered yes to half of these, you have a moderate to low tolerance. You should assess your own score in light of your financial goals.

Figure 1.2   Measure your risk tolerance. *Source:* The Center for Real Estate Studies.

If you devote sufficient time and effort, you will be able to enjoy not only the wealth-building period of your life, but you will be able to look forward to the next chronological stage, the asset conservation period.

The Best Investment Strategy over Age 50

The asset conservation period usually starts in the early fifties and extends until you're "pushing up daisies." Your investments should be primarily in federal and state tax-free bonds. Your main goal is tax-free income and preservation of capital. Estate planning should be initiated during this phase of your life. Your investments can be diversified as long as they are conservative and risk free.

By taking controlled risk in the previous period, you won't have to depend financially on the government or relatives. You'll be independently able to maintain yourself during this asset conservation period of your life.

CONQUERING YOUR FEARS OF INVESTING

Often people do not succeed because of fear. Why do people have a fear of investing? Some people are afraid of making decisions because they continually feel they don't have enough information. This is what is called "paralysis by analysis." Subconsciously, they keep on wanting more information to avoid making a decision. Make your decisions based on the information you have diligently gathered and on the trust you have in yourself and others.

Do you have a fear of failure? If you do not act because you're afraid of failure, you've lost your opportunity. Everyone fails at one time or another. That's part of being human. The only way to conquer this fear is to keep trying. It doesn't matter how many times you fail. What matters is that you just keep trying and never give up. This is what life is all about. This is how to get ahead.

Strange as it may seem, many people have a fear of becoming wealthy. They fear losing friends by moving to a different socioeconomic level, and they fear that others will only like them for their money. If you lose friends because you become wealthy, they weren't true friends to begin with. Real friends like and need you for what you are, not how wealthy you are.

People coming from countries where the government maintains complete control over them from cradle to grave have difficulty dealing with such freedom. Financial freedom works in the same way. People don't know what to do with their time or their money. There are too many choices. They become confused and withdrawn. Just remember all the things you wanted to do and all the people you wanted to help. Take one day at a time and don't make any major changes in your lifestyle.

Expressing your fear of expanding your horizons by continually adhering to an ultra-conservative philosophy is self-limiting. Bargain shopping is a prime example. I've seen people spend countless hours saving pennies when they could have used the same time making dollars. Using your time and money to create wealth has limitless potential. Don't get caught up in petty economics. Expend your valuable resources of time and money for more rewarding goals.

BECOME A GOLD MEDALIST IN INVESTING

The purpose of this investment philosophy is to make you extremely wealthy by taking controlled risks and aggressively concentrating your resources. Make a firm commitment to succeed, the same that is made by an Olympic gold medalist. If you're willing to make that commitment, then the information in this book will help make that goal a reality.

In going for the top, you won't have to quit your job. However, you should be prepared to work at least half a day to accomplish your goals. How much is half a day? Well, when the CEO of a Fortune 500 company was asked by a reporter how he accomplished so much, he responded, "I only worked half a day." The reporter commented, "That doesn't sound like much." He said, "I agree with you. Twelve hours a day isn't much work at all." Seriously, you don't have to work half a day. Work only long enough to get the job done. You be the judge. I'll give you the tools. You will make the sincere effort.

SUMMARY

Your net worth and financial goals will determine how and when you should make your moves. Investments should be timed accordingly.

Financial independence means having enough money. It's that simple. Amass enough capital during the asset-accumulation period so that you can aggressively invest during the wealth-building period to eliminate money worries while you're in the asset-conservation period. It sounds elementary, and it is.

In his book, *In Search of Excellence,* Tom Peters noted that the best strategy for success is, "Ready, fire, and aim." (As opposed to ready, aim, fire.) If you're "ready," then you're ready to fire. Just get out and do it. Fine tune it later. Most people spend so much time aiming, they never pull the trigger.

2

Why Real Estate Is Your Best Investment

Years ago, I discovered that real estate was the best investment to control risk and create wealth. The *Real Estate Digest* reports that seven out of ten millionaires made their money in real estate, and *Forbes* magazine states that there is a three times greater chance of becoming wealthy through real estate than with any other type of investment.

USING REAL ESTATE TO CONTROL RISKS

Real estate allows you to *control your risk* because you can actively participate in the decision-making process. Passive investments such as stocks don't give you this opportunity. Movements in real estate values are less erratic than in the stock market. Most people don't understand the economic forces influencing the market. Since real estate is less volatile, it's easier to control and to understand.

Real estate is tangible. You can touch it, you've been exposed to it all your life, and you can identify with it. As a result of this familiarity, you are better able to understand it.

Effectively Reducing Your Taxes

Real estate ownership continues to be the most popular form of investment because of its potential for substantial tax savings. Since you are able to actively participate in the management of real estate, the Internal Revenue Service (IRS) currently allows qualifying individuals to write off up to $25,000 per year against salary and other income. No other investment gives you this capability. In addition, you can defer paying income taxes on profits indefinitely by using tax-deferred exchanges.

Leveraging That Works

Real estate is the only major investment that gives you the ability to acquire ownership with very little money down. This degree of leveraging allows you to amplify profits by using other people's money. The more assets you are able to control, the more opportunities you have to succeed.

The degree of leverage is calculated by dividing the total purchase price of the property by the amount of funds used to purchase it. Thus, if a down payment of $10,000 plus a $90,000 loan is used to purchase a property, a 10 to 1 leverage ratio has been achieved.

The greater the leverage, the more equity will increase or decrease with the change in value of the property. The affects of leverage are shown in Figure 2.1. Notice that at 20 percent appreciation, it takes seven times longer to double net equity using no leverage compared to using a 10 to 1 ratio.

WHY REAL ESTATE INVESTMENT IS "SMART"

Figure 2.2 shows that over 50 percent of the wealth of the world was in real estate in 2000. In the United States, real estate accounted for 48.2 percent of the wealth (of which residential real estate represented 36.7 percent). Equity investments (stocks) amounted to 19.3 percent and bonds 21.1 percent.

REAL ESTATE VERSUS ALL OTHER REAL ESTATE INVESTMENTS

In the past 20 years, residential income properties have delivered the highest average total investment returns of all real estate types. With a built-in hedge against inflation, it's no wonder that multifamily real estate has out-performed all other types of real estate investments with

Appreciation	Months	
Rate	Double	Quadruple
LEVERAGE = 10:1		
5%	23	64
8%	15	40
12%	10	27
15%	8	22
20%	6	16
LEVERAGE = 5:1		
5%	44	113
8%	28	71
12%	19	48
15%	15	38
20%	11	29
LEVERAGE = 3:1		
65%	70	167
8%	44	105
12%	29	70
15%	24	56
20%	18	42
Leverage = 1:1		
5%	167	334
8%	105	209
12%	70	140
15%	56	112
20%	42	84

Figure 2.1 Number of months to double and quadruple your money at selected interest rates. *Source:* The Center for Real Estate Studies.

relatively low risk. Based on supply and demand over the next 10 years, residential income will out pace all other types of real estate investment. Strong demographic and financial indicators along with changing lifestyles should continue to positively influence residential income investments.

With an average unleveraged rate of return of 10.2 percent over the past 20 years, residential income property has proven to be an attractive low-risk investment. Figure 2.3 shows that from 1990 to 2000 residential income investment provided a more consistent higher total average rate of return than all types of properties and with less variance.

Although 10.2 percent is a great rate of return, it won't get me on the dance floor. What will get me dancing is the rate of return using leverage. A rate based on a 25 percent down payment works out to be almost 24 percent. This type of return definitely gets my feet moving.

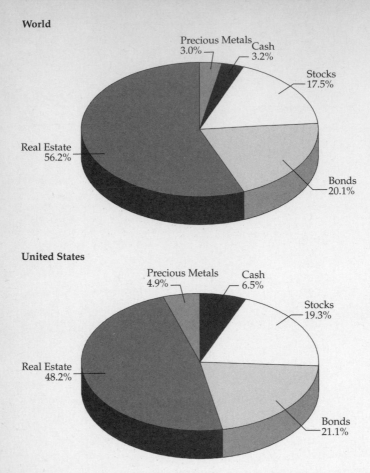

Figure 2.2   Wealth of the world 2000 and wealth of the United States 2000. *Source:* The Center for Real Estate Studies.

Three Advantages Apartments Have over Other Types of Real Estate

Apartments should remain well ahead of other major property types because they are generally more stable. Three important factors account for this stability:

1. They are less dependent on business cycles for occupancy than any other types of real estate investments. It doesn't matter if interest rates and home prices are high or low, apartments are generally more affordable.

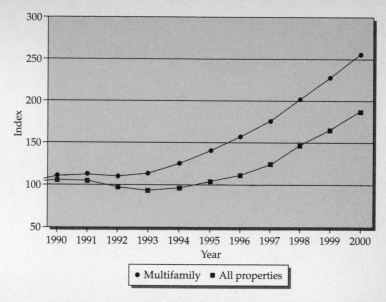

Figure 2.3   Property sector performance 1990–2000. *Source:* National Council of Real Estate Investment Fiduciaries.

2. Apartments have shorter leases; thereby offering greater protection from inflation than the long-term leases associated with other properties. That is, rents can be negotiated more frequently.
3. The pool of tenants is much greater for apartments than other types of properties. This ensures a more consistent occupancy than industrial and commercial properties, which usually have only a few tenants to choose from.

The Building Size That Gives You the Greatest Profit Potential

When investing in apartment complexes, try to find the right building size that makes the best use of your time and gives you the greatest profit potential. Single-family houses and small apartment units do not always work because of the competition and property management problems. Managing property on a day-to-day basis may not be for you. You could spend just as much time on a four-unit building as on a 40-unit complex and not make nearly as much money. In fact, because owners of smaller properties usually become emotionally attached to their property, you tend to spend more time with them telling them that they made the right move. Larger units are the domain of the institutional investors, and you can't compete with their availability of funds. After making many property transactions, you may find, as we did, that mid-size apartment buildings are the right niche.

APARTMENTS—THE COMING BONANZA FOR YOU

Supply and demand play an important role in residential income property value. The demand for rental property is increasing because the number of people entering the rental market is increasing steadily each year. At the same time, construction costs, stricter zoning ordinances, and environmental factors are limiting the new construction of residential income property. Together, these trends bode well for investing in residential income property.

The greatest demand for rental property is being created by the Baby Boomers' children, called Echo Boomers. An analysis from the book by Harry Dent, *The Roaring Twenties,* shows the increasing apartment demand created by Echo Boomers. His cycle is calculated by lagging the birth rate by 25.5 years (Figure 2.4). It shows that the Echo Boomers, who traditionally make up a significant percent of the adult population, are moving more rapidly into the rental market (Figures 2.5 and 2.6). In addition, lifestyle changes and elderly preferences are swelling the ranks of renters.

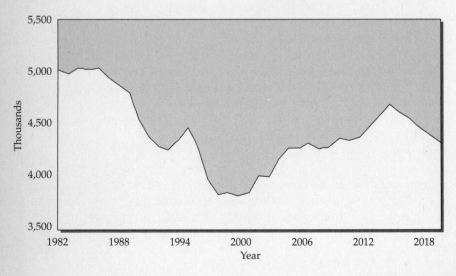

Figure 2.4   The apartment rental cycle for Baby Boomers and Echo Baby Boomers who will typically need these properties between the ages of 16 and 25½.

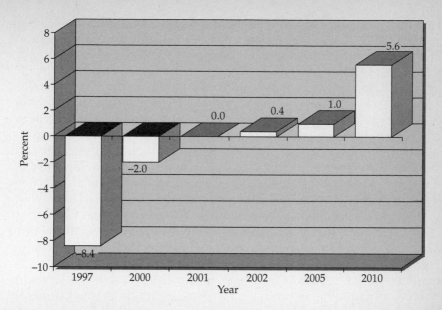

Figure 2.5 Growth in the Echo Boom generation. (Annual change in individuals 20 to 34 years old.)

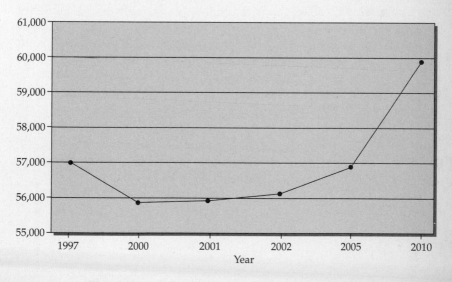

Figure 2.6 Echo Boom population in thousands.

Because the 1997 tax act allows joint owners to exempt capital gains of $500,000, more and more people are selling their homes, saving their money, and moving into rental property. It is estimated that the demand for rentals is likely to increase over 10 percent during the next 10 years. Residential income property offers one of the best protections against inflation. In fact, a study reported by the *Journal of Financial Economics* found that residential real estate is the only investment that offers a complete hedge against both anticipated and unanticipated inflation.

People always need the three basics—food, clothing, and shelter. As the population grows, the need for shelter grows along with it. The hedge against inflation with residential rentals is greater because, unlike long-term commercial leases, they are generally on a month-to-month basis. As prices increase, apartment owners can increase rents more rapidly with month-to-month leases than commercial owners who have long-term leases.

Low-rise developments or garden apartments in suburban communities account for more of the buying and selling transactions than luxury apartments (which have a much smaller market). Remember what we said in Chapter 1—7 out of 10 millionaires made their money in real estate. Shelter is not only vital, but it's often the greatest part of a person's net worth.

Residential income property is one type of investment that is a source of security and stability. Every investment has peaks and valleys, including rental real estate. But over the long-term, it always comes out on top. The key is knowing the right time to buy and sell. That is the golden rule in investing. This book will give you the knowledge you need to invest at the right time and right place.

Table 2.1   Real estate as a portfolio shock absorber 1979–2001.

	United States 1979–2001		
	S&P 500	Russell 2000	Lehman Corp. Bond
Number of times quarterly return is less than −2.5%	16	25	8
Number of times real estate return has been positive in:			
Same period	15	24	8
Lagged 1 period	14	23	8
Lagged 2 periods	14	23	8
Lagged 3 periods	12	22	8
Lagged 4 periods	13	20	8

Source: LaSalle Investment Management.

REAL ESTATE: THE SHOCK ABSORBER

Real estate generally outperforms equities because of its higher yields, greater price stability, and downside protection even in a recession. Table 2.1 shows how many times over the past 20 years real estate has played such a role for investors. When stock markets are down, real estate holds value and produces a positive return. Real estate is less prone to booms and busts than in the past. Residential income-producing real estate is now stronger than it has been in many years.

SUMMARY

Since apartments can be seen and touched—and are not an abstract form of ownership evidenced by a piece of paper—they are *investor friendly*. People can identify with doors and windows, bedrooms and bathrooms, and floors and roofs. They don't feel that the market is being manipulated by programmed buying and selling. They feel they have control over their investments.

Shelter is one of the basic necessities of life. You can't comfortably sleep on gold, silver, or stock certificates, but you can stay warm and dry with a roof over your head. There will always be a need for housing. And midsized apartments fit the bill.

3

The New Approach to Investing in the 21st Century

FORECLOSURES—THE BIG ILLUSION

Periodically, governmental agencies advertise real estate foreclosure auctions that result from various liens (real estate taxes, IRS audits, and criminal attachments, for example). Let me tell you about my experiences with one of these foreclosure auctions.

It all began when I called a telephone number in an advertisement, and requested a list of the properties to be auctioned. The agency handling the sale recommended that I inspect the properties before attending. There were at least 500 properties listed. I only found 10 that even came close to fitting my standards for investment-grade rentals. Most of the properties were single-family residences. There were no midsize apartment buildings, so I had to settle for smaller units.

For six weeks before the auction, I attempted to inspect the properties I'd selected. This proved very difficult. Most of the time I had to return a second or a third time to look inside the building. I was unable to inspect all 10 units.

In attempting to complete my homework, I was able to obtain comparable sales information on most of the buildings. No money was spent to secure independent appraisals. With my real estate background, I felt capable of determining market values. I did incur some costs by having a contractor inspect a few buildings, however. Determining the cost of repairs necessary to collect market rents would be important in deciding how much to bid at the auction.

When trying to secure loans, I found many lenders were not interested in these kinds of properties. Those that were interested, wanted huge down payments, some as high as 50 percent. One lender wanted to cross-collateralize my other properties as additional security to make the loan. Because obtaining the loan was becoming a problem, I turned to the agency conducting the auction; perhaps they would assist in the financing.

I reviewed all the paperwork several times to make sure I had not forgotten anything, and the day before the auction I was confident everything was in order. I had spent much time and some money to make sure my figures were correct. I was ready for the big day. I thought I was on my way to becoming a millionaire. I wasn't thinking about all the effort I had spent just to be able to make a bid at the auction. My thoughts were on the millions of dollars I was going to make. At the time, if I had known what my chances were of actually purchasing any of the buildings, I wouldn't have wasted my time or money. Unfortunately, the only thing I saw was unbridled opportunity. I was blinded by my hopes and ambitions to the realities of the situation.

The auction was held at a convention center in an enormous building that was capable of holding at least 50,000 people. I arrived at 7:30 in the morning, hoping to gain the early bird advantage. There were at least 2,500 people ahead of me. I had to pay a fee just to enter, then a 50-page brochure describing all the properties was handed to me.

I began orienting myself as to the layout of various booths and scheduled activities. The crowd, which was milling around, got larger and larger as the morning wore on. I was able to locate the booths where the properties on my list were to be auctioned. While making note of auction times in my brochure, an auctioneer handed me a piece of paper. Its contents nearly bowled me over. The heading read "PROPERTIES TO BE DELETED FROM AUCTION." At first, it appeared that all the properties were deleted because the list was so long. Approximately 400 were removed, and that meant only about 100 were left. I looked at all the people scurrying around at the auction, and I was devastated. In an effort to try to salvage my dream of becoming a millionaire, I began to check the properties on my list against the ones that were deleted. After several anxious moments, I was able to find two properties that weren't on the deletion list. I didn't know whether to laugh or cry. "Well," I thought, "since I'm down here anyway, I'll just stay for the two. At least it won't be a complete waste of time."

I spent the rest of the afternoon attending both auctions, and I didn't get either property. They were sold for prices far beyond what I had calculated as being reasonable. There were too many people bidding, and crowd emotions rather than reasoning prevailed.

What They Don't Tell You about Foreclosures

What happened? Why were so many properties deleted from the list? I later discovered many owners either reinstated their loans or initiated legal proceedings to stop the sale. In checking further, it became apparent that in most auctions, the better properties end up this way—they never get to the sale. The properties that finally do get auctioned have justifiable reasons for ending up on the auction block. Most either have significant physical problems, or they don't make sense economically. By trying to invest in these kinds of properties, I would be throwing my money out the window. In fact, according to Daniel Furniss, an attorney who filed a class-action suit involving price-fixing in foreclosures, 85 percent of home foreclosures in the state of California end in redemption rather than sales. According to figures published by Experian Real Estate Information Services, the five counties in California with the highest number of Notices of Default (Los Angeles, San Diego, Riverside, Orange, and Santa Clara) had only 12 percent of the properties go on sale. With so many people trying to buy so few foreclosures, it became apparent that this gigantic illusion was not for me.

Foreclosure "experts" suggested that I try buying preforeclosure properties by contacting owners in distress. Contacting apartment investors didn't bother me—they had invested knowing the risks. But contacting someone whose home was about to be taken away was a different story. I know the anguish that I would feel if someone was trying to take away my home. I just couldn't do it! I believe that, in life, people who continually try to become rich on other people's personal misery end up miserable themselves.

Someone tried to convince me that if I got to the owner before the sale, both of us would benefit. I wanted to verify this. After talking with professionals in the field, I discovered that preforeclosure properties could have undisclosed contingent liabilities. That is why financial institutions, in order to clear title, take back properties through foreclosure proceedings rather than buying them directly from the owner before the sale. Even with title insurance, the financial institutions want this additional protection. I felt the same. Not only would I be buying the property, it was possible I could also be buying someone else's problems, and clear title might be obstructed. It was possible that I could end up losing the property to creditors or spend time in court fighting countless legal battles.

In addition, many states have consumer protection laws dealing with foreclosures. Failure to comply with these laws will get you into a great deal of trouble.

WHY APARTMENTS ARE THE BEST INVESTMENT

Basic reasons why midsize apartment buildings make the best investments include:

1. *Competition:* Usually there are fewer qualified buyers for midsized or larger apartments than there are apartments available. Result: You have a few people chasing very good opportunities.
2. *Limitations:* Because of the economy of scale approach, there are fewer limitations as far as location is concerned in buying rental property. You can buy anywhere these pockets of opportunity exist because of the economy of scale.
3. *Frequency:* You do not have to do as many transactions because you're dealing with larger properties, therefore, reducing your chances of making the wrong decisions. You have more time to analyze each deal to make the best decisions.

Working Smarter Not Harder

Some people believe constant movement equates to productivity. They believe, if they work harder than the next guy, they'll succeed. Hard work is important, but working smarter is better. The smarter you work, the greater likelihood you'll succeed.

Instead of spending countless hours driving around areas within your city looking for good buys, spend a fraction of the time finding good locations in other cities, states, or countries by using the simple techniques introduced in this book.

How many times have you heard, "I don't get involved in the big deals. They are out of my ballpark." These people have been afflicted with the disease that I call "smallitis." Just because they have fewer investment dollars than the big guys, they feel they have to settle for smaller properties. If they only knew that with as little as $6,000, they could be *three* deals away from being a millionaire, I wonder what they would do. What would you do? Would you take the cure or not?

If you want to become successful, *don't follow the crowd.* Don't scurry around continually chasing financial fads. Eventually you will become weary and give up. You must force yourself to sit down and analyze your moves. If you have *smallitis,* this book will cure it. I will show you how to become financially healthy taking just a few doses of the miracle remedy.

BECOME A MILLIONAIRE IN ONLY THREE MOVES

You can become a millionaire starting with just $6,000, and you can do it in only three moves: Start by researching midsize apartment buildings. By midsize apartment buildings, I am referring to the number of units in a complex, not the height or square footage. Typically, a midsize apartment building has anywhere from 18 to 100 units.

You've heard the old saying, "It takes money to make money." Believe me, it's true. Money working for you can earn more than you working for money. Ask yourself, would 10 years of paychecks turn you into a millionaire? Investing wisely could! You need to invest in something that is going to yield the rate of return that's required to become rich. That something is rental real estate, and apartment buildings give you the best opportunity with the lowest possible risks.

The problem most people have with investing in rental real estate is that they don't have enough money to buy midsize apartment buildings on their own. Consequently, many end up buying single-family residences or smaller properties. While these sometimes can be good investments, many more moves are required to be successful, thus increasing the risks and chances of failure.

Some real estate investors try to circumvent their lack of money by attempting to buy smaller properties using the tactics preached by some "no-money-down gurus" at their seminars. Innocent people have fallen prey to these charlatans, and they have ended up not only losing money, but also, and most importantly, their own self-confidence.

GROUP INVESTING

There is a better way to invest when you have limited funds. You should combine your investment dollars with others to form an investment pool to purchase midsize apartment buildings. Chapter 13 shows you the easy-to-learn techniques of creating such an investment pool. This approach protects each individual's interest and creates many new tax benefits. The concept of pooling money is known as *group investing.*

Group investing allows you to gather adequate funds to purchase a midsize apartment building. Midsize buildings make economic sense because of the concept of "economies of scale." The cost per square foot of investing in and operating midsize apartment buildings is typically much less than smaller buildings. For example, assume you wanted your fourplex painted. The painter is going to quote you a much higher square foot price for the 4-unit building than if you asked for a quote on a 40-unit building.

The same holds true with vacancies. If one unit is vacant in a four-plex, there is a 25 percent vacancy factor. In a 40-unit building, one vacancy is only 2.5 percent. Units in midsize buildings tend to rent for more than those in smaller complexes because they typically have more amenities, such as swimming pools, landscaping, and recreation and laundry facilities, for example.

Midsize buildings are also less management intensive than smaller ones. The cost of hiring a property manager for many single-family residences is more than any cash flow it may generate. Even in a duplex or a fourplex, the costs are usually high. Managing the property yourself is not the answer. You'll quickly find out how much of your own labor is involved in keeping the complex running. Giving a tenant a small break on the rent to act as a manager can open you to potential liability.

Most part-time resident managers have little or no experience managing property, and they lack the knowledge of the legalities involved. They may learn from their mistakes, but it could be very costly to you. A midsize apartment building purchased correctly has sufficient rental income to support an expert property management company. Their expertise will make your property run at its best. Chapter 10 covers what you need to know to direct your property management company to be sure it is doing a good job. You'll find it's a lot less work managing a property management company than it is managing your property.

The number one question for you to consider is where to buy your property. There are many apartment buildings in the world. You need to find a location that has the greatest potential for appreciation, because that's where the real money is. Try to find areas that are currently economically depressed, and that are projected to begin recovering. Buy a midsize apartment building in this type of market and you're on your way to becoming wealthy. How do you find these kinds of locations?

Step 1: Research

The first part of becoming a real estate millionaire is research. Chapter 5 describes how to perform the kind of research needed. The goal of this research is to determine future values in various real estate markets.

In 1981, my investment group made its first move at the culmination of a tremendous amount of research. In the beginning, the bulk of my research centered around finding the right clues needed to evaluate various markets. Thirteen different variables in over 200 Metropolitan Statistical Areas (MSAs) were tracked for 15 years by my real estate research department. We discovered that vacancy rate movements were the best indicators of the health and potential profitability of the market. In addition, vacancy rate trends were found to predict future rental rates. Since apartment building values are heavily influenced by rental rates, having an accurate prediction of future rental rates gave advanced notice of potential price changes. This meant that we had the capability of making moves before others.

We further analyzed the effects that various combinations of data had on changes in vacancy rates, and meaningful prediction equations began to emerge. If we could successfully predict changes in vacancy rates, we could then predict future rental rates. Once we predicted future rental rates, we had a handle on future apartment prices. Having this much lead time in the apartment market would give us the opportunity to jump into a market just before it turned hot (before the rush of other investors) to gain the greatest economic benefit. It would also allow us to leave a market before it turned cold.

There were a number of areas that exhibited predicted favorable changes in vacancy rates. An area that showed a great deal of promise was Phoenix, Arizona. Our equations predicted a 29.3 percent drop in the vacancy rate would occur in 1982. In addition, building permits for this area had peaked at 11,421 in 1979 and were starting to decline, suggesting that an overbuilding situation was ending. With these factors in mind, we decided to look in Phoenix for a midsize apartment building to purchase as our first move.

To analyze the property, we had to find out what type of financing was available. Based on data from comparable sales in the area, we were able to determine the availability of various financing packages. Since seller financing was feasible, we opted to use it in our analysis. Using seller financing produced more leverage, an increased cash flow, and greater tax benefits.

The purchase of a hypothetical apartment building for $600,000 on January 1, 1981, was our first model. Our group had 10 investors, each contributing $6,000. The $60,000 pool was then used as a 10 percent down payment on the property.

The purchase price of $600,000 was determined by dividing the total amount of money pooled by 10 percent, the amount of the down payment ($60,000/10%). Total building square feet of 20,000 was calculated by dividing the purchase price of $600,000 by the acquisition price per square foot of $30 (provided by *Commercial Leasing Update* in Volume V, No. 2 [February 1990] by Kammrath & Associates).

The total number of units in the complex was based on comparable sales data of $23,000 per unit for a total of 26 units. To achieve maximum rental income, it is important to have the correct type of units (called the *unit mix*). The most desirable unit mix for this area was two to one. In other words, for every one-bedroom unit there should be at least two two-bedroom units. Preferably, the average one-bedroom unit should be 650 square feet and the two-bedroom units should be 825 square feet. Our sample building contained 18 two-bedroom units and 8 one-bedroom units.

The financial aspects of the acquisition were as follows:

Purchase price	$600,000	
First mortgage	420,000	
Second mortgage	120,000	
Down payment	60,000	
Total purchase price		$600,000

With 70 percent of the purchase price covered by the first trust deed and 20 percent by seller financing, only 10 percent down was required to purchase the property. The first mortgage was at 11 percent amortized over 30 years with payments of $4,000 per month. The seller financing available for the second mortgage was structured differently. For the first two years, the seller accrued all interest at 10 percent due at maturity. This interest did not compound. For the next two years, the seller accrued 5 percent interest and was paid 5 percent interest ($500) per month. The accrued interest was due at maturity, and it did not compound. For the final two years, the seller was paid interest at 10 percent ($1,000 per month) with no accrual. At the end of the sixth year, the principal balance and accrued interest were due and payable.

Operating income and expense per square foot were compared to those published by both local real estate associations and the Institute of Real Estate Management (IREM). Local property management firms were consulted to evaluate operating conditions, assist in the estimates, and verify ratios. Based on our findings, the following net cash flow projections were made:

First year	$21,375
Second year	22,377
Third year	13,479
Fourth year	14,274
Fifth year	12,776
Total cash flow	$84,281

After three years, it was anticipated that the initial cash outlay would be repaid. In addition, the projected cash generated from operations would be entirely tax free for the first two years. For years three through five, only $1,000 to $2,000 of the cash flow would be taxable—a very small amount indeed.

Since the average rental rate for a unit was $327 a month, our annual rental rate for all 26 units was $102,024.

Per IREM's reports, projected annual operating expenses of 35 percent on this project were broken down as follows:

Administrative expenses (6.9%)	$ 7,050
Operating expenses (9.2%)	9,400
Maintenance expenses (7.2%)	7,350
Taxes/Insurance (8.3%)	8,450
Recreational/Amenities (.2%)	200
Other payroll (3.2%)	3,250
Total annual expenses	$35,700

Using a computer program developed by The Center for Real Estate Studies, we monitored the local market conditions on a quarterly basis. At the same time, we monitored other areas in case other investment opportunities became available.

In 1982, the Phoenix vacancy rate dropped by 30.6 percent; outstandingly close to our projection of 29.3 percent. Using the 1982 data, we expected to see another 5 percent decrease in the vacancy rate in 1983. Actual data from 1983 shows that there was no change in the vacancy rate between 1982 and 1983. The expected decrease in vacancy rates did not occur because of an unexpected doubling of the number of building permits issued in 1983. These extra units started to come on line toward the end of the year and prevented a further decrease in the vacancy rates. Rental rates for the area continued to rise during the year to 4 percent, which was an improvement over the prior year. Our estimates for 1984 predicted a rise in the vacancy rate of 31 percent. At first glance, our inclination was to sell the property as soon as possible. However, further analysis told us to take a wait-and-see approach.

Building permits and rents were expected to continue to increase despite the rise in vacancy rates. We decided to hold on to the property for one more year to make sure we did not sell too soon. In 1984, the actual vacancy rate only went up 23.8 percent. While quite high, it was not as bad as we had feared. Property values increased 10.3 percent. Apparently, we had made the right choice not to sell. It was predicted that 1985 was to have another increase in the vacancy rate, but this time it was accompanied by a drop in building permits (indicating the beginning of a slide in the market), and a decrease in rents (also a bad sign for an area). Based on these predictions, we decided it was time to move from Phoenix to a better market.

Current sales conditions in Phoenix were still good based on sales activity. There appeared to be a number of serious buyers on the market, and although prices had leveled off, they had not yet started to slip. Scrutinizing comparable sales data confirmed financing was not a problem. We were selling at the right time in the apartment cycle.

A selling price of $860,000 was calculated by multiplying the total square footage by the selling price per square foot of $43, as provided by the *National Real Estate Index*.* Total cash flow from the operations of the property combined with the equity from the sale yielded a total of $354,650, as of December 31, 1985. Each of the 10 investors in our pool netted $35,465 on their $6,000 investment. This represents an annual rate of return of nearly 100 percent for each of the five years the property was owned (see Figure 3.1).

Step 2: Decreasing the Group Size

The time was ripe to make the second move on our quest to become millionaires. The proceeds from the first sale were traded, without paying taxes, to another property. By keeping up with the research, we knew exactly where to purchase the next apartment building.

Since we did so well on our first move, we were able to make the second move with a smaller group of investors. From the very beginning,

*The *National Real Estate Index* (Liquidity Fund, Emeryville, CA) reported only average apartment prices for Class A garden-style complexes. Within any given city, there are many locations and different classes of apartment buildings that provide even greater opportunities to improve on this rate of return.

Phoenix
Purchase of 26 Units

Purchase price (1/1/81)	$ 600,000.00
Loan proceeds	−540,000.00
Net cash outlay	$ 60,000.00

Sale of Property

Selling price (12/31/85)	$ 860,000.00
Closing costs	−25,800.00
Pay off balance of loans	−563,832.75
Cash received before taxes (tax-deferred exchange)	$ 270,367.25

Date	Net Operating Income	Debt Service	Taxes	Net Cash Flow
Year 1	$66,900.82	$47,997.00	$ 2,471.38	$ 21,375.20
Year 2	68,177.65	47,977.00	2,197.24	22,377.89
Year 3	69,454.55	53,997.00	−1,977.68	13,479.87
Year 4	70,729.53	53,997.00	−2,458.11	14,274.42
Year 5	72,000.44	59,997.00	772.85	12,776.29
Total cash flow from property				$354,650.92

Figure 3.1   Phoenix purchase of property. *Data Sources:* The Center for Real Estate Studies; Residential Property Analysis; square foot data from *National Real Estate Index,* published by Liquidity Fund, Emeryville, CA (800-992-7257); per unit sales data from Kammrath & Associates, *Commercial Leasing Update,* February 1990.

the ultimate goal was to end up as sole owner of a very profitable mid-size apartment building.

Our second move involved a property that would require a $175,000 down payment. Consequently, we needed only half of the original group to reinvest in the second property since each of the original investors now had $35,465 instead of the original $6,000. So, with a group of five members we made our second move.

In making the second move, we discovered that Boston, Massachusetts, had the profit potential we were looking for. Our equations predicted a 7.6 percent rise in the vacancy rate in 1986. This is usually an indication of a softening market, but market conditions indicated otherwise. In 1985, there was a sudden jump of 9,653 building permits—almost triple the number of permits from the year before. This was at least double every other prior year's building permits over the past six years. This sudden construction boom led to the increase in vacancy rate in the following year, but it was not projected to continue. Future building permits were expected to drop off over the next few years. In addition, other factors indicated that the demand for apartments would be increasing at an above-normal rate for the next two years. Without a huge inventory of new units coming on line, the increased demand was projected to force the vacancy rate down.

One of the factors indicating an increased demand for apartment units was the *median home price.* The median home price had jumped almost 35 percent in 1985. Compare this to a household income that had barely changed during the same period. Without a higher income, many people who would normally have purchased a home were forced to stay in apartments. By not leaving the market as they had done in the past, the demand for apartments was anticipated to increase. Employment and the number of households were projected to continue to grow as well. All these factors indicated that the increase in the vacancy rate would be temporary.

As with the Phoenix area, market conditions indicated that seller financing was available in Boston. There were many different types of financing packages to choose from, but our cost analysis pointed us to seller financing. In fact, seller financing is usually the most economical method to use.

The availability or lack of seller financing also gives additional clues as to current market conditions. While seller financing indicates a "soft" real estate market where buyers can make good deals, the lack of seller financing indicates a "hot" market. Since a hot market is one that favors the seller, it usually means that the seller can maximize profits. A hot market is a good time to *sell* real estate, but not a good time to *buy.*

Our second hypothetical apartment building was purchased in Boston, Massachusetts, on January 1, 1986. Our group had five investors, each contributing $35,000. The $175,000 pool was then used as a 10 percent down payment on the property. The selling price of $1,750,000 was reached by dividing the money pooled ($175,000) by the 10 percent down payment.

Total building square footage of 32,258 was calculated by dividing the purchase price of $1,750,000 by the acquisition price per square foot of $54.25, as published by the *National Real Estate Index.*

The total number of units in the complex was based on the total square footage and the unit mix to yield 44 units. The most desirable unit mix for this area was three to one. In other words, for every one-bedroom unit there should be at least 3 two-bedroom units. Preferably, the average one-bedroom unit should contain 600 square feet, and the average two-bedroom unit should contain 775 square feet. Our sample building included 33 two-bedroom units and 11 one-bedroom units.

The financial aspects of the acquisition were as follows:

Purchase price	$1,750,000	
First mortgage	1,225,000	
Second mortgage	350,000	
Down payment	175,000	
Total purchase price		$1,750,000

The first trust deed was 70 percent of the purchase price. Seller financing amounted to 20 percent; therefore, only a 10 percent down payment was required.

The first mortgage was at 11 percent amortized over 30 years with payment of $11,665.91 per month. The seller financing available for the second mortgage was structured as follows: for the first two years, the seller accrued all interest at 10 percent due at maturity. This interest did not compound. For the next two years, the seller accrued 5 percent interest and was paid 5 percent interest ($1,458.33 per month). Again the accrued interest was due at maturity and did not compound. For the final two years, the seller was paid interest at 10 percent ($2,916.66 per month) with no accrual. At the end of the sixth year, the principal balance and accrued interest were due and payable.

Operating income and expenses per square foot were compared to those published by both local real estate associations and IREM. Local property management firms were consulted to evaluate operating conditions, assist in the estimates, and verify ratios. Based on our findings, the following net cash flow projections were made:

First year	$50,632	
Second year	67,483	
Total cash flow		$118,115

By the time the property was sold, over $100,000 of the initial cash outlay had been repaid, and it was entirely tax free.

Gross annual rental income was derived by multiplying the average rental rate of $8.01 per square foot times the total square footage of 32,258 square feet, for a total of $258,387. Per IREM's reports, projected annual expenses of 35 percent of gross income were broken down as follows:

Administrative expenses (7.4%) $19,120
Operating expenses (8.6%)   22,220
Maintenance expenses (5.4%)   13,953
Taxes/Insurance (9.7%)   25,064
Recreational/Amenities (.4%)   1,034
Other payroll (3.5%)   9,044

Total annual expenses $90,435

Working with the same computer program, we continued to monitor local market conditions on a quarterly basis to keep abreast of changes that could affect our investment and to be aware of other investment opportunities as they became available.

In 1986, the Boston vacancy rate rose by 13.2 percent. Using the new 1986 data, we expected to see a 12.1 percent decrease in the vacancy rate in 1987. We were not overly concerned with the vacancy rate since the average rental increase was 9.9 percent in 1986. We reasoned that with a decrease in the vacancy rate, the rental rates would increase even more. Actual data from 1987 shows that there was only a 7 percent decrease in the vacancy rate, but once again the rental rates had increased, this time at an average of 9.4 percent for 1987. Our estimates for 1988 predicted a rise in the vacancy rate of 10 percent. When the second rise in the vacancy rate occurred, we started to make plans to sell. Our research had shown us that the Seattle, Washington, area was developing extraordinary potential.

Boston's median home price was predicted to level off in 1988, and household income was expected to rise—an indication of a renter exodus into single-family houses in the near future. There were no other indications that this loss in demand would be offset by any other factors. Unfortunately, the potential increase in the vacancy rate was real. We decided to leave the uncertainty in the Boston market for the greater potential in Seattle.

Sales conditions in Boston were very good. The recent drop in the vacancy rate drew many sellers back into the Boston market. It was definitely the right time to sell.

A selling price of $2,325,000 was calculated by multiplying the total square footage of the property (32,258) by the selling price per square foot of $72.13, as listed in the *National Real Estate Index* for Boston. Total cash flow from the operations of the property combined with the equity from the sale yielded a total of $740,574 as of December 31, 1987. Since there were now only five investors in our pool, each investor netted $148,115 for each $35,000 invested. This represents a return of over 323 percent, or approximately 162 percent per year (see Figure 3.2).

Boston
Purchase of 40 Units

Purchase price (1/1/86)	$ 1,750,000.00
Loan proceeds	−1,575,000.00
Net cash outlay	$ 175,000.00

Sale of Property

Selling price (12/31/87)	$ 2,325,000.00
Closing costs	−69,750.00
Pay off balance of loans	−1,632,790.38
Cash received before taxes (tax-deferred exchange)	$ 622,459.62

Date	Net Operating Income	Debt Service	Taxes	Net Cash Flow
Year 1	$178,153.67	$139,992.00	$12,470.05	$ 50,632.19
Year 2	202,060.83	139,992.00	5,413.74	67,483.04
Total cash flow from property				$740,574.85

Figure 3.2 Boston purchase of property. *Data Sources:* The Center for Real Estate Studies; Residential Property Analysis; square foot data from *National Real Estate Index*, published by Liquidity Fund, Emeryville, CA (800-992-7257).

At the end of the second move, some people might be tempted to stop here, count their winnings, and leave the real estate game. For those of you who wish to make the last move and gain real financial independence, please follow along.

Now it is time for the third move to make $1 million. The proceeds from the second sale were reinvested, through the use of a tax-deferred exchange, into another property. Relying on our research, we knew exactly where to buy the next apartment building. The $145,000 received from the sale of the second property was used for the purchase.

The acquisition price was calculated by dividing the $145,000 by a 10 percent down payment, or $1,450,000 ($145,000/10%). Total building square feet of 30,039 were determined by dividing the purchase price of $1,450,000 by the acquisition price per square foot of $48.27 as provided by the *National Real Estate Index*.

The total number of units in the complex was based on the total square footage and the unit mix to yield 40 units. The most desirable unit mix for the Seattle area was three to one. Again, for every one-bedroom unit there should be at least three two-bedroom units. Preferably, the average one-bedroom unit should contain 600 square feet and the average two-bedroom unit should contain 800 square feet. My sample building contained 30 two-bedroom units and 10 one-bedroom units.

The financial aspects of the acquisition were as follows:

Purchase price	$1,450,000	
First mortgage	1,015,000	
Second mortgage	290,000	
Down payment	145,000	
Total purchase price		$1,450,000

The first mortgage was 11 percent amortized over 30 years with payment of $9,666.08 per month. Seller financing for the second mortgage was structured as follows: for the first two years, the seller accrued all interest at 10 percent, due and payable at maturity. Interest did not compound. For the next two years, the seller accrued 5 percent interest and was paid 5 percent interest ($1,208.33 per month). Again the accrued interest was due at maturity and did not compound. For the final two years, the seller was paid interest at 10 percent ($2,416.66 per month) with no accrual. At the end of the sixth year, the principal balance and accrued interest were due.

Operating income and expenses per square foot were compared to those published by both local real estate associations and IREM. Local property management firms were consulted to evaluate operating conditions, assist in the estimates, and verify ratios. Based on the findings, the following net cash flow projections were made:

First year	$59,526	
Second year	64,777	
Third year	46,304	
Total cash flow		$170,607

By the end of three years, the initial cash down payment had been repaid. The projected cash generated from operations for the first two years was entirely tax free and only 20 percent of the cash from operations in the third year would be taxable.

The projected annual rental income of $261,340 was derived by multiplying the average rental rate of $8.70 per square foot by the total rentable square feet of 30,039.

Per IREM's reports, projected annual expenses of 35 percent of gross income were broken down as follows:

Administrative expenses (8.8%)	$22,998
Operating expenses (8.1%)	21,169
Maintenance expenses (4.8%)	12,544
Taxes/Insurance (8.7%)	22,737
Recreational/Amenities (.3%)	784
Other payroll (4.3%)	11,238
Total annual expenses	$91,470

By using the computer program, we were able to monitor the local market conditions on a quarterly basis while still keeping track of the pockets of opportunity as they became available.

Step 3: Sole Investor

For the third move, I predicted that Seattle, Washington, had the greatest potential in 1988. The econometric computer model forecasted a 13.5 percent drop in the vacancy rate in 1988. This drop was anticipated even though building permits were projected to increase from the 8,000 to 10,000 range to between 12,000 to 13,000. Actual figures for 1988 show the vacancy rate dropped 12.8 percent, and the building permits jumped to 11,939. While rents only went up 4 percent in 1988, selling prices of comparable buildings increased as well. My projections for 1989 called for a 26.3 percent increase in the vacancy rate, to about 5 percent. Although it was a major jump, the overall vacancy rate was still predicted to be quite low. My forecast was that property values would continue to increase, as would rental rates. In 1989, rental rates jumped another 7.5 percent and property value jumped 17 percent. Indications were that the market was going to start slowing down and that it might be time to start looking elsewhere. Predictions for 1990 estimated the vacancy rate climbing to 43.2 percent despite heavy employment growth.

I decided to hold onto the property until the end of 1990, for several reasons. The vacancy rate increases would not really impact the market until the fourth quarter of 1990. Consequently, rental rates and property values would continue to increase until then. Additionally, my predictions showed that I should be able to meet my target goal of $1 million without making any additional moves. Actual figures for 1990 proved me right. Though the vacancy jumped a whopping 52.6 percent in 1990, the property values did not level off until the end of the year. For the year, rents climbed only 1.3 percent, but property values increased 13.8 percent.

As of December 31, 1990, the selling price was calculated to be $2,267,043, that's the total square feet of 30,039 times the selling price

Seattle
Purchase of 38 Units

Purchase price (1/1/88)	$ 1,450,000.00
Loan proceeds	−1,305,000.00
Net cash outlay	$ 145,000.00

Sale of Property

Selling price (12/31/90)	$ 2,267,043.00
Closing costs	−68,011.29
Pay off balance of loans	−1,361,643.88
Cash received before taxes (tax-deferred exchange)	$ 837,387.83

Date	Net Operating Income	Debt Service	Taxes	Net Cash Flow
Year 1	$173,081.81	$115,993.00	$ 2,436.98	$ 59,525.83
Year 2	180,266.63	115,993.00	503.76	64,777.41
Year 3	187,744.09	130,493.00	−10,947.02	46,304.07
Total cash flow from property				$1,007,995.12

Figure 3.3   Seattle purchase of property. *Data Sources:* The Center for Real Estate Studies; Residential Property Analysis; square foot data from *National Real Estate Index,* published by Liquidity Fund, Emeryville, CA (800-992-7257).

per square foot of $75.47, as provided by the *National Real Estate Index* for the Seattle area. Total cash flow from operations and equity totaled $1,007,995. Since I was the sole owner, it meant that my $145,000 investment earned an annual return of 200 percent each year (see Figure 3.3).

I reached my goal. I had successfully turned a $6,000 investment into $1 million in only three moves. The entire process took just 10 years. You too can do it using the exact same methods.

SUMMARY

Don't be misled by the financial fads in foreclosure and distressed properties. With the number of people looking for these kinds of investments, it's nearly impossible to find anything worth buying. There is simply too much competition to make it profitable.

Don't limit your investments to a short driving distance from your house. Expand your choices of locations by purchasing in areas where pockets of opportunity exist.

Spend time on a few good properties to make you wealthy instead of buying and selling many single-family houses and smaller units. Having to continually make investment decisions on numerous smaller buildings doesn't leave you much time to spend on each one; thereby, increasing the probability of making errors.

Analytically proven methods of finding good locations gives you the ability to concentrate your efforts. In so doing, the likelihood of becoming really wealthy is enhanced.

Remember, all you need to do is to make the right moves. It has been done before. It will continue to be done in the future. Are you the one who will do it?

4

How to Effectively Employ Consultants

ADVANTAGES OF A TEAM APPROACH

By investing in midsize apartment buildings, you will be able to use the services of many consultants economically. Relying on a qualified group of specialists will give you the added advantage of a *team approach*. When buying larger properties and using as much leverage as possible, you'll need competent input from qualified professionals. At this level, you can't afford to "shoot from the hip." There's too much at stake.

Paraphrasing an old saying: If you act as your own attorney, you have a fool for a client. This could also apply to the person who tries to be his or her own property manager, real estate broker, accountant, escrow officer, building inspector, loan broker, and/or appraiser. It takes many skilled people to make a winning team. If you try to become proficient in all of these areas, you will go through a very expensive learning curve. More importantly, you will waste valuable time. Instead, spend your time and effort learning how to acquire and direct a team of experts.

39

PICKING THE RIGHT CONSULTANT

When choosing members for your team, be sure they are qualified to handle matters pertaining to your investment. Search for professionals who have education and experience in the real estate field, in general, and midsize apartment buildings, in particular. Don't let a property management company that caters to single-family residences manage your midsize apartment building. Don't employ a family law attorney to read rental contracts. Be sure you find the right consultant for each job.

Begin your search for real estate experts by asking for referrals from local real estate-oriented banks in areas where you plan to invest. Banks frequently use real estate consultants. Check with title companies and real estate associations for additional names.

Professional designations such as CPA (Certified Public Accountant), CPM (Certified Property Manager), CCIM (Certified Commercial Investment Member), or MAI (Member, Appraisal Institute) give additional assurance of qualifications. National associations will be able to provide you with local names and addresses of its members.

Another certified professional you should consider when planning investment strategies is the Certified Financial Planner (CFP). These experts can help you determine whether or not this type of real estate investment is right for you. They have the professional background and education to properly evaluate your financial goals.

For additional help in locating consultants, look through local telephone directories in the cities where you plan to invest. These directories can be found in the local library. Pick out names, addresses, and telephone numbers of local consultants, and send them a letter of inquiry like the one in Figure 4.1.

Once you've received your replies and have identified a number of prospects, make a list of the ones you would like to interview. To save time, try preinterviewing them by telephone before you set up an appointment. If they sound knowledgeable, request a resume. Consultants not qualified or interested should be weeded out immediately to avoid wasting time.

Always verify references. Even if you've been given the names of friends or relatives, check them out anyway. Most people are honest. You'll be able to read between the lines. For additional background information, check with the local Better Business Bureaus, credit reporting agencies, and professional associations representing the consultant's designation(s).

Date

Name
Company Name
Address

Dear Consultant,

   I am interested in purchasing a midsize apartment complex in your area.

   As part of my investment plan, I will be employing the services of qualified consultants, I am considering your firm. I have enclosed a questionnaire to assist me in evaluating your company.

   Please complete and return it as soon as possible in the prepaid envelope. Your cooperation will be greatly appreciated.

Sincerely,

Your Name

Questionnaire

1. What services will you provide for me?
2. What types of clients do you generally serve?
3. What size and kind of real estate do you most often handle?
4. What type of reporting will you provide?
5. How are you compensated, and how do you set your fees?
6. Does your firm have affiliates? If so, who are they, and how do they affect our relationship?
7. What are your educational credentials and business experience?
8. What licenses and/or certificates do you hold?
9. How do you keep up-to-date in your field?
10. What references do you have?

Figure 4.1   Sample consultant letter.

Beware of "Know It Alls"

Let consultants know up front that you're interested in investing in mid-sized apartments. Don't employ anyone who says, "Real estate is real estate. It doesn't matter what the type or the size, I can do the job!" Be aware of the consultant who is willing to give you advice on any and all subjects. Rather than appear dumb, people will expound on anything and everything, even if unqualified or unknowledgeable. I can't count the number of times I've heard attorneys elaborate on real estate market conditions, knowing all too well that they were completely off in left field. Beware of the "shade-tree" mechanic. Always make sure you have people working for you who have the expertise to get the job done.

GETTING THE MOST OUT OF YOUR CONSULTANT

The best way to get the most out of your meetings with consultants is to record them. You will be surprised to find how much you didn't hear when you play it back. Let the consultant know before you begin that the meeting is being recorded and get approval. If there are any objections, get another consultant.

Controlling Fees

Your tape recorder can also help you control billing costs. Consultants who bill on an hourly basis should give you a breakdown of hours (or a fraction thereof) based on specific matters. For example:

Realty Law Corporation (monthly billing)	
Phone conversation with client	0.25 hr.
Read contract	3.50
Prepare sales contract	2.75
Total	6.50 hr.
Amount due @ $250/hr.	$1,625

Make note of the hours on the tape recorder each time you use the consultant's services. Then when you receive the bill, compare the hours. If the bill doesn't agree with your figures, ask to see supporting documentation, such as copies of telephone bills and employee time sheets.

Avoiding Unnecessary Billings

Remember, you're working with an expert. Don't be afraid to ask, "Why do you have to research everything?" You're absolutely right in thinking they should have a strong background in the area of their expertise. The more research, the more billable hours. Be careful!

Beware of the consultant who charges a flat work fee. I've talked with attorneys who charge $200 per hour for their time. But if you ask the same attorney to prepare a living trust, the attorney might quote you a flat fee of $5,000, knowing full well that with the help of a secretary and a word processor, actual billable time won't come close to that figure.

Insist on getting a written cost estimate before any work is performed. An experienced consultant should be able to do this. If the consultant cannot, find out why not. Unless you're asking the consultant to do something that is outside his or her field of expertise, there shouldn't be any reason why an estimate can't be given. If you are asking for something outside of the consultant's area of expertise, don't. Get another consultant.

Protecting Yourself

All consultant reports should be in writing. Recommendations, estimates, interpretations, and opinions must be written down to avoid any misunderstandings. Your decisions are made based on the consultant's input. Don't be trapped into the "I said this instead of that" or "I meant this instead of that" syndrome. The degree for potential liability is extremely high. Protect yourself by getting everything in writing.

Have the tapes transcribed or make written notes of your meetings with the consultant. Be sure everyone involved receives a copy. The notes must reflect what took place at the meeting (and should also include telephone conversations), the plan of action, and who is responsible for what. Always protect yourself from other peoples' failures. Having it down in writing helps.

Fee versus Commission

Always be cautious of the consultant that wants you to go in on his or her deal. The degree of objectivity becomes questionable, at best. Working on a fee basis rather than on a commission reduces this conflict of interest also. It establishes a higher degree of independence among the parties, which is extremely vital in this kind of relationship.

Keeping Control

Probably the most important rule to remember while working with consultants is to maintain complete control. Consultants provide the support for the decision-making process. It's up to you to maintain control by making the decisions. Don't relinquish command to anyone. If you lose authority, you'll end up losing your money.

The questionnaire that appears in Figure 4.1 will assist you in evaluating consultants.

YOUR KEY CONSULTANT

The key consultant to your success is the property manager. In terms of overall real estate background, the property manager is best suited for the pivotal role and is captain of your team of experts. Working on a day-to-day basis managing the property, the property manager must be able to assist in both the acquisition and sale of your building.

Finding a Good Property Manager

What do you look for in a qualified property management company? The first consideration is location. It is important to use a firm that is located in the same general area as the property. Proximity is important for smooth daily operations.

Be sure the firm you choose does not own apartments in the same area as yours. There could be a conflict of interest, and you might find that your units have a higher vacancy factor and operating costs than the apartments the firm owns. When concentrating on midsize apartments, make sure the management company has experience in this specific field and is currently managing similar properties. Don't be misled by the "you've seen one, you've seen them all" reasoning. There are management procedures and techniques that are unique to different kinds of real estate. Knowing which ones apply to midsize apartment complexes will increase the likelihood of success.

Be Wary of "Mom-and-Pop" Operations

I prefer to use a medium-size property management company, rather than a "mom-and-pop" company. These kinds of operations usually don't have the staff to do an adequate job. In addition to managing smaller units, they are typically involved with real estate brokering. I've actually seen these operators give prospective tenants the key to a vacant unit, rather than showing it themselves. This type of marketing effort won't do if you're trying to keep vacancies down.

Be Just as Wary of the "Giants" in the Field

Larger property management firms are geared to institutional investors. Midsize apartment buildings somehow get lost in the shuffle. Individual attention suffers. The needs of your building might have to wait until those of a much larger complex are met. Your building might be assigned to a new or relatively inexperienced property supervisor to provide training.

Procedure Manuals Are Critical

Ask to see the operations or procedure manual of the firm. Read it and ask questions. You'll get a clear indication of how a property management company manages apartment complexes from the manual. Be leery of the company that doesn't have one. In fact, do not consider using a company unless they have a formal plan on how they manage apartment buildings.

What to Expect from Your Property Manager

Under no circumstances should you run the day-to-day management operations. Your role is to properly monitor the project in order to establish effective policies and to make management decisions.

What support should your property management company provide? Ideally, they should be able to provide all services in the areas of acquisition, operation, and disposition of your property.

After you've pinpointed possible property locations, a good property management company should be able to give statistical, as well as subjective, information concerning socioeconomic, political, and developmental conditions. A quality firm should be capable of preparing physical inspection reports, capital improvement requirements, and an effective operations budget.

During the operations phase, a competent property management company will issue timely monthly operating reports that compare actual income and expenses to budgets. They should be able to give you a detailed explanation of any major variances, and their representative should meet with you periodically.

During the sale phase of your property, your management firm should be able to communicate with the potential buyers on your behalf regarding the building, and to assist in various inspections. They should have no problem providing these services because it gives them the opportunity to display their own expertise to the new buyers.

Controlling Property Management Fees

How much should you pay a property management firm? Payment should be based on the various tasks you want performed. In assisting you with the acquisition, you should contract out on an hourly basis that's comparable in the area. Under no circumstances agree to an inspection contingent on signing a management contract. You can readily see where this could lead. More property managed equates to more income, a flagrant conflict of interest. Work with a reputable company, one that won't recommend you buy the building just to get the management contract.

Management fees are usually based on a percentage of the rents collected. Smaller projects pay a higher percentage than larger ones. Remember, management fees are always negotiable. There are no fixed rates. Make sure all services and related costs are spelled out in writing before you enter into a management contract.

It is important to note that fees based on the percentage of rents collected should not include other items such as total cash collected, projected rents, gross possible rents, security deposits, and laundry income, for example. Be careful. Know exactly what the rate is and how it's applied.

If you want to give additional incentive to the property management company, offer them a bonus based on the building's performance. It could be based on net operating income or the overall improvement of the complex over a period of time, usually one year.

Traps to Avoid in the Property Management Agreement

In the chapter that teaches you how to manage your property manager, various techniques are introduced to assist in monitoring and controlling operations. However, there are some important points that should be emphasized at this time, including:

1. Do not sign a management contract that gives a management company exclusive rights to sell or purchase your property. It will severely limit your ability to market it yourself or to arrange to have others do it for you.
2. Be sure the contract has a provision for immediate cancellation upon written notice. Much can happen while you're waiting for a contract to expire that is based on a 60- or 90-day cancellation clause. Typically, a 30-day cancellation clause is required for most written contracts. That is standard for the industry.
3. Make sure that bills and expenses are specifically delineated to be paid in the following order of priority by the property manager: insurance, all debt service, salaries, utilities and service contracts, and taxes and assessments. The last item to be paid should be management fees and any leasing commissions. You

want to make sure your investment is protected (insurance) and that your mortgage is paid before any other expenses are paid. Some property management companies want to make sure that they and their vendors are paid first, but they will be very motivated to quickly collect rents and fill vacancies if they get paid last.

4. Compare the proposed staffing on your building to that of similar properties in the area to find out what type of arrangements are common. State or local regulations may dictate a resident manager in a certain building size or with a number of units, so be aware of the laws. Make sure that the duties and responsibilities of all staff are spelled out in writing as part of the management contract.

5. The management agreement should specifically state the reports to be provided to the owners (more details on what reports you need can be found in Chapter 10). *You* tell the property manager what reports you need, they don't tell you what *they* provide. If they say they can't provide the information that you want, find another property management company.

FINDING THE BEST ATTORNEY FOR YOU

Your attorney must be familiar with the real estate laws in the jurisdiction of your property. An attorney in one state can't give you good advice on property located in another state unless the attorney knows the laws of that state. A copy of the *Martindale-Hubbel Law Directory*, found in many local libraries, will give you a list of lawyers, their backgrounds, and types of practice to assist you in finding a specialist.

As with property management companies, I prefer to use a medium-size law firm specializing in real estate. You can't be too sure who's handling your work with larger firms.

An experienced firm can actually reduce the total billable hours. Experienced attorneys don't have to continually research areas in their field of expertise.

Use the services of an attorney to assure yourself that all documents accurately represent the agreement, and that you're adequately protected. Your attorney must tell you what your exposure is and how to (1) either eliminate it, or (2) make provisions to deal with it.

Your attorney should be able to review the following important documents: escrow instructions, title reports, lease or rental agreements, loan documents, and any other contract that pertains to the building, such as laundry leases, and pool and landscaping contracts, for example. The attorney's written report must assert that these documents accurately reflect the transaction.

In general, your attorney should point out potential problems on absolutely anything that might be out of the ordinary. Most importantly, your attorney should provide protection in case things go wrong.

Structuring Contracts to Avoid Litigation

All parties lose when they litigate; that is, all parties except the attorneys. To avoid costly litigation, insist that all contracts contain a provision for binding arbitration. Nonprofit groups, such as the American Arbitration Association, the Judicial Arbitration Association, and the Judicial Arbitration and Mediation Service, provide arbitrators (usually retired judges) to settle disputes. Arbitration is relatively quick and inexpensive because it requires less disclosure and fewer legal motions.

If you're forced into litigation, try to assess the strength of your case. A good way to do this is to see if you can find an attorney who will take your case on a contingency basis. If you can't, then seriously reassess your position. The best move you can make before getting involved with the entire legal system is to try face-to-face communication. This is the best and least expensive way to resolve misunderstandings.

THE SECRET TO WORKING WITH ACCOUNTANTS

An accountant can help you with statistical analyses and income tax strategies. The accountant should be able to give you a written report that includes projections and tax implications on your real estate transactions. Most accountants who specialize in real estate have computer programs to facilitate this kind of reporting. In a matter of one or two sessions, the components of your transaction can be inputted into the computer, and with the help of specialized computer programs, the accountant will be able to answer questions as to the "what ifs" scenarios and resulting tax implications.

Accountants, by the nature of their profession, tend to be conservative. Accountants should be employed for their accounting and tax ability, not to decide whether your purchase is a "good deal." Your investments must be extremely aggressive in order for you to become wealthy. Don't be discouraged if your accountant gives your real estate deal a "thumbs down." It's an accountant's nature! The advice is given out of the fear of being aggressive rather than the investment itself.

Remember, by conscientiously applying the lessons in this book, you will acquire the knowledge needed to make the right decisions. Never be afraid to act on this knowledge and your own convictions.

GETTING THE MOST FROM THE ESCROW AND TITLE COMPANIES

The key to getting a good escrow company is complete independence. Use a national title company to escrow the transaction whenever possible. Smaller local companies are more susceptible to playing favorites to selected clients. In addition, if interstate transactions are involved, communications improve when you use the services of a national firm. Again, use a company experienced in apartment transactions. A competent escrow company must display a high degree of proficiency in tax-deferred exchanges, bulk sales transfers, prorations, and various forms of ownership.

Another advantage in using a national title insurance company to escrow your transaction is the cost. As an incentive to purchase title insurance, some companies reduce escrow fees. If the quality of the service remains the same, it's an excellent opportunity to save money.

THE CONSULTANT WHO WILL SAVE YOU THE MOST TIME AND MONEY

The one consultant who can save you the most time and money is a real estate investment broker. Notice we said investment broker. Once again we ask you to work with a specialist. All real estate brokers do not have the same qualifications. A real estate professional who you can rely on has the Certified Commercial Investment Member (CCIM) designation. This designation is the result of a strenuous program of certification that is granted by the Realtors National Market Institute (RENMI). For a list of all CCIM real estate agents in an area, write to RENMI, 630 North Michigan Avenue, Chicago, IL 60611 (or call 312-440-8000).

You should be able to delegate many of the tasks involved in buying and selling to a qualified real estate investment broker. However, keep in mind their services are not free. This has to be taken into consideration when calculating a rate of return. If the selling broker is also the listing agent, according to agency law, the broker/agent primarily acts on behalf of the person or entity to whom the broker/agent is contractually obligated. So, if the selling broker is functioning as a listing agent, the broker/agent is primarily representing the seller. If you, as the buyer, want independent representation, consider employing the services of a real estate licensee using the sample contract shown in Figure 4.2.

An Effective Way to Save on Commissions

There is no such thing as a standard broker's commission. Commissions are negotiable. Generally, the higher the selling price, the lower the commission. A reputable broker will not sell you a piece of property just to earn a commission. But, always be careful and analyze all potential conflicts of interest.

Remember, agents working strictly on a commission basis, do not get paid until the sale occurs. It's important to negotiate the commission and the services to be performed up front before anyone starts working.

Understanding How Multiple Listing Services Work

Most larger apartment buildings do not get put into the multiple listing service (MLS) book. Members who belong to the MLS are required to submit all new listings, and/or changes, to the board of realtors literally within hours so that it can be disseminated to other board members quickly. However, not all "hot" listings get on the board or, when they do, it occurs in a matter of days, not hours.

The MLS book provides information on real estate activity for Realtors. It is distributed by the local MLS boards to members who subscribe to the service. Some real estate boards make this information available to the general public.

A knowledgeable investment real estate broker who belongs to the MLS service normally is in the best position to find properties. The broker's continual full-time effort to stay abreast of market conditions provides a decisive edge in finding the best deals.

If you decide to use the services of a real estate investment broker, work with several. You should be exposed to as many properties as possible. Be sure to let the broker know your parameters (building size, price range, down payment, age, unit mix, and so on). A good relationship with a qualified real estate investment broker can be your best ticket to wealth.

WHAT TO TELL THE BUILDING INSPECTOR BEFORE AN INSPECTION

If the property management company does not have anyone on staff to do a physical property inspection, use the services of a building

NCR (No Carbon Required)

BUYER'S BROKER EMPLOYMENT AGREEMENT

The undersigned _____, hereinafter designated as CLIENT,
hereby employs _____, hereinafter designated as BROKER,
for the purpose of exclusively assisting Client to locate property of a nature outlined below or other property acceptable to Client, and to negotiate terms and
conditions acceptable to Client for purchase, exchange, lease, or option of or on such property. This agreement shall commence this date and terminate at
midnight of _____, 19_____.

GENERAL NATURE, LOCATION, AND REQUIREMENTS OF PROPERTY.

_____
_____
_____
_____
_____
_____
_____
_____

PRICE RANGE, AND OTHER TERMS AND CONDITIONS.

_____
_____
_____
_____
_____
_____
_____
_____
_____
_____
_____
_____

COMPENSATION TO BROKER. Client agrees to pay Broker, as compensation:

a) For locating property acceptable to Client and for negotiating the purchase or exchange, a fee of $_____ or _____% of the acquisition price, or $_____ per hour.

b) For obtaining an option on a property acceptable to Client, a fee of $_____, and to pay Broker the balance of a fee equal to _____% of the purchase price in the event the option is exercised or assigned prior to expiration of the option.

c) For locating a property acceptable to Client and negotiating a lease thereon, a fee of _____;

IF:

1. Client or any other person acting for Client or in Client's behalf, purchases, exchanges, obtains an option for, or leases any real property of the nature described herein, during the term hereof, through the services of Broker or otherwise.

2. Client or any other person acting for Client or in Client's behalf, purchases, exchanges, obtains an option for, or leases any real property of the nature described herein, within one year after termination of this agreement, which property Broker, Broker's agent, or cooperating brokers presented or submitted to Client during the term hereof and the description of which Broker shall have submitted in writing to Client, either in person or by mail, within ten (10) days after termination of this agreement.

NOTICE: The amount or rate of real estate commissions is not fixed by law. They are set by each broker individually and may be negotiable between the buyer and the broker.

AGENCY RELATIONSHIP. Broker agrees to act as agent for Client only in any resulting transaction, provided that Broker may cooperate with other brokers and their agents in an effort to locate property or properties in accordance with this agreement, and may divide fees in any manner acceptable to them. If Broker receives compensation from anyone other than Client, Broker shall make full disclosure, and such compensation shall be credited against Client's obligation hereunder.

In addition, Broker will provide appropriate Agency Disclosure as required by law.

BROKER'S OBLIGATIONS. In consideration of Client's agreement set forth above, Broker agrees to use diligence to achieve the purpose of this agreement.

CLIENT'S OBLIGATIONS. Client agrees to provide Broker, upon request, relevant personal and financial information to assure Client's ability to acquire property outlined above. Client further agrees to view or consider property of the general nature set forth in this Agreement, and to negotiate in good faith to acquire such property if acceptable to Client. In the event completion of any resulting transaction is prevented by Client's default, Client shall pay Broker the compensation provided for herein upon such default.

ATTORNEY FEE. If any action is brought to enforce the terms of this agreement, or arising out of the execution of this agreement, or to collect fees, the prevailing party shall be entitled to receive from the other party a reasonable attorney fee to be determined by the court in which such action is brought.

ENTIRE AGREEMENT. Time is of the essence. The terms hereof constitute the entire agreement and supersede all prior agreements, negotiations and discussions between the parties. This Agreement may be modified only by a writing signed by each of the parties.

Receipt of a copy of this agreement is hereby acknowledged.   DATED: _____ TIME: _____

Buyer's Broker: _____   _____ Client

By: _____   _____ Client

Address: _____   Address: _____

Phone: _____   Phone: _____

FORM 100 (6-90)   COPYRIGHT © 1988, BY PROFESSIONAL PUBLISHING CORP, 122 PAUL DR, SAN RAFAEL, CA 94903 (415) 472-1964   **PROFESSIONAL PUBLISHING**

Figure 4.2 Buyer's broker employment agreement.

51

inspection company. Be sure you let them know before they do the inspection that they will not be contracted to do any of the repair work recommended on their inspection report. This will avoid any conflicts of interest.

The report should list all items to be repaired or replaced, including itemized costs and estimated dates the work should be performed. These items should be broken down on a unit-by-unit basis. This information will be useful when preparing budgets and when negotiating. If you question anything on the report, get a second opinion. Narrative data detailing potential problems should be included in the report.

Whenever possible, use a local building inspector. The inspector should be knowledgeable about local codes, costs, and conditions affecting the building.

SAVING MONEY USING AN APPRAISER

The professional designation given to qualified real estate appraisers is MAI (Member, Appraisal Institute). Their reports give present market value as of a specific date. Keep in mind, however, your main concern is with *future market value.*

The appraisal report will assist you in negotiating price and terms, applying for loans, and preparing budgets. A qualified appraiser should provide you with a detailed cost breakdown of repairs and replacements.

When planning the financing of your acquisition, save time and money by employing an appraiser approved by the lender. Be certain that the appraiser works for and is paid by *you,* not the lender. You want the appraiser to act on your behalf. Always have the appraisal company keep several copies of the report on file so that original signed copies can be sent to other lenders without incurring additional costs. Appraisals are very expensive. Make sure you verify with lenders that your appraiser is on their recommended list.

You can find professional appraisers listed in the Yellow Pages of the telephone book, or you can write to the American Society of Appraisers, Dulles International Airport, P.O. Box 17265, Washington, DC 90041 for a list of appraisers in your area.

WORKING WITH LOAN BROKERS

Depending on market conditions, it may or may not be easy to get a loan. Normally you can save money on points (fees for obtaining the loan) by dealing directly with the lender. However, the savings on points may be more than offset if you end up with a bad loan. Loan brokers can usually obtain better financing for you because of their knowledge of the mortgage markets.

First, try to obtain a loan directly from a lender. Compare the lender's fees to those offered by the loan broker, and choose the least expensive one. Some loan brokers want an up-front fee for shopping for the loan. Try to get them to accept your credit report instead. When a broker presents you with a legitimate loan commitment from a lender, a good faith deposit may be requested. You shouldn't give the broker any money until you've verified the commitment with the lender.

Any questions regarding a loan broker's contract or the commitment letter, should be referred to your attorney before you sign any documents.

SUMMARY

One of the advantages of buying midsize apartment buildings is that you can economically employ the services of qualified professionals. Knowing how and when to use them both effectively and efficiently saves you time and money. These experts help you reach your goals faster and with fewer headaches.

Under no circumstances should you abdicate control. This is the key to effectively managing consultants. It is up to *you* to make the final decisions based on the recommendations and information supplied by your team of specialists. Remember, the buck stops with you. Don't pass it on, or you will lose it!

5

Buying in the Right Place at the Right Time

TWO RULES FOR BUYING AND SELLING

How many times have you heard it said, "The three most important things to remember when investing in real estate is location, location, location"? Or, "If I'd bought that property 10 years ago, I would be a millionaire today." Knowing what, when, and where to buy is not only the key to sound real estate investing, it is the key to all investing.

John Paul Getty said, "Buy when everyone is selling and sell when everyone is buying." This simple statement represents the cornerstone of our investment philosophy. When buying, find out where everyone is selling, evaluate the area, and negotiate the best deal possible. Sell when everyone else is buying. This is our Standard Operational Procedure (SOP). In this chapter, you learn how to apply this SOP.

THE BENEFITS OF BOTTOM FISHING

Remember, there are always pockets of opportunity for real estate investments. Good markets exist all over the world at varying times. Concentrate on weak markets, not weak properties. A weak market is the most favorable condition in which to buy. Prices are depressed and profit potential is high. Sellers just want to get out. Buying in a depressed market is called "bottom fishing."

The Key to Evaluating Locations

Focus on areas where the local economy is basically strong and the current downturn is caused primarily by overbuilding. The U.S. Bureau of the Census publishes building permit activity for buildings five units and up for Metropolitan Statistical Areas (MSAs). Identify markets with the largest gains in building permits from one year to the other. If you discover a "construction bubble," it could mean you've located an ideal market. With a diversified local economy, the overbuilding should be absorbed. A weak market caused by conditions other than overbuilding should be scrutinized carefully.

Apartment buildings often make money for the *second* owners in overbuilt markets, not the first. Builders get paid for building and they will keep on building as long as they get paid. More often than not, banks are the ones doing the paying.

The market becomes deluged with an excess of inventory. This is when you should step in.

Employment Trends

Base employment is probably the single most important factor contributing to the economic health of an area. In evaluating employment trends, be careful of construction employment. During boom-and-bust building activity, the labor base can become distorted by construction related jobs. If possible, eliminate construction employment figures when plotting trends. Predicting growth industries and where they will be located can give you a further indication of where future employment growth will take place.

Talk with the local city planner to determine the direction of city growth. Plans for shopping malls, universities, and business parks create a potential demand for employment and desirable apartment locations.

Demographic Factors Affecting Apartments

Demographic factors are also important in evaluating demand. People tend to marry later and divorce is on the increase, both of which result in a larger single population. In addition, people are living longer, and we have the empty nest syndrome, as grown children move away from the family home usually into apartments. The parents no longer need a large private home and many choose an apartment as well. The number of households is increasing, and the size is decreasing. The affordability of single-family homes is also decreasing.

Demographically, look for an area in which there is a higher percentage of females to males, younger and/or older adults as opposed to middle aged, singles rather than marrieds, smaller families over larger families, and renters over nonrenters in evaluating favorable rental areas.

APARTMENT BUILDING CYCLES

The "when" to buy and sell is just as important as the "where." With bad timing you'll strike out every time. To improve your timing, you must become familiar with apartment cycles.

Cycles result from the influence supply and demand have on the marketplace. Economists spend countless hours trying to accurately predict them, and gurus for the current year are the ones who guessed correctly the previous year. As long as their crystal ball remains clear, they will continue to be called on for their advice. One false prediction and they are ousted from the Nostradamus Hall of Fame.

Apartment cycles are difficult to forecast. Yet, it's essential to have projections when buying and selling. Understanding them will give you the insight to make intelligent decisions.

Figure 5.1 shows the five phases of the apartment cycle. Note the most desirable times to purchase and sell.

The Five Phases of an Apartment Cycle

The five phases in an apartment cycle are a result of the interplay of supply and demand. They are:

Phase 1. Population increases, incomes rise, and the picture for employment is rosy. As a result, vacancies are decreasing and apartment rents rise sharply. New apartment complexes have been planned.

Phase 2. Apartment project starts increase rapidly. All market indicators—rents and prices, recordings of deeds and building permits—reach high levels. Existing apartment complexes are being purchased in a bidding war. To maximize profits, sell in this phase.

Phase 3. Apartment projects come onto the market all at once. Inflation has increased quickly. The Federal Reserve Boards try to stop

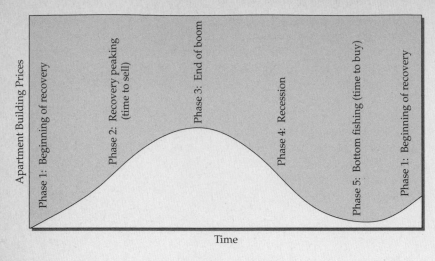

Figure 5.1   Five phases of an apartment cycle. *Source:* The Center for Real Estate Studies.

inflation by increasing interest rates. Vacancy rates begin to creep up. Prices begin to level.

Phase 4. Builders are having trouble selling their properties. Higher interest rates result in high holding costs. Landlords are competing for tenants because of the overbuilding. Foreclosures become more frequent.

Phase 5. Both unemployment and inflation continue at record rates. Renters double up to save money. Effective demand is decreasing. How far this phase will continue depends on the degree of over-building and lending policies. This stage will end and a new phase 1 will begin when the general business economy starts to improve. The ideal time to purchase is during this phase.

MASTER APARTMENT ECONOMICS

Understanding the relationships between supply and demand is essential when determining location and timing in the apartment market. Figure 5.2 shows how the interaction of supply and demand affects prices. The various markets are shown. The equilibrium point is P-1, the current price. Increases in population due to a favorable job market is curve D-2, with prices rising to P-2. A continued increase in population results in a new demand, indicated by D-3, with a resulting price of P-3. Higher prices result in building and a new supply curve, S-2. The additional supply reduces demand, so prices drop to

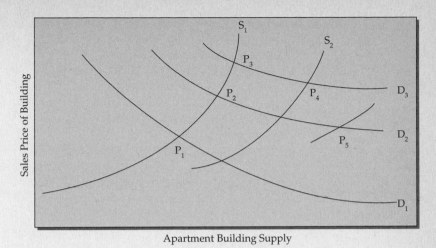

Apartment Building Supply

Figure 5.2 Apartment building supply and demand. *Source:* The Center for Real Estate Studies.

P-4. The supply and demand relationship continues to change prices, which produce P-5 and so on.

To assess the supply side of the apartment cycle, these questions need to be answered:

- Where and when has construction taken place?
- What has been built—apartments, commercial buildings, or single family units?
- What is the number of existing apartment permits?
- What is the likelihood of more permit requests as a result of construction costs?
- How do local ordinances affect the issuance of permits?
- What are the environmental factors?
- Is construction expanding the city or is it in-fill?
- How much buildable land is available?
- Is the squared footage available for rent increasing rapidly?
- Is in-fill causing the supply to remain level as older units are being demolished?

Theoretically, as long as the supply is below the demand, the value of the real estate will increase because of the ability to increase rents. If supply is greater than demand, the reverse is true; therefore, the ability to raise rents is impaired. In fact, rents do tend to come down.

An overabundance of buildable land is a negative factor in projecting potential supply. Excess buildable land causes rapid market changes when builders decide it's profitable to start building again.

In picking locations within a city, choose apartments that have a certain degree of resilience even in down markets. Complexes near public transportation, urban centers, and beachfront property fare much better than ones located elsewhere. The closer an apartment complex is to employment areas, the more desirable it is.

Demand for apartments is created by increases in certain segments of the population. Low-paying jobs tend to create a larger supply of renters than higher-paying jobs. As a result, buying apartments in blue-collar neighborhoods is preferable. Wages paid in these neighborhoods are more compatible to paying rent than they are to paying mortgages.

The single most important factor in gauging demand is job creation. Cities that foster an atmosphere that will bring about greater employment will increase the demand for apartments.

Demand for apartments is also related to changes in affordability. The fewer people able to purchase homes, the greater the demand for rentals and vice versa. Another important factor affecting supply and demand is the availability and cost of mortgage money. Interest rates play an important role in determining demand. When rates are high, fewer people can afford to buy houses, and the demand for mortgage money decreases. Higher interest rates also prevent builders from building, thereby reducing supply. Lower interest rates, on the other hand, tend to increase building activity, and buyers can qualify for loans more readily and are more able to buy. Demand for houses increases, while for apartments it will decrease.

All Markets Rebound Eventually

Knowing the elements of supply and demand is both informative and educational. Knowing how to apply them is what makes you wealthy! The procedures in this chapter help you determine the best locations and time to purchase midsize apartment buildings.

It's important to note that virtually all markets will rebound in one way or another. Sooner or later the economies of supply and demand will take over to create opportunities for the smart investor.

THE ANALYTICAL APPROACH TO LOCATING GOOD AREAS

Many real estate books recommend buying property in good areas, but they fail to tell you where they are or how to locate them. The ability to accurately project vacancies and rental rates is the key to finding good locations. The more proficient you become at forecasting, the greater your chances are for success.

Where do you start? Start with building permits. A construction bubble or sudden increase in total building permits may be an indication of a good area. The Bureau of the Census publishes several pertinent reports. Write to the Bureau of Census, U.S. Department of Commerce, Superintendent of Documents, U.S. Government Printing Office, Washington, DC 20402, and ask for the *Bureau of the Census Guide to Programs and Publications, Subjects and Areas*. This guide contains charts that describe the statistical information available in various Census Bureau publications since 1968 and is fully indexed.

Once you've identified locations based on building permits, compare current selling prices of apartment buildings with replacement costs. If selling prices are below replacement costs, it may be that the area has potential. Local building and real estate associations should be able to provide you with data on selling prices and building costs. Marshall & Swift publish a book, *Residential Cost Handbook,* that details the costs of various apartment buildings based on locations throughout the United States and Canada. It can be found in many local libraries.

Always supplement statistical data with information from newspapers and business and real estate publications. Knowing where jobs are being created and where layoffs are occurring is vital in determining location. Projections on growth rates, cost of living, and quality-of-life surveys are also helpful.

Determining the Best Time and Place to Buy and Sell

The following historical (six years or more) data, as well as forecast (one year or more) data, should be used in computing good locations:

1. Building permits
2. Employment
3. Household income
4. Number of households
5. Median house prices
6. Vacancy factory
7. Rental rates

Be careful when gathering data. You will need reliable, accurate information. The sources listed in each of the following categories are recommended. Please use them whenever possible. Data must also be compatible. For example, when working with employment statistics, make sure your figures include similar employment classifications from year to year. That is, don't use military employment in one report and exclude it in another, or the medium home price can then change to average home price. Be consistent.

BUILDING PERMITS   Permits issued each year for apartments (five units and up) will assist in tracking building cycles (Figure 5.3). Since a time lag exists between issuance and completion, having advance notice of what's coming is important.

> *Sources:*   Two good sources are local city planners and *Housing Units Authorized by Building Permits and Public Contracts* found in either your local library or Department of Commerce, Bureau of the Census, Building Permit Division, Washington, DC 20230, (301) 763-7244.
> *Forecast:*   Local planning departments, banks, colleges, building associations, and chambers of commerce provide projections. If forecasts are not available, estimate permits based on historical cycles.

EMPLOYMENT   Employment is a key figure. Look at the number of people who are employed rather than the unemployed. A new job

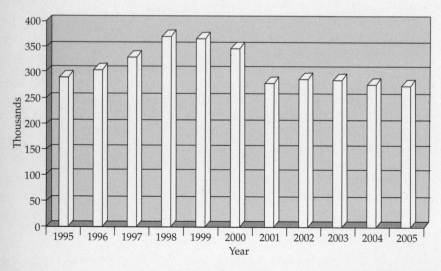

Figure 5.3   Multifamily housing permits. *Source:* The Center for Real Estate Studies.

created in one area of employment results in additional jobs in other areas. For example, each time a factory worker is hired, it creates additional work (and jobs) for the baker, grocer, mechanic, doctor, builder, and so on.

Source: *County Business Patterns* can be found in your local library or Department of Commerce, Bureau of the Census, County Business Patterns Branch, Washington, DC 20233, (301) 763-5430.
Forecast: Bureau of Labor Statistics (BLS) in your local area, the local department of employment, or local chamber of commerce are good sources.

HOUSEHOLD INCOME Household income influences the value of apartments. As income rises, tenants' ability to pay higher rents increases, which, in turn, increases the value of the property. There is, however, a point at which household income will rise sufficiently to afford a mortgage payment rather than rent. At this point, rents will either level off or decline.

Source: *Sales and Marketing Management* published by Bill Communications, 633 Third Avenue, New York, NY 10017, (212) 984-2434. They provide a figure known as Effective Buying Income (EBI) that is excellent for your computation.
Forecast: *Sales and Marketing Management* also publishes a five-year forecast, or try *Editors and Publishers Market Guide,* 11 West 19th Street, New York, NY 10011, (212) 675-4380.

NUMBER OF HOUSEHOLDS Households rent apartments not individuals. A household may consist of one or many people (Figure 5.4). Therefore, using total population will distort the calculation.

Source: *Sales and Marketing Management* published by Bill Communications, 633 Third Avenue, New York, NY 10017, (212) 984-2434. They provide a figure known as Effective Buying Income (EBI) that is excellent for your computation.
Forecast: *Sales and Marketing Management* also publishes a five-year forecast, or try *Editors and Publishers Market Guide,* 11 West 19th Street, New York, NY 10011, (212) 675-4380.

MEDIAN HOME PRICES Median home price levels fall half way between those homes priced above and those priced below. This differs from an average home price, which is derived by dividing the number

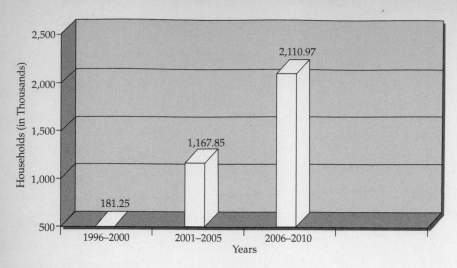

Figure 5.4   Multifamily household formations. *Source:* The Center for Real Estate Studies.

of homes by their total value. An average home price can be easily distorted by extreme values.

> *Sources:*   The National Association of Realtors Library, 430 North Michigan Avenue, Chicago, IL 60611, (312) 329-8200, or Federal Housing Finance Board, 1777 F Street N.W., Washington, DC 20006, (202) 408-2967.
> *Forecast:*   If not available from local sources, base forecast on historical cycles.

VACANCY FACTORS   The goal of this analysis is to project changes in vacancy rates. When vacancy rates increase or decrease substantially in any one year as compared to their historical pattern, it is an indication to either buy or sell (Figure 5.5).

> *Sources:*   Universities and local real estate firms may have data. Department of Commerce, Bureau of the Census, Housing and Household Economic Statistics Division, Washington, DC 20233, (301) 763-8165.
> *Forecast:*   Provided by the analysis.

RENTAL RATES   The final goal of this analysis is to use historical rental rates to project future rents. These rates can then be used to calculate the conservative internal rate of return (IRR).

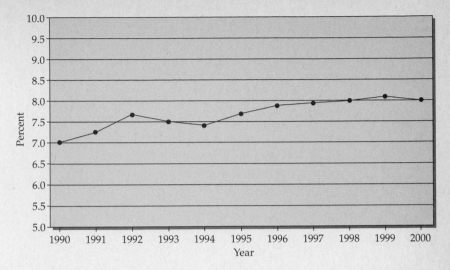

Figure 5.5   Rental housing vacancy. *Source:* The Center for Real Estate Studies.

Source: The American Chamber of Commerce Research Association (703-998-4172) gives the cost-of-living index (rental factor) for various cities.

Forecast: Provided by the analysis.

These seven factors, used in correlation with the least-squares method of projection, give you the ability to forecast both vacancy and rental rates. The computations are time consuming if done manually. The Center for Real Estate Studies (CRES) publishes a quarterly newsletter that projects vacancies and rental rates for many Metropolitan Statistical Areas using similar data. To further analyze local areas, we use CRES's LS STAT analysis program. It is easy to use and designed to forecast both vacancy and rental rates. For more information on the newsletter and software package, see page 226.

SUMMARY

There is no easy way to predict areas of opportunity. This chapter focused on a proven statistical methodology to do so. Correct statistics give you the edge when buying and selling apartment buildings. However, also crucial to your success are the subjective evaluations you make based on your research. The proper use of this methodology will help you determine the areas of opportunity in which to build your fortune.

6

Easy Steps to Locating Good Property

Once you've pinpointed the location, it is time to look for the right property. Where do you start the search? First, find out who's selling. The best place to look is in the classified section of the newspaper under residential income or investment properties. To locate out-of-town newspapers, look in the Yellow Pages of the telephone book under "newspapers" or "news dealers." You can find local papers listed in the *Gale Directory of Publications and Broadcast Media* in local libraries. You can also find out-of-town newspapers in the reference section of the library or on the Internet. If not available there, subscribe to the Sunday editions using the Gale Directory. The majority of real estate advertisements are published on Sunday. By reading about the community, you can begin to formulate your own views of the area.

MAKE THE LENDERS WORK FOR YOU

Contact lenders for additional leads on apartment buildings for sale. Because you are buying in areas where the local economy is currently weak, banks and S&Ls may have property they want to sell.

Lenders are in the business of lending money, not property management. Having an inventory of Real Estate Owned (REOs) ties up funds. As a matter of policy, banks and S&L's profits come primarily from lending, not managing properties.

Some financial institutions have their own real estate and business research departments. They promote community awareness and are instrumental in fostering a healthy business climate. Your questions regarding the local economy can be directed to these organizations.

USE MOTIVATION TO YOUR ADVANTAGE

Owners who advertise and actively market their property are motivated to sell. You will spend less time negotiating with a motivated seller than you would with one who's not. Some owners have egos that continually need stroking. Don't waste your time. It's far better to work with someone who really wants to sell.

THE SECRET OF WORKING WITH REAL ESTATE LICENSEES

Consider using the services of local real estate agents to help you find property. Remember what you learned in Chapter 4 about working with consultants. The secret of working with real estate licensees is to communicate your specific needs. Basically, they should be as follows:

1. Midsize apartments
2. Under 20 years of age
3. Preferably with pitched roofs
4. The correct unit mix for the area
5. Highly leveraged 10 percent down payment (or less)
6. Offering seller financing
7. Deferred mortgage payments

This should give the real estate agent enough to work with to locate the right apartment building for you.

A SAMPLE ADVERTISEMENT FOR BUYING APARTMENTS

If you still are not getting anywhere locating a building, try running a variation of the following ad in the local newspaper for six to eight weeks:

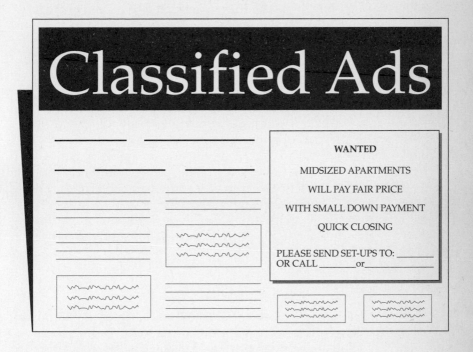

Responses will vary depending on the availability of property and seller motivation. The ad might generate calls from real estate agents wanting to establish your criteria for buying. Be cooperative. You want as many people as possible helping you locate property.

A GOOD SOURCE FOR LEADS

When looking through the classified ads, be sure to turn to the "Apartments for Rent" section. Owners offering free "giveaways" such as rent, vacations, microwave ovens, and so forth, are usually having a difficult time renting. This could be a temporary situation and, depending on what your research has uncovered, you might nab yourself a good deal.

USING ACQUISITION CARDS

Create an acquisitions follow-up file. Ads of interest should be cut out and taped to 3 × 5 index cards. File numerically, according to telephone numbers. Important names, follow-up dates, and comments should be entered on these cards. You will know if the ad changes or when the property is put back on the market simply by checking the telephone numbers. Review your comments. You may want to pursue a lead again. Using this follow-up system will save you a great deal of time and, in some cases, a great deal of embarrassment.

GETTING SELLERS TO TALK TO YOU

Once you have a list of prospective buildings, you should obtain additional information. When you request more details about the properties, you are, in effect, asking for a *set-up sheet* (Figure 6.1).

Sellers will usually ask whether or not you are a principal or a real estate agent. If you hold a real estate license, please so indicate, but let the seller know that you are buying as a principal. Sometimes sellers do not like to deal with real estate agents because they suspect the agents are just trying to get listings. Let the seller know, in no uncertain terms, that you are a qualified principal. Present yourself as a "real player."

Reading a Set-Up Sheet

The set-up sheet simply lists essential information about the property. It gives just enough facts to make a broadbrush determination as to whether or not you are going to proceed further. The standard form in Figure 6.1, or slight variations of it, is used in most states. It is comprehensive enough to do a preliminary analysis of the property.

OPENING STATEMENTS

Location.   The top lines of the set-up sheet give the address of the property. With the help of a local street map, it can be determined if the building is located in a desirable area. In picking locations within a city, try to group them by first choice, second choice, third choice, and so on. Work on the location groups according to preference. Your first choice might not yield any interesting prospects, but you will at least have a basis of comparison with properties in other neighborhoods.

MULTIPLE DWELLING UNITS—APARTMENTS

This is an attachment to a listing contract (A-14/L-11/ACI-14)—read it carefully.
CALIFORNIA ASSOCIATION OF REALTORS® STANDARD FORM

LISTING NO. _____

HAVE _____	CITY _____	NUMBER OF UNITS _____		
ADDRESS _____	CO. _____ STATE _____	LIST PRICE (LP) $ _____		
MOTIVATION _____	DP _____	RPT PRESENT LOANS $ _____		
WANT _____	CAN ADD $ _____	RPT GROSS EQUITY $ _____		

FINANCIAL ANALYSIS (Annual)

RPT. GROSS SCH INCOME (GS)	$ _____
RPT. VACANCY ALLOW _____ %	$ _____
RPT. GROSS OPER INC (GOI)	$ _____
RPT. OPERATING EXP _____ %	$ _____
RPT. NET OPER. INC. (NOI)	$ _____
LOAN PAYMENT (P & I)	$ _____
RPT. GROSS SPEND. INC. (SI)	$ _____
RESERVES (CAP. IMPROV.)	$ _____
CAP. RATE (NOI ÷ LP)	_____ %
GROSS MULTI. (LP ÷ GSI) = _____ X GROSS	

ASS'D VAL. CODE AREA _____ Yr. _____ / _____

LAND	$ _____	_____ %
IMPR.	$ _____	_____ %
PERS. PROP.	$ _____	_____ %
TOTAL	$ _____	

LEGAL DES. LOT _____ BLK. _____

SUBDIVISION _____ MAP NO. _____

(LEAVE BLANK)

Reserved for photograph—printing or writing in this space will not be reproduced. Material for this section should be identified and clipped to the back. This material should be no larger than this blank space. If the material is a map, sketch, or list it should be drawn or typed in black ink (blue will not reproduce). You may use this space for other remarks if no map or picture.

INSTRUCTIONS FOR LISTING

Complete all information requested. Listing may be withheld for clarification if incomplete.
This is an attachment to a listing contract. Read it carefully. If Sale attach A-14, if Exchange or Option attach ACI-14 and if Lease attach L-11.

ABBREVIATIONS, DEFINITIONS

DP = Down Payment	P&I = Principal and Interest
GOI = Gross Operating Income	RPT = Reported
GSI = Gross Scheduled Income	SCH = Reported or Projected by Seller
LP = Listing Price	SI = Gross Spendable Income
NOI = Net Operating Income	

No.	BRS.	BA.	Rms.	RENT PER UNIT	MONTH	RPT. OPER. EXP. ANN.	
				$	$	TAXES EST. ...NEW	$
				$	$	INS.—F & L	$
				$	$	WK. COMP.	$
				$	$	GAS & ELEC	$
				$	$	WATER/SEWER	$
				$	$	TRASH	$
				$	$	SUPPLIES	$
				$	$	ELEVATOR	$
				$	$	CABLE T.V.	$
				$	$	MAINT. _____ %	$
				$	$	PEST CONT.	$
				$	$	LICENSES	$
				$	$	GARDENER	$
			TOTAL	$		POOL	$

LOAN INFORMATION as of _____ , 19 _____

1st TD $ _____ @ $ _____ Loan No. _____ Mo. P & I @ _____ %
Due _____ Lender _____
Assumable _____ VIR/FIXED FEE _____
2nd TD $ _____ @ $ _____ Loan No _____ Mo. P & I @ _____ %
Due _____ Lender _____
Assumable _____ VIR/FIXED FEE _____
Other Terms—Remarks: _____

NO. APTS. LEASED: ____ MO. MO. ____ FURN. ____	MANAGER $ _____
OTHER INCOME $ _____	PROF. MGMT. $ _____
GARAGES NO. ____ @ $ ____ $ ____	FURN. REPL. $ _____
LAUNDRY EQUIP. OWNED $ _____	_____ $ _____
RPT. MONTHLY GROSS SCH. INC. $ _____	TOTAL $ _____

ADDITIONS, ALTERATIONS, REPAIRS YES _____ NO _____
RPT. BLDG. PERMITS AND INSP. YES _____ NO _____
PARKING _____ GARAGES NO. _____ SPACES NO. _____
CARPORTS NO. _____ PATIO _____ RECR. ROOM _____
TYPE PLUMBING _____

ZONING _____ LOT SIZE _____ X _____ NO. BLDGS. _____ AGE _____ TENANTS PAY: GAS _____ ELEC. _____ WATER _____ REFUSE _____
CONST. _____ STORIES _____ SEWER _____ HEAT _____ A/COND. _____ ELEV. _____ FLOORS _____ CARPETS NO. _____ DRAPES NO. _____ RANGES NO. _____ REFRIGS. NO. _____
DISPOSALS _____ CIRC. H/WTR. _____ D/WASH _____ TILE: _____ KITCHEN _____ BATH _____ POOL _____ HEATED _____ SAUNA _____ ALLEY _____ PAVED _____

TO SHOW CONTACT: LISTING OFFICE _____ OWNER _____ OTHER _____ PHONE (_____) _____
PROP. ZIP CODE _____ COMMISSION TO COOP. OFFICE % _____ / $ _____

BROKER _____ ADD. _____ CITY _____ STATE _____
OFFICE PHONE (_____) _____ SALESMAN _____ HOME PHONE (_____) _____
All information is from sources believed reliable but is not guaranteed.
Owner certifies that the above information as to income and expenses is accurate and complete to the best of his knowledge.

OWNER _____ OWNER _____
This listing expires _____ DATE _____

FORM ISMD-11

Figure 6.1 Multiple dwelling units/apartment set-up sheet.

Have and Want.   You can ascertain the seller's plans by reading the "have" and "want" parts of this section. The seller can indicate whether the units are old or new, fixer-uppers or garden type, governmental or nongovernmental assisted. You should be looking for newer garden-type, nongovernmental-assisted rental units. Make this your first choice. Other choices should be combinations of the above. Your last choice should be governmental-assisted programs.

Motivation.   Motivation and wants go hand in hand. The seller might be motivated because business capital is wanted; therefore, the seller needs to be "cashed out." It would be very difficult for this seller to assist in the financing. If the motivation is to reduce taxes, seller financing or a trade might be attractive. Structuring the transaction to fulfill the seller's needs might be the deciding factor to your getting the deal. Understanding motivations and wants will help you formulate the best deal for all parties.

Gross Equity.   The listing price less existing loans represents the seller's gross equity. Knowing this will help you structure the offer. If the seller has a considerable amount of equity, you might be requested to obtain new financing to get more cash for the seller. If the seller doesn't need cash, she or he may be willing to carry paper (loans) and not disturb the existing financing.

Ideally, existing loans with low interest rates should be retained, and a low interest note that accrues should be created for the remaining equity. Sellers who are willing to finance the purchase in this way can do so through the use of a wraparound loan. It can be an excellent method of financing for both the buyer and seller. Sellers get a secure monthly annuity, and buyers are able to use leverage and receive cash flow. Both obtain significant tax savings.

MAKING SURE THE DOLLARS MAKE SENSE   The financial analysis section of the set-up sheet shows the figures that will determine whether or not the dollars make sense. At all times, work with actual figures, not projections or estimates. Some set-ups show projected income and expenses to paint a rosy picture. Make your own projections based on your independent research, not anyone else's.

At this point, you may want to compare the financial information on the set-up sheets with those published by the Institute of Real Estate Managers (IREM), or you may want to confer with your consultant. IREM publishes a detailed annual breakdown of operating income and expenses of apartment buildings by square footage. Information is cross-referenced by:

Furnished units
Building age
Unfurnished units
Building size

This data includes the United States and Canada, and represents information received on over 9,000 buildings. Details on how to analyze these figures will be presented later. Your main objective now is a quick review to determine if you want to write the offer. Don't spend too much time at this point. Wait until the property is under contract.

Capitalization Rate.   This section contains one of the most important figures you will ever use in evaluating apartments. It is called the capitalization rate (*cap rate*). It is calculated by dividing the net operating income by the listing price. The lower the rate, the higher the selling price. Conversely, the higher the rate, the lower the selling price.
    To figure the selling price using the cap rate method of evaluation, apply this formula:

$$\text{Selling price} = \frac{\text{Net operating income}}{\text{Cap rate}}$$

For example, if the net operating income is $100,000 and the cap rate is 10 percent, the selling price would be $1,000,000 ($100,000 ÷ 10%). Lowering the cap rate to 8 percent increases the selling price to $1,250,000 ($100,000 ÷ 8%). Raising it to 12 percent reduces the selling price to $833,333 ($100,000 ÷ 12%).

Gross Rental Multiplier.   The gross rental multiplier (GRM) or gross times factor computation is also shown in this section of the set-up sheet. It is calculated by dividing the listing price by the gross scheduled income. It is a simple, quick, rule-of-thumb approach to evaluating property.
    In order to make a fast evaluation of the selling price, multiply the GRM by the gross income generated by the property. Use the formula below to calculate selling price:

$$\text{Selling price} = \text{GRM} \times \text{Gross income}$$

If the property generates a gross income (includes all income—rents, laundry rooms, and so forth) of $100,000 per year and the GRM is 9, then the selling price would be $900,000 ($100,000 × 9). By lowering the GRM, you also lower the selling price. For example, if the GRM is 7.5, the selling price would be $750,000 ($100,000 × 7.5). As a rule of thumb, stay away from properties with a GRM higher than 7.5 unless you can be convinced you got a real good deal.

Since income items included in gross scheduled rents are not standardized on all set-ups, we prefer using the cap rate to make out preliminary evaluations.

Assessed Valuation.   Based on the property tax records, approximate values for land and improvements (the building) can be calculated. There is a correlation between assessed value and market value. Knowing what it is will give you an indication of the value of the property. Your consultant or the property tax assessor should be able to assist you further.

For depreciation of improvements, the Internal Revenue Service (IRS) applies the same ratio of land to building as shown on the property tax bill. Have a qualified appraiser value the improvements, also. The IRS will accept such an appraisal. If it comes in higher, you will be able to deduct more for depreciation, giving you a greater tax savings.

Legal Description.   This section contains a legal description of the property. When obtaining a preliminary title report, knowing the legal description will help the title company in the title search. It's vital to know the exact location of the property and who the recorded owners are when negotiating.

Make your offer directly to the owner unless you are certain the owner is being legally represented by an agent. Agents sometimes purport to represent sellers when, in fact, they don't. This is done so that they can get in on the deal hoping to make a commission. Remember, you have more flexibility on price when commissions don't have to be paid.

Title reports give the legal location of a building. A set-up might show that the property is located in one city, but the title report shows another location. The title report has a higher degree of accuracy. Why is this critical? If a property is located in the "wrong" city, even if it's just across the street, market values can change drastically. The preliminary title report lets you know the legal location of the property.

It will also reveal other items affecting the title, such as mortgages, mechanic liens, judgments, and restrictions. Knowing what's on the title has a bearing on how you write the offer. If you've established a good relationship with a title company, preliminary title reports can be obtained free of charge.

MAXIMIZING GROSS RENTAL INCOME

Schedule of Income. Rental income plays an important role in evaluating apartment complexes. You should know what the going rents are in areas under consideration. Your property manager will be able to help you determine this.

When analyzing locations with a high percent of families, the unit mix should show more three-bedroom units and fewer single units. The opposite applies to senior citizens. Knowing the household size will dictate the most desirable unit mix.

If children are in the complex, it should be close to schools, parks, and day care centers. Adult complexes rent better close to shopping, recreation, and services. Senior citizens prefer living near medical services, community centers, and bus lines.

A building on a main street has more visibility than one set back or on a dead-end street. The more visible it is, the easier it is to rent.

Apartments in good neighborhoods close to shopping centers, employment, and churches command higher rents. The further outside these neighborhoods, the lower the rents. Properties located in areas where there is little or no room for development, such as shorelines or hillsides with views, also tend to command higher rents.

Rent per square foot is a good method of evaluating properties. Set-ups showing rent per square foot can be compared for credibility using IREM's figures. Square foot rents are generally higher for newer and smaller units.

Rents for furnished units will be higher than unfurnished. When calculating the market value of an apartment, discount rents attributable to furnished units. Income generated by the furnishings can be determined by comparing differences in rents between furnished and unfurnished apartments or by contacting a furniture rental company.

Depending on location, it may be necessary to furnish units just in order to rent them. However, remember that there are fewer managerial problems renting unfurnished units than there are renting furnished ones. Furnished units historically have higher turnover rates. Higher turnovers equate to higher maintenance costs.

The GRM method will produce a higher valuation for furnished apartment buildings than for unfurnished ones if the rental value of the furniture is included in gross income. Be aware of this.

HANDLING OTHER INCOME   There are two theories on classifying other income for valuation purposes:

1. The apartment should be valued based on unit rents only.
2. All income regardless of its nature should be used.

When computing the cap rate, net operating income is used. The entire apartment complex generates both income and expenses; therefore, including all income will not distort the computation. If the GRM method is used, only include income attributable to rental units. Other items of income, such as laundry revenues, interest income, or garage income, are not directly related to a unit itself and will distort comparisons.

Apartment Operating Expenses.   The set-up should show only actual figures; no projections.

When you purchase an apartment building, a change of ownership is recorded, which sometimes triggers a reassessment of property values that, in turn, affects property taxes. Don't forget to estimate what these new taxes will be when calculating operating expenses.

Preferably, tenants should pay all utilities. Avoid master metered buildings. Due to the problems associated with the energy crisis, utility bills are, and will continue to be, a constant managerial headache. Newer buildings are usually constructed with this in mind. Older buildings were often not. Consider having metering devices installed in master metered buildings to allocate utility costs to tenants.

Always include a charge for management expense, even if it's not shown in the set-up.

Loan Information.   This section contains several areas to help evaluate the property. Knowledge of the existing loans will help determine how you structure the offer. If the underlying loans can be left in place and the terms are acceptable, consider either assuming the existing loans or taking them subject to. Have your consultant calculate what the new monthly mortgage payments will be. It's important to know for cash flow projections purposes.

The less cash paid on the mortgage means the more available for operations. Your goal is to get the highest interest deduction allowable with the least amount of cash outlay. This can be accomplished with the cooperation of the seller. Have the seller carryback secondary financing and accruing as much interest as possible. Then, arrange to have accrued interest paid at a later date after rental income has increased.

Under the subheading "Other Terms . . . Remarks," sellers can indicate their interest in taking stocks or bonds, other property, or professional services as part of the down payment. Agents use this section to disclose any special features. It should be noted that upscale locations require more amenities to attract tenants, such as garages, recreation rooms, weight lifting facilities, saunas, extensive landscaping, and others.

Additional Information.   A picture is worth a thousand words when referring to apartment buildings. Some set-ups include pictures. If they don't, this section will help you at least paint a mental picture of the project. Spaces marked with an "X" indicate a yes answer.

Generally, the newer the building the more desirable and the fewer maintenance problems. Like anything else, however, it all depends on how well the building was maintained. As a rule, try to buy buildings under 20 years of age.

The type of construction affects the operating expenses of the building. Brick has fewer maintenance problems than stucco, stucco fewer problems than wood, stairs fewer problems than elevators, blinds fewer than drapes, pitched roofs fewer than flat, and so forth. Your local consultant will be able to advise you on how climatic conditions affect various types of constructions.

The more landscaped grounds available, the more desirable to the tenant—the more easily rented, and the more expensive to maintain. Knowing the size of the lot(s) and the number of buildings will help you evaluate the open space in terms of landscaping costs.

More amenities mean more maintenance but fewer vacancies. One always has to be weighed against the other when analyzing the bottom line. Favor the buildings with amenities. The more desirable a project is, the fewer tenant problems.

Broker Information.   The bottom section of the set-up sheet tells who to contact regarding the property. If you're being represented by an agent, your agent should work directly with the listing agent. The fewer agents involved in the transaction, the fewer the problems regarding commission splits. I've seen agents lose a deal, rather than agree to a commission split. Not only did they lose, but the buyers and sellers lost as well. Fewer is better!

SUMMARY

In this chapter, you've learned how to read a set-up sheet that is designed to give you the highlights of a property. Your initial review should be broadbrush. You want to look at as many set-ups as possible. Don't spend too much time on any one. You're only trying to decide whether or not you want to make an offer. Even in a down market, good properties tend to move quickly. If you're spending countless hours analyzing set-up sheets before you make an offer, you might lose a profitable opportunity. Remember, if you look too long, you'll never leap! How you make that leap is covered in the next chapter.

7

Writing an Offer That Will Be Accepted

After you've looked at several set-ups and have established a priority system, you should make contacts regarding the property—preferably with the owner. If the contact is an agent, find out who will make the final decisions. Here are four questions to ask prior to writing the offer that firmly establishes your parameters for buying:

1. Will the seller allow me to buy the property either subject to or to assume the existing loan(s)?
2. Can I pay 10 percent (or less) as a down payment?
3. Will the seller take back paper (assist in the financing) and accrue monthly payments?
4. Can I make the offer based on a favorable capitalization rate of 8.5 percent or more?

If the answer is yes to most of these questions, prepare an offer immediately. If the answer is no, thank the seller for the time, and leave your telephone number in case the situation changes and the seller changes his or her mind.

Don't be discouraged if you get all negative answers. Remember that you're buying in a down market—make some slight modification in either the price and/or terms based on responses, and submit an offer. Desperate sellers won't always let you know how anxious they are to sell; however, they might respond to a written offer.

When talking with sellers, it's possible to ascertain their degree of motivation. Knowing how "hot" or "cold" they are helps establish a starting point in your negotiations.

WHEN TO USE THE 80 PERCENT RULE

Try to get the seller to reveal the lowest price and terms that would be acceptable before making your offer. If the price fits within your parameters, submit the offer at that price. If not, start at 80 percent of the listing price (the price shown on the set-up sheet).

Your acquisition plan is to use as much leverage as possible. Try not to purchase a property with more than 10 percent down. We prefer paying slightly more for an apartment complex rather than increasing the down payment. Make the price flexible; not the terms. The number of properties and active buyers in the market should determine whether or not you perform a perfunctory or detailed analysis of the apartment complex. Few properties and many buyers won't allow much time for research and a detailed property analysis. If the conditions dictate, make the offer as quickly as possible using the 80 percent rule. If you have more time, prepare a more detailed analysis.

GETTING THE SELLER'S ATTENTION

When talking with sellers, let them know you've researched their property. If convenient, either you or your consultant should do a drive by (look at the property) before making contact. Sellers don't like to receive offers from buyers who haven't at least seen their property. They feel that you're wasting everyone's time just "throwing out" offers.

Use a Written Offer

Why do you write an offer in the first place? Why not go directly into escrow? Buyers write offers to make sellers aware of their intentions. It's as simple as that. If the seller's expectations are the same as the buyer's, they have a legally enforceable contract. Right? Wrong! Only when both parties agree in writing does a legally binding contract exist.

Never forget that. There are some exceptions, but if you stick to this rule, you will eliminate a lot of grief.

You want a written contract because people change their minds. It's expensive to make a conscientious effort to perform a *due diligence* (discovering everything you possibly can about a property), and then find out that the seller has different thoughts. When properly written, the offer to purchase will prevent this. Any changes can only be made with the mutual consent of all the parties.

While under contract, the seller is prevented from selling the property to someone else. The contract gives you certain enforceable rights in the property.

A PURCHASE OFFER DESIGNED FOR SUCCESS

Figure 7.1 is a sample offer. Note its conciseness. It is not a legal-size, eight-page, small-print, initial-here document to scare away sellers, or to send them running to their attorney. Professional investors like the format. Its easy in understanding and straightforward approach account for the favorable acceptance it has received.

When making an offer, we send a package that contains our financial statement, track record, covering letter, and the deposit check. We include as much information as possible on our financial capabilities so as to establish creditability.

Key components of the offer are:

Date: The date establishes the beginning of the acceptance period. Acceptances received after the expiration period can either be accepted or rejected by either party. However, if the offers/counteroffers are accepted within the allowable time frame, a legally binding contract is created.

Address: Using the street address at this point is acceptable. Later you will want to verify the legal description by reviewing the preliminary title report.

Property: Use the name of the complex for further identification. List the number of units (by bedrooms and baths) as shown on the set-up sheets. It puts the seller on notice that you're relying on that information. Be aware of the neighborhood. Large concentrations of families require more bedrooms per rental unit than singles.

It's important to have the right unit mix to keep vacancies low. However, don't keep them too low at the expense of aggressive rent raises. Always try to be the rent leader rather than a follower. The ultimate value of the building depends on ambitious rent raises.

Date

OFFER TO PURCHASE

ADDRESS: (as shown on set-up sheet)
PROPERTY: (name of complex)
                               (number of apartments according to bedrooms and baths)
PURCHASE PRICE: (80 percent of asking price or lower)
DOWN PAYMENT: (10 percent of purchase price or lower)
DEPOSIT: (1 percent of purchase price)
FINANCING: Buyer to purchase subject to the existing financing. Seller to take back equity in the form of an assumable mortgage at _____ percent interest. First 24 months interest to accrue; next 24 months, pay _____ percent, accrue _____ percent; the remaining 36 months pay _____ percent. Principal and accrued simple interest due at maturity.

THIS OFFER TO PURCHASE IS SUBJECT
TO THE FOLLOWING CONTINGENCIES:

1. Approval of title report, books and records, physical inspection reports, and loan documents, or any other information requested by buyer within 10 (ten) working days from the receipt of same.

2. Seller shall furnish a report from a licensed pest control operator showing property to be free and clear of any visible infestation from termites, dry rot, and fungi. Escrow holder is instructed to pay for said report and/or work completed (including all direct and indirect costs resulting from tenting) from funds due Seller at close of escrow.

3. Buyer's rights hereunder may be assigned to a partnership, corporation, or other party, and any such transfers shall have all the benefits including rights of specific performance, damages, and enforcement of warranties, that Buyer has under this agreement.

4. Buyer to have final approval of any rental agreements, service contracts, and/or leases during escrow period.

5. Seller to deliver marketable title and warrants at closing that, to the best of the Seller's knowledge, no part of the property is in violation of any existing codes, health or safety regulations, and is not involved in any governmental or judicial proceedings.

6. Buyer has the right to extend the date for closing of escrow by releasing the Seller through escrow an amount equal to one-quarter of one percent of the purchase price for each 30 day extension requested, to be applicable to the purchase price, with Buyer to maintain at all times the current deposit, as set out in this Agreement, in escrow.

Figure 7.1   Sample purchase offer.

7. Seller warrants that at the close of escrow all plumbing, heating, cooling, electrical, appliance, and mechanical apparatus to be in working order, and roof(s) to be in proper repair and free from leaks.

8. Seller is not aware of any structural defects or adverse geological and/or environmental conditions affecting the property.

9. Evidence of title is to be in the form of an owner's ALTA (American Land Title Association) policy of title insurance.

10. The undersigned agree that any unresolved disputes will be submitted to either the American Arbitration Association or the Judicial Arbitration and Mediation Service for binding arbitration.

FOR SELLERS: It is understood that Buyer is purchasing and Seller is selling subject complex at a minimum scheduled gross income of $_____ per year (or greater), as if the complex were 100 percent occupied.

ESCROW PERIOD: 60 days or sooner by mutual consent. Escrow to open without any contingencies.

COMMISSION: Buyer is a licensed Real Estate Broker. This offer includes a _____ percent commission to _____ Realty Co.

This constitutes an offer to purchase the described property. Unless acceptance is signed by the Seller and delivered in person or by mail to the address below within 10 (ten) working days, this offer shall be deemed revoked. Buyer acknowledges receipt of a copy hereof:

SELLER:_____   _____   BUYER: _____   _____
            date   date

Figure 7.1 *Continued*

Purchase price: As a rule of thumb, the price should not go below a 8.5 cap rate. Since it may or may not be the final purchase price, it's best to start at about 80 percent of the asking price. Always leave room for further negotiations.

Down payment: Keep the down payment as low as possible. Notice I didn't say "cash" down payment. There are assets other than cash that can be used as a down payment. (Refer to Chapter 9 on negotiations for additional sources.) Remember, the more cash invested in a project, the more it has to appreciate to maintain the same rate of return. Consider using a part or all of the down payment for repairs rather than toward the selling price. It'll give you more leverage and provide the seller with additional security if he assists in the financing.

Deposit: Send a deposit check of approximately 1 percent of the offer price with your offering package. On the back of the check write, "Not to be deposited until all parties have signed escrow instructions." This will prevent your check from being deposited before contingencies have been removed. Deposits placed in escrow usually get eaten up with fees for a myriad of trivial matters. You can be assured that this will happen, even if the deal doesn't go through. The deposit check must remain uncashed until escrow instructions have been signed and contingencies have been removed.

Financing: The financing package shown in the sample offer to purchase provides adequate leverage and monthly mortgage payments designed to create cash flow plus the maximum tax savings. Sellers may not want to leave the existing mortgages in place. Make the initial proposal anyway, especially if existing rates are below market. You won't know what the seller will accept unless you try.

It's difficult to get financing in a weak economy. Try to keep the existing loans. Additional costs associated with getting new financing such as points, appraisal fees, and escrow charges are expensive. Be absolutely certain, however, that the existing financing is less expensive. The mortgage markets can be volatile. To save money, it's to your advantage to keep abreast.

By leaving existing financing in place, the loan qualification process is eliminated, saving you additional time and expense. Also, you will gain control of more property by not having to pledge your assets as security for obtaining new loans.

Never forget this basic rule: Use as little cash as possible to control as much property as possible whenever possible. Try to get the seller to accrue as much of the monthly payments as you can. When accruing all or a portion of the monthly mortgage payment, current cash requirements are reduced. Based on the sample offer, interest is scheduled to be paid when rents are projected to increase.

Have the seller take back the note for a minimum of two years past the date you either plan to sell or refinance the property. This gives you breathing room. Also notice in the sample offer that the seller is asked to take back an assumable loan. If the property is sold before the note comes due, the new buyer won't have any problems with the assumption. It can be assumed without qualification or paying nay additional costs. This important clause makes your property more marketable when it comes time to sell.

Remember, more cash equates to less leverage. Less leverage results in fewer assets under your control. Fewer assets reduce your potential profits.

Item 1. If the property doesn't pass your inspection, this provision gives you the opportunity to cancel the contract. It's sometimes referred to as the escape clause and details contingencies:

- *Title report:* You need to approve the title report. It is best to have your attorney review it. Your attorney should be able to tell you if there is anything that would adversely affect the property. He or she must be able to comment on each item in the report and how it affects your transaction. Make sure you get the attorney's interpretations and recommendations in writing.
- *Books and records:* Have your accountant examine the books and records for at least a minimum of three years. Five years is preferable. The accountant should be able to report, in writing, on the income and expense trends and to compute ratios. Records must reflect actual figures not estimates. All figures should be compared to actual tax returns, and any differences must be explained. Also, make a comparison with those published by local property management organizations and/or the Institute of Real Estate Management (IREM) for credibility.
- *Physical inspections:* Physical inspections must be done by qualified consultants (see Chapter 4). To assure that tenants are properly notified of all inspections, work with your property manager. Insist that all inspection reports be in writing and include data on local climatic conditions affecting the property. Every unit must be inspected. Do not, under any circumstances, exclude a single unit. It will come back to haunt you. Estimates of repair and/or replacement costs must be included in the report. Roof(s), plumbing, mechanical, and electrical have to be inspected. Repair costs should be itemized separately from replacement costs. The "written report" is essential when negotiating and preparing budgets.

  Try to obtain copies of earlier inspection reports from the seller. They can save you time and money and will prove invaluable in disclosing any problem areas. If there have been previous roof inspections, it could mean they are in bad shape. These reports, compared to your own, will give you a clear understanding of the condition of the building.
- *Loan documents:* Loan documents should be read by an attorney. You must determining the following:

Is there a due-on-sale clause (can the loan be called up if the property is transferred)?

Are there any balloon payments? When?

What will the monthly payments be over the life of the loan? (An accountant can give you this information, also.)

Do these payments change? When?

Are there any restrictions in transferring the loan?

Do the terms comply with local lending laws?

It's difficult to read and interpret lengthy loan documents yourself. It is best to have your real estate attorney do it and supply you with a written report. This report becomes your safeguard if disputes arise later.

Item 2.   All inspection reports should be approved in writing within 10 days of receipt thereof. Written approval or rejection should be sent to the escrow company and a signed receipt of delivery should be obtained. The seller is responsible for getting the information to you as quickly as possible. If you don't receive it on time, contact the seller. Remember that in a down market, time is on your side. The seller does not benefit from delays. However, both parties should be cooperative. Be careful dealing with partnerships. Managing general partners may want you to remove all contingencies before getting the limited partners' approval to sell. Don't do it under any circumstances! You're leaving the door open for the seller to back out of the deal.

The seller must pay for this report and any work to be done if the report from a licensed pest control operator provision is accepted. If the property has to be tented and accommodations have to be made for the tenants, it is the seller's responsibility to pay.

The termite provision is especially important when applying for new loans or assuming existing ones. Lenders do not like to lend unless the building has a clean bill of health from a qualified termite company.

Item 3.   When forming a group to purchase property, this provision allows you to transfer your position in the contract to other entities. It also gives you a simple way to determine the current market value of the apartment complex. Here's how it works. While under contract, advertise the property for sale. Place your advertisement in a newspaper with a large circulation (*Wall Street Journal*) on the day that real estate advertisements are run. The amount and kind of activity generated is an indication of demand, hence value.

The advertisement may generate offers to buy. If you decide to sell your position in the contract, this proviso gives you that right. Many fortunes have been made using this technique without risking a dime.

You may also want to sell because a more desirable property is now available. With this assignment provision it can be done. Having the flexibility to transfer ownership interests increases the likelihood of success.

If you locate a buyer for the property while under contract and, as a real estate licensee, you want to limit your involvement, simply introduce the buyer to the seller, using the sample agreement of introduction (Figure 7.2).

AGREEMENT OF INTRODUCTION

I hereby employ you as a Broker for the period beginning _____, and ending at midnight on _____, called the listing period for the purchase of a certain real property described as follows:

_____
(Property address)

Broker's only obligation under this agreement is to introduce me to the Seller and I shall be solely responsible for all due diligence and for negotiating the price and terms for purchase of the property.

I agree to pay Broker as a commission _____ percent of the selling price, if, during the listing period or any extension of it, I or any affiliate purchases the property, or if I, in a capacity as broker, procure a Buyer on any terms acceptable to Seller. The commission shall be payable on the close of escrow or on failure to close if failure is due to my default or lack of good faith.

If I have not entered into a contract to purchase the property within _____ days from the execution of this agreement, Broker shall be allowed to market the property to others without terminating my obligation to pay Broker a commission pursuant to this agreement.

If, within _____ days after the termination of the listing period or any extension of it, I or an affiliate acquire the property or I procure a Buyer for the property, Broker shall be entitled to a commission in the amount and on terms specified in this agreement.

_____   _____
Buyer   Date

_____   _____
Broker   Date

Figure 7.2 Sample agreement of introduction letter.

Concurrently, send the sample letter (Figure 7.3) to the seller having the seller acknowledge and consent to your acting as an agent for the new buyer.

Item 4.   During the escrow period, it's important to maintain as much control over operations as possible. A seller could make long-term commitments to either tenants or vendors that might adversely affect your investment. This provision will prevent it from occurring.

With the cooperation of the seller, tenant/owner personality conflicts can be reduced by having the seller implement rent increases before escrow closes. Tenants will probably be more receptive to having the existing owner institute increases than you. Negatives associated with such a move should be avoided whenever possible.

Date

Dear Seller:

RE: Notice of agency and commission

This letter will confirm that I called you and disclosed that I had entered into a contract with (*buyer*) to act as their agent in the purchase of your property located at (*location*). As you know, I am a licensed real estate agent. By this letter it is my intention to put you on notice that:

1. I shall act solely as the buyer's agent.
2. I will receive a commission from the buyer if this transaction is consummated.

Please sign the acknowledgment below and return a copy to me for my files. If you do, in fact, object, please so state in writing within 5 days.
I look forward to working with you in the future.

Sincerely,

Broker

I hereby acknowledge and consent to (*broker*) acting in the proposed transaction solely as agent and broker for (*buyer*). I further agree that (*broker*) may receive a real estate commission from the buyer and that I will have no such financial obligation.

_____   _____
Seller   Date

Figure 7.3   Sample letter of acceptance.

Item 5. The purpose of this provision is to make sure the seller has the authority to transfer title. It could be that the seller doesn't, and you will want to know immediately. The seller may need approval from a trustee, partners, or an attorney. To avoid spinning your wheels, be sure you're working with the person(s) who can legally sign all documents.

Governmental and judicial agencies can cloud title. This provision puts the seller on notice that any pending complications are to be disclosed. A preliminary title report might now show these potential snags. Having the seller's warrant will help if disputes arise. In areas where there are high ratios of renters to owners, local governments might be considering rent controls. If there is anything brewing, you must be made aware of them before escrow closes.

Item 6. This provision allows you to extend the escrow closing period by depositing additional funds in escrow. Sometimes totally unexpected things can come up that delay a closing. If escrow cannot close on a specific day, this clause gives you the ability to extend it.

Theoretically, with this provision you can literally keep making these deposits of principal and extend the closing until the apartment building is paid in full.

Item 7. It's important to have express warranties. They are guarantees, specific as to the contract. Express warranties can extend the time of implied warranties. They can provide protection in areas not normally covered by implied warranties such as the quality of the work done and the life of certain fixtures. In addition, express warranties can include remedies for losses not normally found in implied warranties.

What are implied warranties? Implied warranties are those for which the law will hold the builder or seller accountable even though no promises are written in the contract. Implied warranties must be honored since they can seldom be limited or eliminated in a contract.

There are three implied warranties in real estate:

1. The property purchased is constructed in good and skillful manner.
2. The property is habitable.
3. The property will be reasonably fit for the intended purpose.

Implied warranties are subjective and can be interpreted loosely. The more specific the warranty the more enforceable it becomes.

Item 8.   The purpose of this provision is to make the warranty more specific. Potential problems usually don't appear in title reports. It is best to protect yourself in case something comes up later. For example, adverse soil conditions, flood control areas, or a toxic waste dump can put a damper on any improvements or additions to your apartment complex. This provision puts the seller on notice that any and all knowledge possessed in this area must be disclosed.

Item 9.   Coverage under the American Land Title Association (ALTA) policy is designed to protect the buyer. It covers legal fees for defending title and defects in the title prior to purchase. In some areas, you can obtain additional insurance for easements and items not shown on the title report.

Title company sales representatives are very helpful in answering questions regarding title insurance. They also aid in obtaining preliminary title reports and property profiles (ownership and legal data) on various properties for you. The service that they provide gives them an opportunity to generate goodwill, and hopefully, you will purchase title insurance from their company.

Item 10.   The benefits of arbitration far exceed those of litigation. This provision nails down the procedure for resolving disputes. A judge once told me, "The most equitable resolution of any disagreement occurs when both parties walk away unhappy!"

> *For sellers:* This statement lets the seller know that your computations are based on the seller's gross income figures. Gross income is a very important component in determining selling price. Making the seller aware of it, up front, will help in negotiations if gross income cannot be substantiated.
>
> *Escrow period:* The escrow opening date should be tied to the removal of contingencies. For example, if escrow is to open after all contingencies have been removed, don't open sooner. Sellers usually want the escrow to open immediately. This provision in the sample offer gives them that additional motivation to get all the paperwork in on time. Don't forget, opening escrow without contingencies is less cumbersome and costly. Prematurely opening escrow frequently results in numerous changes. Don't cause extra headaches and expense by rushing into escrow. Keep it simple.
>
> *Commission:* Real estate licensees may only want to receive their commissions in cash. However, if the buyer's cash is limited, it may be a

good idea to take your commissions in paper (a note) to make the deal work.

If you're a real estate agent and you're buying the property, consider reducing both the price and down payment in lieu of commissions. You can save money on your taxes by not having to report any income.

If commissions have to be paid, reducing the down payment and selling price accordingly, guarantees the buyer will be paying less. Remember, the savings on commissions should benefit both parties. Whether you agree to split the savings on commissions or not, always look to the internal rate of return, irrespective of commissions, when making investment decisions.

Closing paragraph: Don't give the seller too much time to think about your offer. A time limit of approximately 10 working days from the date of the offer should be sufficient. Technically, without it a response could be made at any time and still be valid. Legally, if a response is not made in the time allotted, a binding contract does not exist. However, if the seller answers after the deadline and you accept the counteroffer within the allotted response time, the contract then becomes binding.

Make Sure Your Contract Is Legally Binding

To be assured that a legally binding contract is in effect, proper procedures must be followed. Documents must be signed and delivered on a timely basis to the right parties. Timely delivery is very important. Without it you do not have an enforceable contract. To be assured that delivery is made on time, a signed receipt of delivery is recommended.

A SUREFIRE COVERING LETTER When sending an offer to purchase, accompany it with the sample letter (Figure 7.4) and a check for approximately 1 percent of the offer price. Also include the following information:

1. Your financial and business qualifications
2. Your after-tax internal rate of return requirements (don't disclose what it is)
3. Your knowledge of current market values
4. Financing package limitations

Your address

Date

Dear (seller or agent):

RE: (property address)
    Enclosed please find our offer to purchase, our track record (*or your financial statements*), and deposit check.
    After completing an analysis and drive-by inspection, we believe the enclosed price and terms are reflective of current market values in the area.
    Based on our after-tax internal rate of return requirement, we are limited to the proposed financing package.
    We would appreciate hearing from you as soon as possible due to our relatively short time frame. If you have any questions, please call.

Sincerely yours,

(Your name)

Figure 7.4   Sample offer letter.

Time is of the essence in getting a counteroffer. The seller cannot sit on your offer waiting for others so that one can be played off the other. Let the seller know you're making offers on other properties.

WHEN DEALING WITH SELLERS, ONLY GO AROUND ONCE

Depending on *very* unusual circumstance, always make it a rule never to write a second offer on the same property without first receiving a written counteroffer. Sellers will say, "I can't accept your offer, it's too low. Why don't you just write another one." Your reply should be, "Since I spent a good deal of time and money submitting this offer, I would appreciate the professional courtesy of having you write a counteroffer." If the seller refuses, go on to the next deal. It has been our experience that the few times we've submitted a second offer without first receiving a written counteroffer, we never heard from the seller again.

If the seller counters and it is not acceptable, try some preliminary negotiations, based on the following market conditions:

Weak Buyers Market

If there are a number of buyers bottom fishing, quickly submit an offer that will tie up the property. Initiate further negotiations, if necessary, after completing all inspections.

Strong Buyers Market

Time is on your side. Wait until the seller calls before making your next move. If the seller doesn't call, wait and make contact again in about three weeks. Maybe the seller will be more receptive to negotiating then.

We have purchased property where offers and counteroffers have flown back and forth at least a dozen times. You'll discover that in down or weak markets time is really on the buyer's side. Never be overly anxious to accommodate the seller's time schedule.

A UNIQUE ACCEPTANCE LETTER THAT EFFECTIVELY TIES UP PROPERTY

When an acceptable offer is received, call the seller to advise that you've accepted it. Immediately mail, receipt requested, an originally signed copy with an acceptance letter (Figure 7.5). Be sure the date of acceptance is within the allowable time. A late acceptance makes the contract voidable.

Critical Documents for Due Diligence

There are many critical pieces of information enumerated in the sample acceptance letter (Figure 7.5) that are needed to perform an acceptable due diligence.

Copies of tax returns tend to be less creative than in-house income and expense statements. It's always good practice to find out where the differences lie and why. For comparison, use the information on the set-up sheet to verify inspection reports, rent rolls, and financial statements.

Try to obtain information on items not covered in the title reports, such as lawsuits, pending rent control ordinances, governmental-assisted rent programs, and so forth.

Verify the size of the units by looking at floor plans. Building inspectors can give more accurate estimates of repairs and replacement costs with a set of floor plans.

Your address

Date

CERTIFIED MAIL

Dear (seller or agent):

RE: (property address)
    Enclosed please find acceptance of the offer (or counteroffer) dated
_____.
    To proceed rapidly, please send us copies of the following information
regarding the subject property:

1. Last five (5) years year-end financial statements and tax returns
2. Title report
3. Current inspection reports
4. Current appraisals
5. Current rent roll
6. Current financial statements
7. All existing loan documents
8. Litigation (existing and pending)
9. Floor plans
10. Sales comparables
11. Demographics
12. Local business conditions
13. Interior and exterior pictures
14. Name, address, and telephone number of property manager
15. Name, address, and telephone numbers of vendors
16. Last 12-months utility bills
17. All service contracts
18. Insurance policies
19. List of all personal property
20. Current and last two years tax bill

Your cooperation in supplying this information as soon as possible will be
greatly appreciated.

Sincerely yours,

(Your name)

Figure 7.5 Sample letter of acceptance.

Whenever possible try to obtain as many photographs as you can of both the interior and exterior of the building. These will help clarify many questions, especially if you haven't seen the building.

Any information that can be provided directly by the seller will save you time and money by not having to obtain it from other sources.

SUMMARY

If I had to answer, "What is the most important thing to remember in this chapter?" I would say, "Always get it in writing." Write as many offers as you possibly can, but don't lose credibility. If too many offers are received from you by the same person or company, your ability to perform might be questioned. Be selective and know the parties involved.

Make every attempt to get a signed counteroffer. In doing so, the property will be under your control. You will have the time you need to complete your due diligence and to negotiate further, if necessary.

The only way to get experience is to get out there and do it. You may make a few mistakes, but you'll learn in the process. The most important thing to remember is to keep trying. You'll improve each time, and you'll find yourself securely on your way to becoming financially independent.

8

Highly Effective Techniques for Analyzing Properties

Only after the property is under contract should you prepare a comprehensive analysis, as shown in this chapter. Don't waste time and money before you legally control the apartment building.

THE KEY FIGURE IN EVALUATING INVESTMENTS

The key figure is the internal rate of return (IRR) after taxes. By comparing this figure with the IRRs from other investments, you will be able to determine the best investment for you.

It is critical to understand why the IRR is important when analyzing property. The IRR shows the time value of money, and it reflects cash flows based on present values. Return on investments, in terms of purchasing power, might actually be less, depending on how the cost of living has changed. Knowing the IRR will help to further quantify your investment opportunities.

Your analysis should be based on two types of returns, *growth rate* and *replacement costs*. Growth rate projections are based on historical trends. An analysis performed using this rate will give you a conservative IRR. An aggressive IRR is obtained by projecting a future selling price based on future replacement costs. Use both when analyzing apartment buildings. Knowing both will give you an edge when negotiating.

What you should be looking for is *steep* growth. Buy apartment complexes below the cost of replacement. Sell them when values are at least equal to or greater than replacement costs. This is how to become wealthy!

A SOUND DOWN-MARKET STRATEGY

In a down market, your strategy is to buy as far below current replacement cost as possible. To determine the current replacement cost, consult local building associations or your local library for the Marshall & Swift Valuation Service (M&SVS). M&SVS provides information on the construction costs of different types of apartment buildings throughout the United States. Figures 8.1, 8.2, and 8.3 (pp. 100–105) show how costs differ based on style for three types of apartment buildings. Local square footage costs can be calculated using the conversion chart applicable to each area.

ANALYZING PROPERTY

The methods to analyze property depend on the availability of information. They are as follows:

- Qualified appraisers
- Comparable sales data or "comps"
- Gross multiplier approach
- Capitalization rate method
- Essentials of property analysis software

We prefer using a specially designed computer program in conjunction with input from consultants and comparable sales data. Since the final decision rests with us, we want to be absolutely certain of our sources.

Qualified Appraisers

Appraisers use three appraisal techniques to establish the current market value of apartments. They are the (1) cost, (2) income, and (3) market data approaches. The cost approach establishes market value based on what it would cost to replace a reasonable facsimile. The income approach is designed to calculate the market value based on the expected future income. And the market data approach uses information gathered from recent comparable sales to determine value.

The appraiser considers all three methods when making a final determination as to current market value.

Comparable Sales Data or "Comps"

In a weak market, it is difficult to use comparable sales data to determine market value. Sales figures may not be available or may be stale because properties aren't moving. Prices, under these circumstances, usually have no bearing on current market conditions. At best, comparables will give an indication of trends.

A sample of comparable sales information from the CoStar Group (Figures 8.4 through 8.8, pp. 106–120) shows how the information is presented. Local real estate boards can be of further assistance.

Gross Multiplier Approach

The gross multiplier approach is the ratio between the gross rents and the selling price. By comparing gross multiples of other properties in the same general area, a rule-of-thumb determination of market values can be made.

Capitalization Rate Method

The capitalization rate is the ratio between the net income and the selling price. This rate can also be compared to those of other buildings in the same neighborhood. Capitalization rates should be adjusted to reflect the following:

- *Liquidity:* How fast can you get your money out?
- *Risk factors:* What is the degree of safety?
- *Tax benefits:* How much money will you save on taxes and when?
- *Ability to borrow money:* Is it easy to get loans on the property?
- *Degree of management activity:* How much time do you have to put into managing your investment?
- *Expectation of appreciation:* What is the potential of this property?

We generally don't purchase apartment buildings with a capitalization rate under 8.5 percent. However, depending on the weight of these factors, we would consider a lower capitalization rate. Adverse

MULTIPLE RESIDENCES
(Pages Mul-8, Mul-9)

Figure 8.1 Multiple residences (fair quality). Reprinted by permission of Marshall & Swift.

FRAME AND STUCCO MULTIPLE COSTS: Per Building

Total Floor Area	NUMBER OF UNITS									
	3	4	8	12	16	25	40	60	80	100
2,000	$40.88	$42.61	-----	-----	-----	-----	-----	-----	-----	-----
3,000	37.91	39.15	-----	-----	-----	-----	-----	-----	-----	-----
4,000	35.88	36.75	$42.46	-----	-----	-----	-----	-----	-----	-----
5,000	35.03	35.62	39.98	$44.91	-----	-----	-----	-----	-----	-----
6,000	34.19	34.87	38.40	42.31	$46.60	-----	-----	-----	-----	-----
8,000	-----	33.96	36.52	39.27	42.24	-----	-----	-----	-----	-----
10,000	-----	33.40	35.39	37.16	39.76	$45.32	-----	-----	-----	-----
12,000	-----	-----	34.64	36.37	38.18	42.58	-----	-----	-----	-----
16,000	-----	-----	33.66	34.90	36.22	39.34	$42.09	-----	-----	-----
20,000	-----	-----	33.02	34.00	35.02	37.42	41.79	-----	-----	-----
25,000	-----	-----	-----	33.25	34.08	35.92	39.23	$44.16	-----	-----
30,000	-----	-----	-----	32.72	33.36	34.90	37.57	41.49	$45.81	-----
40,000	-----	-----	-----	-----	32.57	33.70	35.62	38.36	41.33	$44.53
50,000	-----	-----	-----	-----	-----	32.91	34.41	36.56	38.81	41.18
60,000	-----	-----	-----	-----	-----	32.35	33.59	35.32	37.12	39.04
80,000	-----	-----	-----	-----	-----	-----	32.53	33.77	35.09	36.45
100,000	-----	-----	-----	-----	-----	-----	31.82	32.80	33.81	34.87

FRAME: Plywood/Hardboard, - 1%; Siding/Shingle, + 1%; Masonry Veneer, + 9%
MASONRY: Common Brick, + 13%; Face Brick/Stone, + 16%; Concrete Block, + 3%
For senior citizens' buildings, add 8% to the basic multiple costs above.

SQUARE FOOT ADJUSTMENTS

ROOFING: (Divide by number of stories)
Comp. shingle/built-up rock		(base)
Wood shingle	+	$1.03
Wood shake	+	1.20
Composition roll	-	.63

SUBFLOOR:
Wood subfloor		(base)
Concrete slab	-	$1.83

FLOOR COVER:
Allowance (if not itemized)	+	$1.43
Carpet and pad	+	1.42
Ceramic tile	+	7.65
Resilient floor cover	+	1.49
Wood flooring	+	5.51
Parquet blocks	+	6.66
Light-weight concrete	+	.79

FLOOR INSULATION:
Mild climate	+	$ .72
Moderate climate	+	.90
Extreme climate	+	1.12
PLASTER INTERIOR:	+	$1.66

HEATING/COOLING:
Forced air		(base)
Oil-fired	+	$ .20
Floor or wall furnace	-	1.49
Electric, radiant		.13
Baseboard or panel	-	.22
Hot water, baseboard	+	1.41
Warm and cooled air	+	1.37
Heat pump, packaged	+	1.62
Individual wall units	+	.15

ENERGY ADJ: Moderate Climate (base)
Mild climate	-	$ .31
Extreme climate	+	.49

FOUNDATION ADJ: (Divide by no. of stories)
Moderate climate		(base)
Mild climate	-	$ .63
Extreme climate	+	.74
Hillside, moderate slope	+	.52
Hillside, steep slope	+	1.15

SEIMIC/HURRICANE (WIND) ADJ.:
Zone 2 range	$ .33	- $ .46
Zone 3-4/wind range	.63	- .73

LUMP SUM ADJUSTMENTS PER UNIT

PLUMBING: 5 fixtures
		(base)
Per fixture	+ or -	$520
Per rough-in	+	270

FIREPLACES:
Single, one-story	$1,250 -	$1,875
Double, two-story	2,350 -	3,500
Triple, three-story	3,200 -	4,825

BASEMENTS: For sprinklers, add $1.95/sq. ft.; for mechanical vent, add $ .67/sq. ft.

BUILT-IN APPLIANCES:
Allowance (if not itemized)	+	$975
Range and oven	+	675
Hood and fan	+	180
Dishwasher	+	525
Garbage disposer	+	190
Exhaust fan or bath heater	+	110
Radio-intercom	+	390
Wall air conditioner, ½ ton	+	600

BASEMENT TYPE	3000	6000	9000	12000	15000	18000	21000	24000
Unfinished, conc. walls	$12.31	$11.54	$11.08	$10.79	$10.53	$10.36	$10.22	$10.08
Finished basements	19.45	18.17	17.48	17.01	16.63	16.37	16.12	15.92
Parking garage*	14.74	13.79	13.26	12.88	12.60	12.37	12.20	12.04

*When concrete roof of garage is utilized as a court deck on the top side, add $9.05 per sq. ft.
Where utilized as first floor of apartments, add $4.15 per sq. ft. to basic floor cost.
BALCONIES AND STAIRWAYS: See Page Mul-18.   GARAGES AND CARPORTS: See Page Mul-19.

Figure 8.1 *Continued*

MULTIPLE RESIDENCES
(Pages Mul-10, Mul-11)

Figure 8.2   Multiple residences (average quality). Reprinted by permission of Marshall & Swift.

FRAME AND STUCCO MULTIPLE COSTS: Per Building

Total Floor Area	NUMBER OF UNITS									
	3	4	8	12	16	25	40	60	80	100
2,000	$47.16	$49.15	------	------	------	------	------	------	------	------
3,000	43.73	45.16	------	------	------	------	------	------	------	------
4,000	41.39	42.38	$48.98	------	------	------	------	------	------	------
5,000	40.41	41.08	46.11	$51.80	------	------	------	------	------	------
6,000	39.43	40.21	44.29	$48.80	$53.75	------	------	------	------	------
8,000	------	39.17	42.12	45.29	48.72	------	------	------	------	------
10,000	------	38.52	40.82	42.86	45.85	$52.27	------	------	------	------
12,000	------	------	39.95	41.95	44.03	49.11	------	------	------	------
16,000	------	------	38.83	40.26	41.78	45.38	$48.54	------	------	------
20,000	------	------	38.09	39.22	40.39	43.16	48.20	------	------	------
25,000	------	------	------	38.35	39.30	41.43	45.25	$50.93	------	------
30,000	------	------	------	37.74	38.48	40.26	43.34	47.85	$52.84	------
40,000	------	------	------	------	37.57	38.87	41.08	44.25	47.68	$51.36
50,000	------	------	------	------	------	37.96	39.69	42.17	44.77	47.50
60,000	------	------	------	------	------	37.31	38.74	40.73	42.82	45.03
80,000	------	------	------	------	------	------	37.52	38.96	40.47	42.04
100,000	------	------	------	------	------	------	36.70	37.83	39.00	40.21

FRAME: Plywood/Hardboard, - 1%; Siding/Shingle, + 1%; Masonry Veneer, + 8%
MASONRY: Common Brick, + 11%; Face Brick/Stone, + 15%; Concrete Block, + 4%
For senior citizens' buildings, add 5% to the basic multiple costs above.

SQUARE FOOT ADJUSTMENTS

ROOFING: (Divide by number of stories)
Comp. shingle/built-up rock		(base)
Wood shingle	+	$1.06
Wood shake	+	1.24
Composition roll	-	.69

SUBFLOOR:
Wood subfloor		(base)
Concrete slab	-	$2.02

FLOOR COVER:
Allowance (if not itemized)	+	$1.92
Carpet and pad	+	1.74
Ceramic tile	+	8.35
Resilient floor cover	+	1.85
Wood flooring	+	6.18
Parquet blocks	+	7.22
Light-weight concrete	+	.85

FLOOR INSULATION:
Mild climate	+	$ .72
Moderate climate	+	.90
Extreme climate	+	1.12
PLASTER INTERIOR:	+	$1.97

HEATING/COOLING:
Forced air		(base)
Oil-fired	+	$ .22
Floor or wall furnace	-	1.62
Electric, radiant	-	.14
Baseboard or panel	-	.22
Hot water, baseboard	+	1.44
Warm and cooled air	+	1.47
Heat pump, packaged	+	1.73
Individual wall units	+	.16

ENERGY ADJ.: Mod. Climate
		(base)
Mild climate	-	$ .37
Extreme climate	+	.55

FOUNDATION ADJ.: (Divide by no. of stories)
Moderate climate		(base)
Mild climate	-	$.73
Extreme climate	+	.86
Hillside, moderate slope	+	.60
Hillside, steep slope	+	1.33

SEISMIC/HURRICANE (WIND) ADJ.:
Zone 2 range	$ .33 -	$ .46
Zone 3-4/wind range	.63 -	.73

LUMP SUM ADJUSTMENTS PER UNIT

PLUMBING: 5 fixtures
		(base)
Per fixture	+ or -	$615
Per rough-in	+	300

FIREPLACES:
Single, one-story	$1,475 -	$2,200
Double, two-story	2,700 -	4,075
Triple, three-story	3,725 -	5,575

BASEMENTS: For sprinklers, add $2.10/sq. ft.; for mechanical vent, add $ .75/sq. ft.

BUILT-IN APPLIANCES:
Allowance (if not itemized)	+	$1,625
Range and oven	+	775
Hood and fan	+	230
Dishwasher	+	600
Garbage disposer	+	220
Exhaust fan or bath heater	+	130
Radio-intercom	+	440
Wall air conditioner, ¾ ton	+	775

BASEMENT TYPE	3000	6000	9000	12000	15000	18000	21000	24000
Unfinished, conc. walls	$13.33	$12.48	$11.98	$11.67	$11.41	$11.21	$11.06	$10.91
Finished basements	21.12	19.74	18.99	18.47	18.07	17.77	17.49	17.28
Parking garage*	16.03	15.00	14.42	14.01	13.71	13.47	13.27	13.11

*When concrete roof of garage is utilized as a court deck on the top side, add $9.40 per sq. ft.
Where utilized as first floor of apartments, add $4.40 per sq. ft. to basic floor cost.
BALCONIES AND STAIRWAYS: See Page Mul-18.   **GARAGES AND CARPORTS:** See Page Mul-19.

Figure 8.2 *Continued*

MULTIPLE RESIDENCES
(Pages Mul-12, Mul-13)

Figure 8.3 Multiple residences (good quality). Reprinted by permission of Marshall & Swift.

FRAME AND STUCCO MULTIPLE COSTS: Per Building

Total Floor Area	NUMBER OF UNITS									
	3	4	8	12	16	25	40	60	80	100
2,000	$61.93	$64.55	-----	-----	-----	-----	-----	-----	-----	-----
3,000	57.43	59.31	-----	-----	-----	-----	-----	-----	-----	-----
4,000	54.35	55.66	$64.32	-----	-----	-----	-----	-----	-----	-----
5,000	53.07	53.95	60.56	$68.03	-----	-----	-----	-----	-----	-----
6,000	51.79	52.81	58.17	64.10	$70.59	-----	-----	-----	-----	-----
8,000	-----	51.45	55.32	59.48	63.98	-----	-----	-----	-----	-----
10,000	-----	50.59	53.61	56.29	60.22	$68.65	-----	-----	-----	-----
12,000	-----	-----	52.47	55.09	57.83	64.49	-----	-----	-----	-----
16,000	-----	-----	50.99	52.87	54.87	59.59	$63.75	-----	-----	-----
20,000	-----	-----	50.02	51.50	53.04	56.69	63.30	-----	-----	-----
25,000	-----	-----	-----	50.36	51.62	54.41	59.42	$66.89	-----	-----
30,000	-----	-----	-----	49.57	50.54	52.87	56.92	62.84	$69.39	-----
40,000	-----	-----	-----	-----	49.34	51.05	53.95	58.11	62.61	$67.46
50,000	-----	-----	-----	-----	-----	49.85	52.13	55.38	58.80	62.39
60,000	-----	-----	-----	-----	-----	49.00	50.88	53.50	56.23	59.14
80,000	-----	-----	-----	-----	-----	-----	49.28	51.16	53.16	55.21
100,000	-----	-----	-----	-----	-----	-----	48.20	49.68	51.22	52.81

FRAME: Plywood/Hardboard, - 2%; Siding/Shingle, + 2%; Masonry Veneer, + 7%
MASONRY: Common Brick, + 9%; Face Brick/Stone, + 13%; Concrete Block, + 3%
For senior citizens' buildings, add 1% to the basic multiple costs above.

SQUARE FOOT ADJUSTMENTS

ROOFING: (Divide by number of stories)
Wood shingle		(base)
Wood shake	+	$ .19
Concrete or clay tile	+	3.48
Composition roll	-	1.95
Comp. shingle / built-up rock	-	1.12

SUBFLOOR:
Wood subfloor		(base)
Concrete slab	-	$2.46

FLOOR COVER:
Allowance (if not itemized)	+	$3.26
Carpet and pad	+	2.61
Ceramic tile	+	9.94
Resilient floor cover	+	2.85
Wood flooring	+	7.78
Parquet blocks	+	8.47
Light-weight concrete	+	.99

FLOOR INSULATION:
Mild climate	+	$ .72
Moderate climate	+	.90
Extreme climate	+	1.12
PLASTER INTERIOR:	+	$2.74

HEATING/COOLING:
Forced air		(base)
Oil-fired	+	$ .22
Floor or wall furnace	-	1.78
Electric, radiant	-	.12
Baseboard or panel	-	.25
Hot water, baseboard	+	1.46
Warm and cooled air	+	1.57
Heat pump, packaged	+	1.86
Individual wall units	+	.18

ENERGY ADJ.: Mod. Climate
		(base)
Mild climate	-	$ .46
Extreme climate	+	.63

FOUNDATION ADJ.: (Divide by no. of stories)
Moderate climate		(base)
Mild climate	-	$ .98
Extreme climate	+	1.19
Hillside, moderate slope	+	.83
Hillside, steep slope	+	1.84

SEISMIC/HURRICANE (WIND) ADJ.:
Zone 2 range	$ .33	- $ .46
Zone 3-4/wind range	.63	- .73

LUMP SUM ADJUSTMENTS PER UNIT

PLUMBING: 7 fixtures
		(base)
Per fixture	+ or -	$875
Per rough-in	+	335

FIREPLACES:
Single, one-story	$2,025	- $3,050
Double, two-story	3,650	- 5,450
Triple, three-story	4,975	- 7,450

BASEMENTS: For sprinklers, add $2.45/sq. ft.; for mechanical vent, add $ .91/sq. ft.

BUILT-IN APPLIANCES:
Allowance (if not itemized)	+	$2,350
Range and oven	+	1,075
Hood and fan	+	400
Dishwasher	+	800
Garbage disposer	+	295
Exhaust fan or bath heater	+	185
Radio-intercom	+	570
Wall air conditioner, 1 ton	+	1,025

BASEMENT TYPE	3000	6000	9000	12000	15000	18000	21000	24000
Unfinished, conc. walls	$15.62	$14.61	$14.05	$13.67	$13.37	$13.14	$12.92	$12.78
Finished basements	24.91	23.28	22.39	21.77	21.32	20.95	20.63	20.36
Parking garage*	18.99	17.76	17.07	16.59	16.24	15.95	15.70	15.51

*When concrete roof of garage is utilized as a court deck on the top side, add $10.20 per sq. ft. Where utilized as first floor of apartments, add $4.90 per sq. ft. to basic floor cost.
BALCONIES AND STAIRWAYS: See Page Mul-18. **GARAGES AND CARPORTS:** See Page Mul-19.

Figure 8.3 *Continued*

4689 Roswell Rd NE *Published*
Park Village Apartments
Atlanta, GA 30342 -3056
Multi Family - 68 Units of 56,800 SF Sold for **$2,800,000**

buyer

Charles X Lin
4565 River Masions Cove
Duluth, GA 30096
(770) 248-0731

seller

Park Village Associates (LLC)
c/o George Rohig & Gary Pollack
247 Barlett Ave
Atlanta, GA 30305
(404) 237-4415

vital data

Sale Date:	**01/23/2003**	Sale Price:	**$2,800,000**
Escrow/Contract:	**N/Av**	Status:	**Confirmed**
Days on Market:	**N/Av**	Building SF:	**56,800 Approx**
Exchange:	**No**	Price/SF:	**$49.30**
Conditions:	**None**	Price/Unit:	**$41,176**
0 Bedroom:	**0**	No Units:	**68**
1 Bedroom:	**24/ 35% (1+1)**	GRM:	**N/Av**
2 Bedroom:	**38/ 56% (2+1)**	Down Pmnt:	**$735,000**
3 Bedroom:	**6/ 9% (3+2)**	Pct Down:	**26%**
Other:	**0**	Doc No:	**34082-0363**
Year Built:	**1964 Age 39**	Trans Tax:	**N/Av**
Parking Spaces:	**Not Available**	Corner:	**No**
Parking Ratio:	**N/Av**	Zoning:	**RM75, County**
Lot Dim:	**Irregular**	Improv Ratio:	**86%**
Land Area SF:	**119,742**	Submarket:	**Central Perimeter**
Acres:	**2.749**		
Comp No:	**FNA-17032-02-0320**	Property Type:	**Apartment**

income/expense

Listing Broker reported that the property sold at a 7% cap rate based on income at time of sale. There was a 90% occupy rate at time of sale.

Cap Rate: **7.0%**

listing broker

Southeast Apartment Partners
3400 Peachtree St Ste 1035
Atlanta, GA 30326
(404) 442-5600

Joshua Goldfarb

buyers broker

None involved per principal

financing

1st Summit National Bank(due in 10 yrs)
   Bal/Pmt: **$2,065,000**
Net Spendable (rate):**N/Av   (7.0%)**

Figure 8.4   Comparable sales information for Atlanta apartment building. *Source:* Copyright© 1999–2002 CoStar Realty Information, Inc. All rights reserved. Information obtained from sources deemed reliable but not guaranteed. Phone: (800) 204-5960.

unit mix

Units	Type/Description	Bath	Min Rent	Max Rent	Min SF	Max SF	Remarks	Vacant
8	1 Bedroom	1				500 net		
16	1 Bedroom	1				650 net		
38	2 Bedroom	1				950 net	townhouse	
6	3 Bedroom	2				1,050 net		

Total Units: **68**

building

Address	Yr Built	Serial	SF	Bldgs	Stories	Construction	Roof	Foundation	Condition	Comments
	1964		56,800	12	2	Mixed const			Average	

Total Buildings: **12**
 Building Class: **C**

plat map

Map: **738-K/9** Legal: **Land Lot 94, District 17**

Comps No: **FNA-17032-02-0320** Parcel Number: **17-0094-0005-033** Title Co: **Calloway**

No Plat Map Available

site map

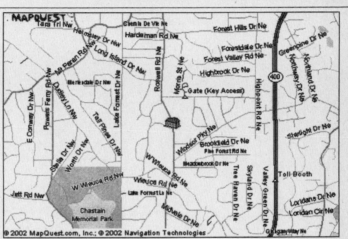

This site map is derived from MapQuest.com Inc. No opinion is expressed concerning the accuracy of any information contained herein.

Figure 8.4 *Continued*

description

```
* additional contacts
Rental Office

(404) 252-5833

Financing:
1st   Summit National Bank   $2,065,000      due in 10 yrs

* Notes: This is the sale of a 68 unit apartment community in Atlanta. The
buyer is a local private investor.

Total Assessed: $2,244,000
Year Assessed: 2002

Doc Num / Transfer Tax
34082-0363  (N/Av)

Recording Date: 01/23/2003

Confirmed by: Rose Filmore
Date: 02/19/2003
Email: qualitycontrol@costar.com
Phone: (888)636-8389
Deed Date: 01/23/2003
Updated Date: 06/17/2003
```

Figure 8.4 *Continued*

8490 E Old Spanish Trl *Published*
Tucson East Senior Apartments
Tucson, AZ 85710 -4313
Multi Family - 52 Units(Senior) of 34,706 SF Sold for **$2,100,000**

buyer

Rae Shel One (LLC)
c/o Sheldon J Larson (Pres)
7301 E 22nd St
Tucson, AZ 85710
(520) 885-9316

seller

Tucson East Apartments (LLC)
c/o James T Szymanski
P.O. Box 19376
Fountain Hills, AZ 85269

vital data

Sale Date:	06/30/2003	Sale Price:	$2,100,000
Escrow/Contract:	N/Av	Status:	Confirmed
Days on Market:	N/Av	Building SF:	34,706 Rentable
Exchange:	No	Price/SF:	$60.51
Conditions:	None	Price/Unit:	$40,384
0 Bedroom:	0	No Units:	52
1 Bedroom:	41/ 79% (1+1)	GRM:	7.20
2 Bedroom:	11/ 21% (2+1) (2+2)	Down Pmnt:	$772,000
3 Bedroom:	0	Pct Down:	37%
Other:	0	Doc No:	12082-0983
Year Built:	1982 Age 21	Trans Tax:	N/Av
Parking Spaces:	106	Corner:	No
Parking Ratio:	2.04/Unit	Zoning:	R-3, Tucson
Lot Dim:	Irregular	Improv Ratio:	86%
Land Area SF:	76,185	Submarket:	East
Acres:	1.749		
Comp No:	TUA-72053-08-0320	Property Type:	Apartment

income/expense

GSI $291,840 derived from rents at time of sale as reported by broker. See description for rent roll. Laundry income of $881 per month, vacancy at time of sale of $19,596 and expenses at time of sale of $126,068 per year reported by broker. The property sold at a 7.46% cap rate based on income.

Gross Income Multiplier:	6.94	
Gross Scheduled Income:		**$302,412**
Vacancy 6.48%:	<	$19,596 >
Effective Gross Income:		**$282,816**
Property Tax :		$23,110
Other Expenses:		$102,958
Total Expenses 44.58%:	<	$126,068 >
($2,424/Unit)		
($3.63/SF)		
Net Annual Income:		**$156,748**
Cap Rate:	7.46%	

listing broker

Marcus & Millichap
6083 E Grant Rd
Tucson , AZ 85712 -2319
(520) 296-3232

Mike McClain

buyers broker

Marcus & Millichap
6083 E Grant Rd
Tucson , AZ 85712 -2319
(520) 296-3232

Mike McClain

financing

1st LaSalle Bank FSB(Assm)
Bal/Pmt: **$1,328,000**
Net Spendable (rate):**N/Av   (N/Av)**

prior sale

Date/Doc No:	10/21/1998 (10906-1733)
Sale Price:	$1,660,000
Comps No:	TUA-62075-12-9819

Figure 8.5 Comparable sales information for Tucson apartment building. *Source:* Copyright© 1999–2002 CoStar Realty Information, Inc. All rights reserved. Information obtained from sources deemed reliable but not guaranteed. Phone: (800) 204-5960.

property characteristics

unit mix

Units	Type/Description	Bath	Min Rent	Max Rent	Min SF	Max SF	Remarks	Vacant
40	1 Bedroom	1		$450 atos		600 net		
1	1 Bedroom	1				756 net	manager's unit	
1	2 Bedroom	1		$570 atos		930 net		
2	2 Bedroom	2		$575 atos		870 net		
8	2 Bedroom	2		$575 atos		910 net		

Total Units: **52**

building

Yr Built	Bldgs	Stories	Construction	Roof	Foundation	Condition	Comments
1982	3	2	Frame/stucco	Flat blt-up	Conc slab	Average	
1982	1	1	Frame/stucco	Flat blt-up	Conc slab	Average	

Total Buildings: **4**

Building Class: **B**

amenities
club house, laundry, pool, rec room

parking

Composition	Open	Open Tandem	Covered	Covered Tandem	Total Spaces	Condition
Asphalt	64		42			106 Average

Garages, 1-car:

2-car:

Total Parking including Garages: **106**

Parking Ratio: **2.04/Unit**

plat map

Map: **109-237/QJ** Legal: **Por blk C Desert Steppes Estates bk 15 pg 47**

Comps No: **TUA-72053-08-0320** Parcel Number: **134-09-005** Title Co: **Fidelity National Title**

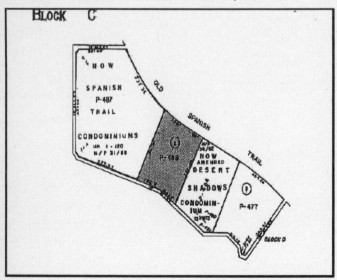

Figure 8.5 *Contnued*

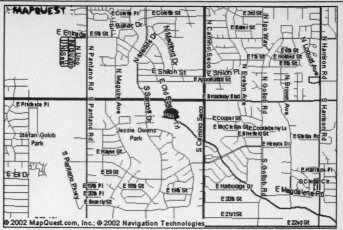

This site map is derived from MapQuest.com Inc. No opinion is expressed concerning the accuracy of any information contained herein.

description

* additional contacts
Subject Property
Tucson East Senior Apartments
(520) 886-6161

Financing:
1st   LaSalle Bank FSB $1,328,000   Assm,

* Bldg SF: Bldg SF shown does not include a 960 SF club house.

* Description: Property is an age restricted 55+ community.

Total Assessed: $1,333,839
Year Assessed: 2002

Doc Num / Transfer Tax
12082-0983   (N/Av)

Recording Date: 06/30/2003

Property Tax: $23,110
Confirmed by: Karen Schutte
Date: 08/03/2003
Email: qualitycontrol@costar.com
Phone: (888)636-8389
Updated Date: 08/06/2003

Figure 8.5 *Continued*

---

buyer

454 NE 23rd St (Ltd)
c/o Constantine J. Scurtis
107 Sarto Ave
Coral Gables, FL 33134
(305) 445-8177

seller

Ms. Celina M Hernandez
7885 Sunset Dr
Miami, FL 33143
(954) 752-3361

---

vital data

Sale Date:	**03/31/2003**	Sale Price:	**$2,975,000**
Escrow/Contract:	**60 days**	Status:	**Confirmed**
Days on Market:	**150 days**	Building SF:	**29,406 Rentable**
Exchange:	**Tax Dfrrd**	Price/SF:	**$101.17**
Conditions:	**Bulk/Portfolio Sale**	Price/Unit:	**$49,583**
0 Bedroom:	**24/ 40% (1+Studio) (1+Studio) (1+Studio)**	No Units:	**60**
1 Bedroom:	**32/ 53% (1+1)**	GRM:	**8.36**
2 Bedroom:	**4/ 7% (2+1)**	Down Pmnt:	**N/Av**
3 Bedroom:	**0**	Pct Down:	**N/Av**
Other:	**0**	Doc No:	**21138-2728**
Year Built:	**1948 Age 55**	Trans Tax:	**N/Av**
Parking Spaces:	**Not Available**	Corner:	**No**
Parking Ratio:	**N/Av**	Zoning:	**R-4, Miami**
Lot Dim:	**Irregular**	Improv Ratio:	**48%**
Land Area SF:	**47,550**	Submarket:	**Biscayne Corridor**
Acres:	**1.092**		
Comp No:	**DDA-36748-04-0320**	Property Type:	**Apartment**

---

income/expense

Listing broker reported rents at time of sale of $29,652 per month. Vacancy at time of sale of 3% & expenses at time of sale of $134,984 per year reported by listing broker. The listing broker reported that the tenants pay for electricity.

Gross Income Multiplier:		8.36		
Gross Scheduled Income:		**$355,824**		
Vacancy 3%:	<	**$10,675**	>	
Effective Gross Income:		**$345,149**		
Property Tax :		**$56,913**		
Other Expenses:		**$78,071**		
Total Expenses 39.11%:	<	**$134,984**	>	
($2,249/Unit)				
($4.59/SF)				
Net Annual Income:		**$210,165**		
Cap Rate:		**7.06%**		

listing broker

Marcus & Millichap
5900 N Andrews Ave Ste. 100
Fort Lauderdale, FL 33309
(954) 463-2400

Andrew Jordan, Greg . Celentano

buyers broker

Marcus & Millichap
5900 N Andrews Ave Ste. 100
Fort Lauderdale, FL 33309
(954) 463-2400

Andrew Jordan, Greg . Celentano

---

financing

Net Spendable (rate): **$210,165   (7.06%)**

Figure 8.6   Comparable sales information for Miami apartment building. *Source:* Copyright© 1999–2002 CoStar Realty Information, Inc. All rights reserved. Information obtained from sources deemed reliable but not guaranteed. Phone: (800) 204-5960.

unit mix

Units	Type/Description	Bath	Min Rent	Max Rent	Min SF	Max SF	Remarks Vacant
6	0 Bedroom Studio	1		$410 atos			
10	0 Bedroom Studio	1		$430 atos			
8	0 Bedroom Studio	1	$330	$420 atos			
21	1 Bedroom	1	$450	$560 atos			
3	1 Bedroom	1		$535 atos			
6	1 Bedroom	1		$575 atos			
2	1 Bedroom	1		$525 atos			
4	2 Bedroom	1		$630 atos			

Total Units: **60**

building

Address	Yr Built	Serial	SF	Bldgs	Stories	Construction	Roof	Foundation	Condition	Comments
	1960		14,780	1	3	Not available	N/Av	N/Av	Average	
	1956		5,211	1	2	Not available	N/Av	N/Av	Average	
	1971		6,225	1	2	Not available	N/Av	N/Av	Average	
	1948		3,190	1	1	Not available	N/Av	N/Av	Average	

Total Buildings: **4**

Building Class: **C**

amenities
A/C Wall

plat map

Map: **32-AA/12** Legal: **Lots 6 & 7 blk 3 Edgewater pl bk 2 pg 31, lots 5 thru 8 blk 3 Bay Breeze pl bk 7 pg 77 & lot 1 less W75' b**

Comps No: **DDA-36748-04-0320** Parcel Number: **01-3230-025-0040, 0060, 026-0140, 028-0010** Title Co: **Not Available**

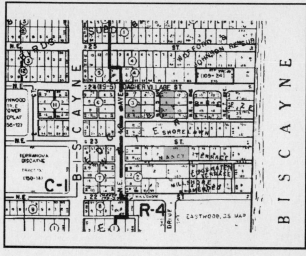

Figure 8.6 *Continued*

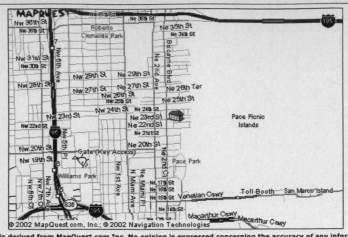

This site map is derived from MapQuest.com Inc. No opinion is expressed concerning the accuracy of any information contained herein.

description

```
* Additional Property Address:
  500 NE 24th St Miami              , FL 33137
  2337 NE 4th Ave Miami           , FL 33137
  2321-2331 NE 5th Ave Miami           , FL 33137
```

* Sale Price: The listing broker had reported that the property sold approximately 10% over the appraised value. No additional information was disclosed by the listing broker.

* Exchange: This was the seller's downleg in a 1031 exchange.

* Description: Reportedly the property is individually metered.

* Notes: The listing broker had stated that the subject property is located 3 blocks from the waterfront and is also located near a new retail redevelopment district. Reportedly, the immediate area is being redeveloped and it is the listing brokers opinion that the rental rates will appreciate by approximately 5% within the next year due to these new redevelopment projects.

```
Total Assessed: $1,954,201
Year Assessed: 2002

Doc Num / Transfer Tax
21138-2728   (N/Av)
21138-2651   (N/Av)

Recording Date: 04/11/2003

Property Tax: $56,913
Confirmed by: Jorge Rosa
Date: 04/14/2003
Email: qualitycontrol@costar.com
Phone: (888)636-8369
Deed Date: 03/31/2003
Updated Date: 08/13/2003
```

Figure 8.6   *Continued*

5712 N 67th Ave *Published*
La Mesa Apartments
Glendale, AZ 85301 -5569
Multi Family - 70 Units of 49,200 SF Sold for **$2,950,000**

buyer

Robert & Patricia Emrish (et al)
173 Magee Ave
Mill Valley, CA 94941

seller

KUMS, Inc.
c/o Rados Stevelich (Pres)
5712 N 67th Dr
Glendale, AZ 85303-4902

vital data

Sale Date:	**06/06/2003**	Sale Price:	**$2,950,000**
Escrow/Contract:	**90 days**	Status:	**Confirmed**
Days on Market:	**N/Av**	Building SF:	**49,200 Rentable**
Exchange:	**No**	Price/SF:	**$59.96**
Conditions:	**None**	Price/Unit:	**$42,142**
0 Bedroom:	**0**	No Units:	**70**
1 Bedroom:	**46/ 66% (1+1)**	GRM:	**N/Av**
2 Bedroom:	**24/ 34% (2+2)**	Down Pmnt:	**$731,600**
3 Bedroom:	**0**	Pct Down:	**25%**
Other:	**0**	Doc No:	**0734483**
Year Built:	**1985 Age 18**	Trans Tax:	**N/Av**
Parking Spaces:	**120**	Corner:	**No**
Parking Ratio:	**1.71/Unit**	Zoning:	**R-3, Glendale**
Lot Dim:	**Irregular**	Improv Ratio:	**97%**
Land Area SF:	**108,159**	Submarket:	**Glendale**
Acres:	**2.483**		
Comp No:	**PXA-59836-07-0320**	Property Type:	**Apartment**

income/expense

The broker reported that the property sold at a 5.7% cap rate based on pro forma income at time of sale. Tenants pay electricity.

Cap Rate: 5.7%

listing broker

Marcus & Millichap
4040 E Camelback Rd Ste. 130
Phoenix, AZ 85018 -8351
(602) 952-9669

Richard Butler

buyers broker

Marcus & Millichap
4040 E Camelback Rd Ste. 130
Phoenix, AZ 85018 -8351
(602) 952-9669

Richard Butler

financing

1st ABN Amro Mortgage
     Bal/Pmt: **$2,218,400**
Net Spendable (rate):**N/Av   (N/Av)**

prior sale

Date/Doc No:	**06/12/1998 (501908)**
Sale Price:	**$1,750,000**
Comps No:	**PXA-26314-09-9819**

Figure 8.7 Comparable sales information for Glendale apartment building. *Source:* Copyright© 1999–2002 CoStar Realty Information, Inc. All rights reserved. Information obtained from sources deemed reliable but not guaranteed. Phone: (800) 204-5960.

property characteristics

unit mix

Units	Type/Description	Bath	Min Rent	Max Rent	Min SF	Max SF	Remarks	Vacant
46	1 Bedroom	1		$475 avg		600 net		
24	2 Bedroom	2		$550 avg		900 net		

Total Units: **70**

building

Address	Yr Built	Serial	SF	Bldgs	Stories	Construction	Roof	Foundation	Condition	Comments
	1985		49,200	6	2	Frame/stucco	Flat blt-up	Conc slab	Average	

Total Buildings: **6**

Building Class: **C**

amenities

balcony, covered parking, laundry, patio, pool

parking

Composition	Open	Open Tandem	Covered	Covered Tandem	Total Spaces	Condition
Asphalt	50		70		120	Average
	Garages, 1-car:					
	2-car:					

Total Parking including Garages: **120**

Parking Ratio: **1.71/Unit**

plat map

Map: **124-156/LQ** Legal: **E533' S460' S2 NE4 NE4 sec 13 T2N R1E (exc pors)**

Comps No: **PXA-59836-07-0320** Parcel Number: **144-25-008E** Title Co: **Fidelity**

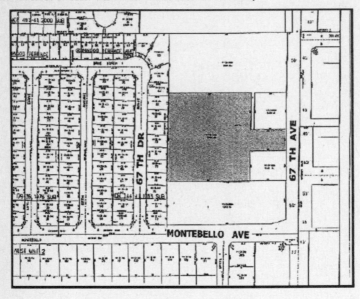

Figure 8.7 *Continued*

site map

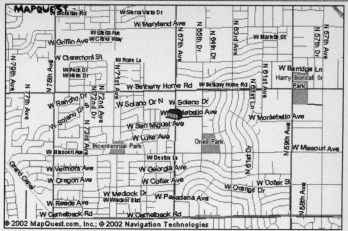

This site map is derived from MapQuest.com Inc. No opinion is expressed concerning the accuracy of any information contained herein.

description

```
Financing:
1st   ABN Amro Mortgage    $2,218,400

* Description: The property is comprised of 6, two-story frame & stucco
apartments.

Total Assessed: $1,720,500
Year Assessed: 2002

Doc Num / Transfer Tax
0734483   (N/Av)

Recording Date: 06/06/2003

Confirmed by: Phil Majarucon
Date: 07/10/2003
Email: qualitycontrol@costar.com
Phone: (888)636-8389
Updated Date: 07/11/2003
```

Figure 8.7   *Continued*

Miami, FL 33155 -4888
Multi Family - 62 Units of 42,256 SF Sold for **$2,975,000**

buyer

62 Bird (LLC)
c/o Sergio Concepcion - Mayor Realty
7207 Coral Way
Miami, FL 33155
(305) 267-0208

seller

Dalma, Inc.
c/o Nikolaus Szentpaly
6150 Bird Rd Ste. A-4
South Miami, FL 33155

vital data

Sale Date:	**03/17/2003**	Sale Price:	**$2,975,000**
Escrow/Contract:	**N/Av**	Status:	**Confirmed**
Days on Market:	**N/Av**	Building SF:	**42,256 Rentable**
Exchange:	**No**	Price/SF:	**$70.40**
Conditions:	**None**	Price/Unit:	**$47,983**
0 Bedroom:	**26/ 42% (1+Studio)**	No Units:	**62**
1 Bedroom:	**16/ 26% (1+1)**	GRM:	**771.12**
2 Bedroom:	**20/ 32% (2+1) (2+2)**	Down Pmnt:	**N/Av**
3 Bedroom:	**0**	Pct Down:	**N/Av**
Other:	**0**	Doc No:	**21120-1242**
Year Built:	**1965 Age 38**	Trans Tax:	**($17,850.00)**
Parking Spaces:	**55**	Corner:	**No**
Parking Ratio:	**0.89/Unit**	Zoning:	**RU-1, South Miami**
Lot Dim:	**Irregular**	Improv Ratio:	**47%**
Land Area SF:	**64,904**	Submarket:	**West Miami**
Acres:	**1.490**		
Comp No:	**DDA-49050-07-0320**	Property Type:	**Apartment**

income/expense

The buyer reported unit mix, please see rent roll information. She also reported that water, sewer, and gas are included in the rent. She stated that there is additional income from laundry, but she could not recall how much.

listing broker

None involved per principal

buyers broker

Mayor Realty
7207 SW 24th St
Miami, FL 33155
(305) 267-0208

Sergio Concepcion

financing

Net Spendable (rate): **N/Av   (0.13%)**

Figure 8.8   Comparable sales information for Miami apartment building. *Source:* Copyright© 1999–2002 CoStar Realty Information, Inc. All rights reserved. Information obtained from sources deemed reliable but not guaranteed. Phone: (800) 204-5960.

unit mix

Units	Type/Description	Bath	Min Rent	Max Rent	Min SF	Max SF	Remarks	Vacant
26	0 Bedroom Studio	1		$650 curr				
16	1 Bedroom	1		$750 curr				
12	2 Bedroom	1		$850 curr				
8	2 Bedroom	2		$900 curr				

Total Units: **62**

building

Address	Yr Built	Serial	SF	Bldgs	Stories	Construction	Roof	Foundation	Condition	Comments
	1965		42,256	2	2	Conc blk/stuc	Flat blt-up	Conc slab	Average	

Total Buildings: **2**
Building Class: **C**

amenities
A/C Wall, pool

parking

Composition	Open	Open Tandem	Covered	Covered Tandem	Total Spaces	Condition
Asphalt	55				55	Average

Garages, 1-car:
2-car:
Total Parking including Garages: **55**
Parking Ratio: **0.89/Unit**

Map: **47-T/17** Legal: **Lots 1 thru 5, blk 1 lots 1 thru 5 (less N 25' lot 4), blk 2, McKeever Terrace, plat bk 9, pg 49.**

Comps No: **DDA-49050-07-0320** Parcel Number: **09-4024-035-0010, 0250** Title Co: **Not shown**

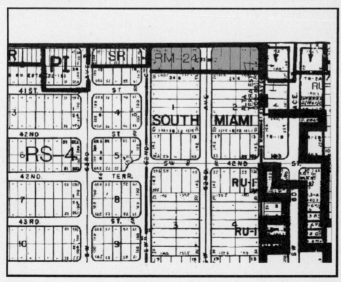

Figure 8.8 *Continued*

site map

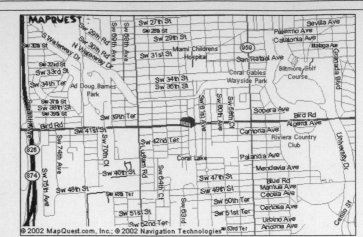

This site map is derived from MapQuest.com Inc. No opinion is expressed concerning the accuracy of any information contained herein.

description

```
* Notes: The buyer's assistant reported that the units are being renovated
as they become vacant.

Total Assessed: $1,108,542
Year Assessed: 2002

Doc Num / Transfer Tax
21120-1242  ($17,850)

Recording Date: 03/25/2003

Confirmed by: Barbara Ciesinski
Date: 07/08/2003
Email: qualitycontrol@costar.com
Phone: (888)636-8389
Deed Date: 03/17/2003
Updated Date: 08/22/2003
```

Figure 8.8 *Continued*

conditions cause the capitalization rate to be adjusted higher; favorable conditions cause it to be lowered.

Essentials of Property Analysis Software

Choose a computer program that fits your needs. We prefer using the program created by The Center for Real Estate Studies (for more information on the software package, see page 226) which is specifically designed to analyze investments in apartment buildings. You should select software capable of providing the following features:

- Projections and analysis of cash flows and tax benefits using the IREM format
- Maximum forecasting flexibility
- After-tax IRR
- User friendly

A computer program that has these features makes it easier to analyze properties. If the data is accurate, your reports will supply you with the necessary facts to make the right investment decisions. Figures 8.9, 8.10, and 8.11 illustrate the kind of analysis used to evaluate apartment buildings.

When inputting data, numerous assumptions must be made. There's an expression that communicates the importance of inputting good data. If data submitted to computer operations came back stamped "verified," it meant it was accepted. Reports stamped GIGO meant the opposite! GIGO stands for "garbage in garbage out." The same applies

Phoenix		Percent of GPI	$/SQFT
Income:			
Gross possible rents	$115,332.24	96.00	5.77
Vacancy/rent loss	−16,699.14	13.90	.83
Other income	4,805.50	4.00	.24
Total Collections	$103,438.60	86.10	5.17
Expenses:			
Administrative	$ 7,783.00	6.48	.39
Operating	9,244.00	7.69	.46
Maintenance	6,613.00	5.50	.33
Tax/insurance	7,965.00	6.63	.40
Recreational/amenities	365.78	.30	.02
Other payroll	4,567.00	3.80	.23
Total Operating Expenses	$ 36,537.78	30.40	1.83
Net Operating Income	$ 66,900.82	55.69	3.35
Debt Service	−47,997.10	39.95	2.40
Cash Flow after Debt Service	$ 18,903.72	15.74	.95
Cash Effects of:			
Tax on Net Operating Income	$−20,739.25	17.26	1.04
Tax on Interest Expense	18,007.67	14.99	.90
Tax on Depreciation Expense	5,202.96	4.33	.26
Net Cash Flow after Taxes	$ 21,375.10	17.79	1.07

Figure 8.9 Sample analysis—Phoenix.

	Seattle	Percent of GPAI	$/SQFT
Income:			
Gross possible rents	$ 273,777.41	96.40	9.11
Vacancy/rent loss	−17,324.09	6.10	.58
Other income	10,224.06	3.60	.34
Total Collections	$ 266,677.38	93.90	8.88
Expenses:			
Administrative	$ 24,241.00	8.54	.81
Operating	21,527.00	7.58	.72
Maintenance	12,729.00	4.48	.42
Tax/insurance	22,837.00	8.04	.76
Recreational/amenities	842.57	.30	.03
Other payroll	11,419.00	4.02	.38
Total Operating Expenses	$ 93,595.57	32.96	3.12
Net Operating Income	$ 173,081.81	60.94	5.76
Debt Service	−115,992.97	40.84	3.86
Cash Flow after Debt Service	$ 57,088.84	20.10	1.90
Cash Effects of:			
Tax on Net Operating Income	$ −53,655.36	18.89	1.79
Tax on Interest Expense	43,518.52	15.32	1.45
Tax on Depreciation Expense	12,573.83	4.43	.42
Net Cash Flow after Taxes	$ 59,525.83	20.96	1.98

Figure 8.10   Sample analysis—Seattle.

to investment data. If the information inputted is garbage, your output will be the same.

The computer program should be designed to give an IRR based on specific assumptions. Confer with your consultants to assist you in making these assumptions. For example, estimates of tax rates and depreciation should be made with the help of your tax advisor. When speculating on general business conditions in the area, your property manager or real estate broker should be consulted for advice. These professionals must be able to provide you with the data needed to make the right assumptions.

THE INTERNAL RATE OF RETURN TO AIM FOR

The IRR should reflect the degree of risk you're willing to take. The more risky an investment, the higher the IRR. If you're purchasing an apartment building that has decreased in value only because of temporary market conditions, your degree of risk might be considered

	Boston		
		Percent of GPI	$/SQFT
Income:			
Gross possible rents	$ 283,227.42	99.40	8.78
Vacancy/rent loss	−14,246.85	5.00	.44
Other income	1,709.62	.60	.05
Total Collections	$ 270,690.19	95.00	8.39
Expenses:			
Administrative	$ 11,937.00	4.20	.37
Operating	35,997.00	12.60	1.12
Maintenance	15,824.00	5.60	.49
Tax/insurance	19,525.00	6.90	.61
Recreational/amenities	3,423.52	1.20	.11
Other payroll	5,830.00	2.00	.18
Total Operating Expenses	$ 92,536.52	32.50	2.87
Net Operating Income	$ 178,153.67	62.50	5.52
Debt Service	−139,991.53	49.10	4.34
Cash Flow after Debt Service	38,162.14	13.40	1.18
Cash Effects of:			
Tax on Net Operating Income	$ −55,227.64	19.40	1.71
Tax on Interest Expense	52,522.38	18.40	1.63
Tax on Depreciation Expense	15,175.31	5.30	.47
Net Cash Flow after Taxes	$ 50,632.19	17.80	1.57

Figure 8.11 Sample analysis—Boston.

moderate. Conservative projections are computed using rental growth and vacancy rates, and they establish the lower limits of the IRR. IRR projections based on replacement costs determine the higher limits of the IRR. Analyzing both rates of return allows you to assess the risks versus rewards relationship of each investment.

REVENUE ASSUMPTIONS THAT MAKE SENSE

Revenue assumptions play an important part of your analysis. In addition to the information provided by consultants, check with local apartment rental firms. They are on top of current trends and demand. Lease agreements should be verified to actual rents for each tenant. Use rental applications to develop tenant profiles. Obtain a signed estoppel from each tenant attesting to the rent paid, occupancy dates, and deposits. Rent raises don't always occur on the first day of the month or in the first month of the year. A careful review of rental agreements will assist in making accurate cash flow projections. Ideally, try to stagger

Life Expectancy Guidelines
Replaceable Components

When capitalizing the income of investment properties, it is necessary to include in the expenses an annual reserve for the replacement of various components which have a shorter life than the building as a whole (see Section 81). To estimate the annual reserve for replacement of a component, divide the estimated years of life into the total cost of the component. The following guide gives the most typical of such items and an estimated life under standard applications in years for each, sub-divided by quality. Individual component lives can have a wide range depending on the loads and conditions placed on them, the method of installation, and appropriate maintenance and warranties. Lives may be shortened under severe requirements due to heavy wear, corrosive contact and/or atmospheric conditions, etc. or lengthened under very light usage, mild circumstances, protective coatings, etc. Costs for the various components may be selected from appropriate tables throughout the manual. The allocation of a component cost over its expected service life can also be used in establishing reserves for condominium or owner's association budgets or sinking funds, etc. and in the evaluation of life-cycle costing for use in the component selection or design alternative process, for financial planning, energy analysis or audits, etc.

Component	Low	Average	Good	Excellent
Appliances				
Major appliances, residential	10	12	15	18
Garbage disposers, washing machines	6	8	10	12
Radio-intercom, paging systems	12	15	19	24
Telephone systems	9	10	11	12
Vacuum cleaning system	12	13	15	17
Floor Covering				
Access (Computer) floor	10	12	15	18
Carpet and pad	4	5	7	10
Carpet tiles	5	6	8	10
Ceramic or quarry tile or pavers	25	30	34	40
Indoor-outdoor carpet	3	5	7	10
Vinyl composition tile or sheet	7	10	14	19
Vinyl or rubber tile or sheet	12	15	19	24
Wood flooring	21	25	30	35
Miscellaneous Interior				
Acoustical ceiling tiles or panels	8	10	12	15
Built-in lockers, mail boxes, etc.	12	15	20	25
Partitions, demountable	16	20	25	30
folding	8	10	12	15
Drapery	6	8	10	12
Paint	3	5	7	10
Wallpaper	7	10	13	18
Wood doors	18	20	22	25
Conveying Systems				
Elevators and escalators	18	20	23	26
Pneumatic tube system	12	13	15	17
Heating, Cooling, and Ventilating				
Forced air heat	12	14	17	20
Heating and combined cooling plants	12	15	20	25
Package heating and cooling	5	8	13	20
Refrigerated air conditioning, central	10	13	16	20
Package refrigeration	5	7	10	15
Refrigerated coolers, window	7	9	11	14
Solar heating systems	5	7	10	15
Unit heaters	8	10	14	18
Wall or floor furnaces	10	13	16	20

Figure 8.12 Life expectancy guidelines. *Source:* Marshall Valuation Service © 1990, Marshall & Swift. Printed in U.S.A.

Component	Low	Average	Good	Excellent
Evaporative coolers	5	6	8	10
Exhaust and ventilating fans	6	9	12	18

For detailed components, see Section 53.
  Storage tanks, see Section 61.

Plumbing and Electrical

Component	Low	Average	Good	Excellent
Plumbing fixtures	17	20	25	30
Faucets and valves	8	10	13	16
Water heaters, residential	2	4	7	12
commercial	8	11	15	20
Light fixtures, residential	15	20	26	35
Light fixtures, commercial	7	10	14	20
Emergency generators	22	25	27	30
Sprinkler and fire protection systems	20	23	26	30
smoke and heat detectors	13	15	17	20
Miscellaneous pumps, motors, controls	3	4	7	10

Roofing

Component	Low	Average	Good	Excellent
Built-up tar and gravel	10	13	16	20
Composition shingles	12	16	22	30
Elastomeric	12	15	20	25
Metal	13	20	30	45
Wood shakes	20	24	29	35
Wood shingles	16	20	24	30
Tile, concrete or clay	30	36	42	50
Slate or copper			50	60

Miscellaneous

Component	Low	Average	Good	Excellent
Store fronts	18	20	22	25
Doors, automatic	7	10	14	20
overhead	8	10	12	15
Storm windows	8	10	12	14

Site Improvements

Component	Low	Average	Good	Excellent
Flag pole	16	20	25	30
Fencing, chain link	13	15	17	20
masonry walls	20	25	30	35
wood	6	8	10	12
wind screens	4	5	6	7
Landscaping, decorative shrubs, trees, etc.	7	10	14	20
Outdoor lighting fixtures	10	13	16	20
Outdoor furniture	3	5	7	10
Parking lot bumpers	3	4	5	7
Paving, asphalt	5	8	11	17
concrete	10	13	16	20
gravel	3	5	7	10
Snow melting systems	8	10	12	14
Sprinklers, galvanized pipe	10	14	18	25
plastic pipe	15	18	22	28
controllers and pumping systems	8	9	11	13
Stairway and decks, wood	7	9	12	15
cement composition	12	15	20	25
Swimming pool, residential	15	18	21	25
commercial	10	15	20	30
mechanical equipment	4	5	6	7
solar equipment	7	10	14	20
Tennis court	18	20	22	25
asphalt/colored concrete resurfacing	3	4	5	7
nets	1	2	2	3
Underground sewer & water lines	22	25	28	32

Figure 8.12 *Continued*

individual rent raises throughout the year. It is less disturbing to the entire complex.

Vacancies vary in seasonal locations like college towns and resort areas. Make provisions for these fluctuations in cash flow projections. Don't assume income will be received evenly month-to-month and year-to-year. Projections based on research will result in a more accurate IRR.

ANALYZE EXPENSES CORRECTLY

When analyzing expenses, refer to the property inspection report. It should detail, by projected date the costs, repairs and replacements for each unit and the entire building. Using a comprehensive computer program will produce accurate operating budgets.

Mechanical equipment such as water heaters, dishwashers, garbage disposals, and pool equipment, for example, have estimated life spans (see Figure 8.12, pp. 124–125). Major repairs and replacements on roofs, plumbing, decking, and cement should be detailed by estimated costs and the dates work is to be started and completed.

As with income, expenses do not occur evenly throughout the year. For example, in cold climates, utility bills are higher in the winter than in the summer. With grounds and pool maintenance, it is just the opposite.

Expense figures should be compared with those published by the IREM. All sizable discrepancies must be explained.

Do not make flat rate projections. Don't apply inflation rates across the board. Projections should be made on an item-by-item basis using the best information available. For example, if the inflation rate of 5 percent is used in one year, don't use it again unless it applies. Actuals should be used whenever possible.

USE THE FEEL-AND-TOUCH ANALYSIS

As part of the analysis, absolutely nothing beats the feel-and-touch approach. A physical inspection of the property and the neighborhood will confirm your consultant's reports. Critical words like good, bad, best, worst, bright, dull, a lot, and a little are subjective. Make sure everyone's singing from the same hymn book when praises to your property are being sung!

Ask yourself the following questions when evaluating the area as part of the physical inspection:

- Would you be willing to live or at least collect the rents in this neighborhood?

- What's the graffiti index?
- How does the landscaping of the other properties compare with the one you're considering?
- Is there debris in the streets?
- Are there cars on blocks?
- Is it completely off the beaten path to major shopping and work centers?
- Is the community growing favorably in the direction of your property?
- Are transportation lines readily available?
- Are schools and recreational facilities nearby?
- What is the ratio of renter- to owner-occupied buildings?

The greater the rental population, the more transient the area becomes and the greater possibility of it being left unkempt. The physical test will give you that personal viewpoint necessary to complete the analysis.

Even in depressed markets you should look for properties in good locations. A cardinal rule is to buy the worst property in the best location, not the best property in the worst location. Buying the poorest property in a good location, at least gives you the opportunity to upgrade it. Whereas, upgrading an entire neighborhood could be difficult, if not impossible. When in doubt, a drive through will help. Contact your local property management company or real estate licensee for assistance.

SUMMARY

The various methods of analyzing property have been discussed in this chapter. Why perform these analyses? Simply to find out how the building should be operating and what the anticipated profits should be.

When estimating profits, use the growth rate for the low or conservative end, and the projected replacement cost for the high end.

The internal rate of return is the key figure to use when evaluating apartments. Comparing the IRRs of other investments will help you determine whether the rewards are worth the risks.

Knowing what to expect from computer software programs and how to input the data correctly will produce meaningful reports for intelligent decision making.

The best approach to analyze midsize apartment buildings is to use a combination of the evaluation methods discussed in this chapter. Doing your own analysis, with the help of your consultants, gives you a better understanding of your investment and its profit potential.

9

How to Become an Outstanding Negotiator

When I first started buying and selling apartment buildings, I put an offer in on an apartment building. I had my appointment set at 1:00 P.M. and I had to wait until 3:00 before the seller would see me. So, I sat in the office for nearly two hours anxious to present my offer. When I finally did get into the seller's office to present the offer, he looked at it and started laughing. He pulled a stack of offers about 3 inches deep out of his lower left-hand desk drawer. He said, "You're kidding. Get me another offer." Right then and there I should have asked for a counteroffer, but still being new at the game, I went back and rewrote another offer. Fortunately, I made money. Appreciation bailed me out!

About a year-and-a-half later, the same seller had another property for sale. I presented the offer, but this time I made sure he was on time. When I presented the offer to him, he started laughing and again he reached in his lower left-hand drawer, pulling out a stack of offers and said, "You're kidding. How can you offer me this; get me another offer." And I said, "May I see them?" He started yanking the stack toward him and I yanked them toward me, I finally yanked them away from him and started looking at some of the offers. They were for other properties and some of them were two or three years old. He was playing "real estate poker."

I sat down with him and said, "If you want to sell, we want to buy, I have offers on two other properties." Actually, we didn't have any. But I was playing real estate poker, too. We negotiated. He got the price he wanted, and I got the terms I wanted. I made a substantial profit on it plus I also saved money on my taxes.

Why is the seller selling? Finding the answer will give you the negotiating edge. For the most part, being in a weak market is enough motivation in itself. However, there are other circumstances beyond depressed market conditions that motivate owners to sell. Some of these circumstances are as follows:

- *Poor management:* It's possible that the owner is doing a terrible job managing the property, and there might be more vacancies than normal for the area. Maybe the building is run down and the seller just doesn't want to put any more money into it. The seller could be an absentee owner without a competent local property management company, or one that simply doesn't know how to delegate.

- *Personal tragedies:* Death, divorce, bankruptcy, or illness could force the sale of a property. These are basically trauma situations for the seller. We're not suggesting that you take advantage of people in distress. You should certainly treat them fairly.

    In personal tragedies, the seller usually wants cash—which is diametrically opposed to your standard operational procedure. Your investment plan calls for leverage created, in part, by seller financing. However, if the price is right, you can still maintain leverage by structuring the transaction with outside financing. You'll probably be negotiating with a trustee, and the trustee's primary goal is to get as much cash as quickly as possible for the beneficiaries. Be prepared to act quickly when working with personal tragedy circumstances.

- *Retirement:* When some people retire, they want to pack it all in. They don't want the problems of management, and collecting monthly income hassles-free rates high on their priority list. The motivational key is the monthly income check. If you can structure your purchase to give the seller the required monthly check, you will have an excellent chance at the deal. Notice I said *re-quired* monthly check. Monthly payments can be in any amount.

However, you must arrange them to give you the maximum cash flow and tax write-offs.
- *Taxes:* Taxes are one of the most compelling motivations in real estate transactions. A seller might want to trade his or her building for another piece of real estate to defer taxes. The seller might want your property or might have another property in mind. If you're able to accommodate the seller in a trade, you might be able to gain advantages in other areas such as price and terms.

The seller might be amenable to selling on an installment basis with little or no money down and carry back accrued paper. This financing package ideally fits into your plans.

Whatever the seller's motivation, be flexible enough to explore all avenues of approach. Try to work and rework the transaction to suit everyone's needs. Your success depends on finding the right motivation and the degree of intensity. Don't attempt to negotiate any real estate transactions unless everyone is motivated. Ideally, the more the other party is motivated, the better it is for you.

THE MOST EFFECTIVE FINANCING STRATEGIES

There are various methods of financing your acquisition. Listed next are three of the most effective strategies used to purchase and/or control property. Also, I've included a few tips that will protect you when negotiating.

Take a Loan "Subject To" Rather Than Assuming It

Depending on mortgage costs, the best method of financing is "subject to." Assuming existing financing or obtaining a new loan requires qualification and additional costs. Taking the loan *subject to* avoids both.

Protecting Yourself When Using an All-Inclusive Trust Deed

Robert Bruss, the National Real Estate syndicated columnist, points out that in selling, owners should consider owner financing because it helps them sell their property faster at a higher price. Generally the sale is conducted through an instrument called an all-inclusive trust deed (AITD).

If the apartment complex can't be purchased *subject to* or the present mortgage cannot be *assumed* the next best method is a *wrap-around loan,* or an AITD. A new note is created encompassing or wrapping the existing loans. Usually, one mortgage payment is made to the noteholder of the AITD, from which the noteholder, in turn, pays the underlying loans. For your protection, use an independent trustee to handle these payments. This method of financing should be reviewed by an experienced real estate attorney. Be careful! A due-on-sale clause provision in any one of the underlying notes could cause them to accelerate, making the entire balance immediately due and payable.

To benefit from any equity buildup on the underlying notes, the borrower should only be liable for current unpaid principal balances.

A Little Known Secret of the Lease Option

The benefits of lease options have been extolled by respected national syndicated real estate columnist Robert Bruss as a way to make a low initial investment to lock in a firm selling price. This gives you the possibility of making a highly leveraged transaction.

At times it's better to negotiate a lease-option agreement to initially finance your purchase, instead of using mortgages. The cost of an option can be paid in installments. As long as there's a balance due, escrow remains open, allowing you to maintain control of the property.

Lease options, when used in conjunction with subleases, can generate significant tax savings. They are based on the *intent* of the parties. Consult a competent tax advisor for additional help.

WHO BENEFITS FROM COMPOUNDING INTEREST

Because it costs more for the loan, borrowers should insist that interest accrue on a simple, rather than a compounded, basis. Lenders, on the other hand, benefit from compounding because interest charged on interest increases their yield. Have you noticed when financial institutions advertise interest rates they show two figures, one represents the actual interest rate, the other the yield? The higher figure is attributable to compounding.

AVOIDING DEFICIENCY JUDGMENTS

Loan contracts should not contain *deficiency judgment provisions*. A deficiency judgment occurs when proceeds are not sufficient to pay off existing loans. For example, if property with an $800,000 mortgage is sold and the net proceeds are only $700,000, a lender legally can demand payment of the $100,000 deficiency.

To avoid these kinds of situations, take the loans *subject to.* They are, in themselves, nonrecourse-no-deficiency loans. The holder of the note has recourse only to the original borrower. On the other hand, when you assume a loan, you become liable for deficiencies. If your loan contains a deficiency judgment clause, have your attorney take it out.

DETERMINING THE COST OF YOUR LOAN

Borrowers sometimes get confused trying to calculate the cost of a loan. To sort things out, forget about the various loan packages available and focus your attention on *present values.* If you concentrate on this figure, you will be able to find out which one is the least expensive.

Have either the lender or loan broker calculate the present value of the loan based on total actual dollars to be paid, including points, appraisal fees, escrow costs, and so forth. Comparisons made on this basis give the true cost of a loan.

RESTRICTIVE COVENANTS

Restrictive covenants could hinder transferability and act as a roadblock to selling your property. Restrictions on specific time limits in refinancing, releases on loans, and due-on-sale clauses, should be avoided whenever possible.

When buying an apartment complex that's built on contiguous lots, try to obtain individual releases as each is paid off. You will have the flexibility to choose what lots you want to own free and clear without having to pay the entire mortgage. A lot in default would not affect the unencumbered parcels.

STOPPING LATE MORTGAGE PAYMENTS

Late payment penalties should be spelled out in the loan. There are two methods of handling late penalties.

One is to include "due on the first, late on the tenth" of each month in the contract. You'll probably get your check closer to the tenth. The other is to have the contract read: "due on the first, in default thereafter." Legally, the property can be put in foreclosure if a payment is not paid on the first of the month. Foreclosure costs only have to be paid once (they are much higher than late penalties), and it won't happen again.

Some states give automatic grace periods before payments are considered late and foreclosure proceeding can begin. If in doubt, contact your local real estate attorney.

ADJUSTING MORTGAGE PAYMENTS TO PRODUCE CASH FLOW

Mortgage payment can be negotiated to produce cash flow. Monthly payments can be tied to fluctuations in income by either increasing or decreasing the interest accruals. All mortgage payments don't have to be paid on the first day of each month. They can be paid annually or semiannually, quarterly, or whatever is agreed upon.

If the seller doesn't want to accrue interest, he or she might agree to amortize the loan over a longer period of time, possibly 40 or 50 years. Highly motivated sellers may even agree to monthly payments that are tied to cash flow. When operations produce cash, all or a portion of the mortgage can be paid. If there's no cash flow, then no payments are made. Interest could either be waived or accrued. You'll be surprised to find just how agreeable motivated sellers can be.

GETTING THE IRS TO PAY FOR YOUR INVESTMENT

Within certain limitations, interest rates and payback periods can be adjusted as an offset to price. Buyers can get a higher interest expense deduction, and sellers get a higher interest rate on a short-term note that will make it more salable.

Lowering the purchase price has a minimal effect on taxable income because the depreciation deduction has been reduced as a result of changes in the tax laws. Discuss this complicated strategy with your tax advisor before implementing.

WORKING WITH CONSTANT CHANGE AND LIMITATIONS

After the property is purchased, monitor all changes that may affect your investment. Never be afraid to ask the holder of the note for better terms. A refusal is the worse that can happen. Things change over time. Motivations change. People change. Always be cognizant of change. You might be able to negotiate a better deal.

Remember, you're attempting to buy in distressed markets due primarily to overbuilding. If you're working with the bank's and savings and loan's real estate owned departments, keep in mind that they are governed by stringent regulatory agencies. They have limitations on the financing proposals they are able to accept. You might not be able to accrue interest, but you may be allowed to extend the life of the loan or pay interest only.

ALWAYS THINK OF THE SALE WHEN BUYING

Always think about how you're going to sell the property while negotiating its purchase. If you incorporate the following strategies, the building will be easier to sell:

- Have the seller take back assumable financing free from any fees and loan qualification requirements.
- Avoid long-term laundry, pool, landscaping, and any other maintenance service contracts. Since you don't know what a subsequent buyer's plans might be, it's best to leave as many options open as possible.

Always think in terms of "how this will benefit the next buyer" when negotiating the purchase.

PRICE STRATEGIES THAT WORK

In negotiating, always remember that *price is inversely related to terms*—the more you insist on your price, the less you will be able to insist on terms (loans). When making a concession on price for better terms, never forget its effect on the IRR. Buyers should always demand low down payments, below market interest rates, longer pay-back periods, and interest accruals.

By putting more cash down, in effect, giving up terms, you're in a better position to dictate price. Unless you're stealing the building, or you can resell it rapidly for a profit, go with the terms. You may run the risk of tying up leverageable assets for longer than may be necessary, if you don't.

Figures Smart Investors Want to See

The asking price should be based on the actual net operating income (NOI) when calculating the capitalization rate—not estimates or projections. If the NOI is lower than what's represented on the set-up sheet, the selling price should be reduced or more favorable terms should be given. Written reports from experts substantiating your figures, will always strengthen your position. Incorporating these findings into your negotiations will give you a winning hand when playing "poker" with the seller.

Never Pay Taxes on Profits Again

The price can be negotiated based on a trade. If both parties want to trade their properties, equities can be adjusted for favorable tax advantages. As long as the transactions are done correctly, you will never have to pay taxes on your profits again. Consult your real estate tax advisor for more details.

Avoiding Mistakes When Negotiating

Don't be fooled by the seller who says, "That's why the price is what it is. I took into account all of those things." To avoid making mistakes when negotiating, never lose track of the IRR. It should always be your reference point. The seller has to prove that your computations are wrong, so just stick to your guns. You'll do fine!

DOWN PAYMENT STRATEGIES THAT WORK

The preferred down payment strategy is *leverage*. However, you must be realistic using this approach. Unless you have information to the contrary, start by offering 10 percent down, and it doesn't have to be cash either. There are other valuable resources that can be used. Here are a few to consider:

- *Create paper:* Prepare a note and secure it with your house, business, or other property.
- *Professional services:* Create a contract for your services as a valuable asset. Agree to repair the building as a down payment. The seller's equity will be more secure if you do.
- *Assign income:* Assign income from rents, commissions, profits, and future income. Judgments, inheritance, and lottery winnings, for example, can also be given.
- *Additional loans:* Loans from family members, credit unions, real estate licensees, insurance policies, or certificates of deposits will work.
- *Partnership:* You can reduce your cash outlay by having each member invest either cash or notes. The financial strength of a group is more substantial than its individual members. Sellers are more likely to accept unsecured paper when issued by a group.

- *Other assets:* Planes, cars, boats, accounts and notes receivable, animals, trade inventory, hobby and athletic equipment, vacation time rentals, land, works of art, season tickets, and cemetery plots might sound outlandish, but you will be surprised at what sellers will take as a down payment if highly motivated.
- *Escrow prorations and credits:* Rental deposits can be credited as part of the down payment, if not restricted by law. Other prorations such as rents and interest can also be used to adjust down payments and loan balances. Credits for work can be completed, prorations of taxes, and insurance reduce cash outlays.
- *Split downs:* If a seller wants 20 percent down instead of 10 percent, try paying 10 percent at the close of escrow and 10 percent later. Compute interest as if it were an 80 percent loan.

There are both advantages and disadvantages in using any of these down payment strategies. Always be careful. Remember, money doesn't always "talk." Buyers and sellers have different needs. Finding and filling them is the key to successful negotiating.

PROTECTING YOURSELF WHEN THE BUYER WANTS YOU TO PAY FOR REPAIRS

When repair work is needed, a credit should be issued toward the down payment. The buyer can take the credit and do absolutely nothing, or get the work done. If the work is completed for less than the amount of the credit, the buyer pockets the difference. The seller is then released from liability.

If the seller continues to have an involvement in the property, by holding a trust deed or management contract, demand should be made that all work be completed. Only in this way will the seller's interest be completely protected.

The best way to account for repair credits is to deposit the required funds needed to complete the work in an interest-bearing fiduciary account. It should be set up under the following terms:

- *Limit your liability:* Agree to maximum dollar and time limit.
- *Specific repairs:* Only do agreed upon specific repairs. Use the inspection report as a reference. Don't be vague. When it says plumbing repairs, it shouldn't mean replace the plumbing in the entire building.
- *Approvals:* Buyer should approve all completed work in writing before dispersing funds. Be sure to get all liens released. Require seller's approval of all work over a stated amount. Inspection

reports from either an inspection company or a property management company will help you negotiate repairs and replacements
costs on an item-by-item basis. It's important to scrutinize each
item on the report. If the seller is in a hurry to sell, opportunities
for concessions may arise.

WHY "AS IS" IS NOW "AS WAS"

Some sellers advertise property on an "as is" basis. Most state laws ren-
der these words meaningless. It's really not a "buyer beware" market
anymore. Don't proceed under this false assumption. Placing this
wording in the contract doesn't automatically release the seller from liability. Be sure all parties agree, in writing, to complete the transaction
based on the knowledge they have of the project. With the proper releases, a nominal sum can be paid as consideration to cover all repair
items. Confer with an experienced real estate attorney in this matter.

POSSESSION BEFORE ESCROW CLOSES— A GREAT STRATEGY FOR WHOM?

If extensive repairs are needed, try to take possession of the property
before escrow closes so that the work can be started immediately. This
is a great strategy for the buyer, as it provides an opportunity to get an
in-depth look at the building before escrow closes. Sellers have an in-
herent danger in this arrangement. Buyers could nitpick the property to
death or uncover reasons not to close. Escrows can be strung out for inconsequential reasons. You've heard it said, "It isn't over until it's over."
Well, it isn't closed until it closes. Don't get trapped by being an overly
accommodating seller.

WHEN YOU SHOULD AVOID RAISING RENTS

If rental contracts do not reflect actual rents collected, the seller must
rectify the situation. It's best to let the seller contact the tenants. You
should always try to maintain a positive relationship with the tenants,
especially during change of ownership.

When rents are low, they should be raised during the escrow period.
The current owner will probably have greater compliance than you. If
rents need to be raised substantially, there might be a number of evictions. This usually causes bad feelings and additional legal costs. It's
better to have the seller deal with these headaches, especially if a rosy
rental picture was painted on the set-up sheet.

As the new owner, you might be able to offer the existing resident manager additional incentives to initiate rent raises. Be careful. If the resident manager is the cause of many of the problems, don't compound the problem. Remove the resident manager and have your property management company find a new resident manager immediately.

AVOIDING SALES TAX PROBLEMS

Valuations of furnishings can be used for depreciation and sales tax purposes. Be careful when making these evaluations. Higher values placed on personal property such as furniture could result in a higher sales taxes liability. It also means a greater deduction for depreciation. The income tax saving must be weighed against the additional sales tax paid when computing the IRR.

Sales taxes should be collected in escrow. Be aware that even though the seller has primary responsibility to pay the taxes, the buyer is not completely off the hook until they are paid.

WHEN TO CLOSE ESCROW TO AVOID COLLECTING LATE RENTS

Try to close escrow at least 15 days after rents are due. This allows some of the "collection dust" to settle, and spares the new owners the task of collecting late rents. Have delinquent rents at the close of escrow charged to the seller; then he is faced with the collection problem. Your property managers can then concentrate on evictions, if necessary. Closing escrow the day rents are due puts the burden on you because, technically, there are no delinquencies.

BEWARE OF INDEPENDENT ESCROW COMPANIES

Knowing how to properly use the services of competent escrow companies will benefit you during negotiations. Be careful when using the other party's escrow company, especially if they relate on a first name basis. Biased interpretations of the purchase contract may end up on the typed escrow instructions. If typed escrow instructions do not correspond exactly to the offer-to-purchase contract, refuse to sign them until they do—no matter how anxious the other party is to close. The delay is not your fault. Remember, time is on your side when the other party is anxious to consummate the deal.

Always negotiate escrow fees to reduce costs. This strategy is often overlooked. There are no firm price tags for escrow services. Fees for recording, typing, and notary can add up. Agree, up front, on one fee to cover *all*. However, using the other party's escrow may work to your advantage. The escrow officer may be willing to reduce fees and provide additional services to everyone as an accommodation.

In circumstances where one party insists on opening escrow before contingencies are removed, be sure to route all correspondence through the escrow company. Inspection reports and approvals should be dated and recorded by the escrow company to properly document compliance with deadlines.

REDUCING THE COST OF TITLE INSURANCE

The cost of title insurance can be reduced considerably if you know what to ask for. Since title policy premiums are usually controlled by state laws, they cannot be negotiated. However, there is a way to reduce them when a short holding period is anticipated. Before escrow closes, ask the title insurance company for a "short rate" or a binder. If the property is sold within the binder period, a new title policy is not required. The cost for the binder at purchase is nominal compared to the cost of a full-blown title insurance policy when you sell.

CONTROLLING ESCROW DEPOSITS

Funds held by the escrow company should be deposited in a bank of your choice earning the highest interest rate possible. If the escrow is canceled, all funds should be returned to you without any offsets. In the real world, this probably won't happen unless it's specifically spelled out in the escrow instructions. The escrow company wants to be paid for its time and effort even if the transaction doesn't close. To avoid this problem, try to remove all contingencies (with the possible exception of the loans) before opening escrow. It's a lot simpler and less costly.

HANDLING COUNTER OFFERS

Make minuscule moves in price and terms when negotiating. If you offer $1 million for a property and the seller wants $1.5 million, don't come back with $1.3 million. It's too big of a jump. Try $1,050,000. Don't get into the habit of splitting the difference and counter with a $1.250 million. A good negotiator will spot this ploy every time and know he or she is dealing with an amateur.

Always know your parameters—"never" adjust them during face-to-face negotiations. If necessary, excuse yourself from the meeting and take time to analyze any new proposals. Everything must be evaluated in terms of the IRR. Give yourself time to do it properly. Don't be afraid to walk away temporarily.

Walking away from negotiations is an effective tactic. It gives both parties time to think, and it creates the impression that you're not motivated. If offers and counteroffers are properly signed, the property is still under contract whether you walk away or not. If something favorable doesn't develop, you can always revert back to your previous agreement.

The one who is the least motivated has the greatest advantage. Never forget that! Buyers should have several properties lined up to project a laissez-faire attitude. To be able to say "So what if I don't buy your property, I'll buy someone else's," or "It really doesn't matter to me," boosts your negotiating position enormously. Sellers, on the other hand, should give the impression that buyers are beating the door down to buy their property.

HANDLING SELLER'S REMORSE

You should be buying in good locations where there's a temporary downturn or weakening of the local economy. The negotiating edge is yours because sellers are highly motivated. Normally, they are amiable to giving excellent terms and price. However, keep in mind that real estate ownership can be extremely personal, even in apartment buildings. Sellers might harbor deep emotional resistance. Although this sentiment is not prevalent with investment property owners, it still exists. Proceed with care. Continually reassure the seller that he or she is making the right move. Always keep the seller informed. Communicate! Communicate! Communicate!

Initial reluctance on the part of sellers may result in offers being rejected. Remember, acquiring a good apartment building is based on numbers. Rejections, negative comments, and apparent lack of progress could cause you to become discouraged. Be persistent! Never lose track of what you're trying to accomplish—financial freedom. It's important to truly believe you're on course. If you stick to the guidelines in this book, you will find a suitable property and make the right deal.

SUMMARY

When do you stop negotiating? Never! Negotiate and negotiate, and then negotiate some more. Keep on negotiating until you can't negotiate any more. You'll find that as long as you have an interest in the property, you'll probably continue to try to strike a better deal.

While negotiating, remember the other party is a competitor not a pal. Stakes are high and the business at hand is negotiating. Stick to business and play your hand properly. At the same time, treat everyone with respect.

10

Managing Your Property Manager

Paramount to the success of any project is the full and proper utilization of a competent property management company. The efficient use of this qualified consultant provides the expertise needed to attain your goals.

Through proficient management, you're able to control risks. These professionals will help you make the correct choices in acquisitions, operations, and selling. With a capable management team at your side, you'll have an effective sounding board for new ideas. Their accurate and timely reports will give you the controls needed to detect problems immediately and take appropriate action.

THE OBJECTIVES OF A GOOD MANAGEMENT PLAN

What do you want to accomplish while you own the apartment complex? This question needs to be answered to formulate an effective plan of action. A *written plan* is essential. Unless they are in writing, specific goals could become blurry. Decisions may become counterproductive without specific objectives.

A good management plan reflects the following investment strategy: Buying midsize apartment buildings in weak markets caused primarily by overbuilding, using little of your own capital, selling at or above replacement costs, and holding on long enough to allow market conditions to improve. To accomplish this, concentrate on:

- Improving physical appearance
- Increasing rental income
- Reducing operating expenses

Information gathered during the inspection phase of the acquisition should provide most of the data needed to prepare a written management plan. Successful management companies have an operations or procedural manual to assist in managing their properties. Use it to formulate your own management plan.

Communicate your management plan to all those involved. Anytime there are changes, make sure everyone is notified. Constant and continual communications are imperative to the success of your project. Periodic meetings and property inspections are also an essential part of your management plan.

Improving Physical Appearance

Concentrate on purchasing newer buildings. There's usually less functional, physical, and economic obsolescence. *Functional obsolescence* occurs when styles or construction methods change. For example, Victorian as opposed to modern, wood shingles to new fire-retardant materials, fuses to circuit breakers, water coolers to air conditioners, and so forth. This type of obsolescence can sometimes be cured by using updated materials and equipment.

Physical obsolescence refers to the day-by-day wear and tear on a building by continual usage and climatic conditions. As things get old, they deteriorate. A determination should be made as to whether or not the deterioration is irreversible. If it is, do not purchase the building. It should be demolished.

Economic obsolescence is a result of circumstances not directly related to the property. It is caused by location problems—a change in the zoning laws from residential to commercial or industrial, for example.

Newer apartment complexes requiring only cosmetic repairs should be your prime target for acquisition. A management plan must rank according to priority those components of repair that will improve cash flow and maintain the building. The less out-of-pocket cash, the less the building has to appreciate to maintain the same IRR.

Expenditures for repairs should be made with an anticipatory pay-back period. If a unit requires paint, carpeting, and drapes, the additional revenue generated must recover these costs as soon as possible. Revenue is generated by reducing vacancies and increasing rents. Major capital improvement such as roofs and major plumbing have much longer pay-back periods.

Based on inspection reports, the management company should present plans to complete all necessary repairs and replacements, including estimated costs, time, and pay-back periods, in effect, creating an itemized monthly budget.

Increasing Rental Income

A marketing plan should be established to fill vacancies. It doesn't make sense to spend money on the building and not have a plan to keep vacancies at a manageable level.

Your management company should know the demographics of tenants interested in renting your apartment complex and target a media campaign accordingly. Program proposals to attract these tenants should detail method(s) of implementation, costs, recommendations, and monitoring procedures.

There are questions that need to be answered: How will the existing tenants be handled? Will management move them out? Will they try to retain present tenants? What type of tenant retention programs and incentives do they specifically plan to use? What are the market tenant retention programs and incentives presently available? The goal in any complex is to create a community of friendly neighbors. People will respond favorably when working toward a mutually beneficial objective. This is the key to successful tenant relations.

Based on previous reports and surveys, detail projections should show rent increases, unit absorption, and vacancies. These figures should be compared to the budget. Variances should be analyzed and adjustments made either in the budget or in marketing procedures.

Make your management company aware that you want your building to be a rent leader rather than a rent follower. You want to be aggressive in rent raises to keep rents as high as possible. The first thing most buyers and lenders look at is rental income. Once the local economy starts to rebound, your rents should be in the top 90th percentile of similar buildings in the area. If they are not, your rents are too low.

Reducing Operating Expenses

An important function of the property manager is to reduce operating expenses. How will they accomplish this? What's their plan? How will it be implemented? Look at each expense item on the statement of operations and ask, point blank, "How do you plan to reduce these expenditures?" Evaluate answers as to credibility by consulting with other experts.

Reducing Insurance and Property Tax Expenses

A unique situation occurs when purchasing apartment buildings in down or weak markets. Property values have decreased. Because of this, assessments tied into these evaluations, such as property taxes and insurance, should be reviewed for potential savings. Overstated property values should be appealed, and your property manager should request a reassessment. If it comes in lower, property tax and insurance bills could be slashed considerably. To assure yourself that you're paying the lowest possible premiums for property insurance, obtain at least three quotes from different insurance companies based on this revaluation.

Comparing Your Apartment's Performance to Other Complexes

Income and expenses should be compared periodically with the "Income/Expense Analysis: Conventional Apartments" published by the Institute of Real Estate Management (IREM). See the sample in Figure 10.1 (pp. 148–149). This comparison will indicate whether or not your figures are in line. Always ask for explanations whenever major differences occur.

PROPERTY MANAGER'S REPORTS

Your property manager should provide monthly operating reports that follow IREM's format. Comprehensive monthly operating statements should include the following information:

- *Receipts:* Whether you call it an income register, a tenant deposit register, or a rent roll, what's most important is that the report contain certain important information. Each apartment unit should be listed numerically by size: number of bedrooms, features (location, patio, and views, for example). Include tenant's name, security deposit, term, rent, date rented, delinquencies, and other income (garage, laundry, security deposits, late charges, and so forth).
- *Disbursements:* Numerical listing of all checks written, vendor amount, account, brief description and listing of unpaid bills, and a copy of the bank reconciliation. One vital portion, often called

an *expense register* must indicate which units that certain expenses pertain to (HVAC replacements, plumbing repairs, carpets, or painting, etc.). This is critical for budgeting and auditing purposes.

- *Operating statement:* On a cash basis, all income and expense items, actual compared to budget, including explanations of all variances. There should be monthly and year-to-date columns for both actual and budgeted amounts.
- *Narrative:* Summation of both current and year-to-date operations, capital improvements, changes, or recommendations.
- *Vacancies/Delinquencies:* A report showing the vacant and delinquent units for the *current operating month.* The vacancy portion should list each vacant unit, condition of the unit, deposits taken/move-in date for new tenant, and when the unit was vacated. The delinquency portion should show the balance due, the unit number, and status (date notice served, court date, lockout date, etc.). This information will tell you how aggressively your manager is collecting rents and renting up units.
- *Market survey:* Your property manager should provide you with a written market survey (quarterly or semi-annually) showing your property as compared to the market. At a minimum, it should compare such factors as rent (by type of unit), required deposits, vacancy (by type), amenities, property conditions, incentives or concessions, and advertising. Knowing how your property "measures up" to your competition is critical to maximizing its performance and value.
- *Annual budget:* Your property manager should prepare a 12-month calendar year budget for all items listed on the operating statement. This budget should be prepared, reviewed and approved before December 1 of the current year (year prior to the budget year).

These reports will help you direct the activities of your property manager. However, burying your head under reams of reports won't get the job done. You can't effectively manage your property unless you use these reports wisely and take an active part in making decisions. As a part of the property management plan, make a commitment to see the building periodically and to actively participate in its operations.

Defining Income and Expense Classifications

To maintain consistency in reporting, classify all income and expenditures according to the chart of accounts shown in Figures 10.2 and 10.3. This will assure "apples-to-apples" comparisons.

Selected Metropolitan Areas—U.S.A. · Median Income and Operating Costs · By Building Type

	Nashville, TN — Low Rise over 24 Units — 5 Blgs. 661 Apts. 562,822 Square Feet				Nashville, TN — Garden Type Buildings — 45 Buildings 10,216 Apartments 9,708,463 Rentable Square Feet								New Jersey Northern — Elevator Buildings — 4 Blgs. 1,056 Apts. 1,131,332 Square Feet			
	Bldgs.	%GPI Med.	$Sq.Ft. Med.	$Unit Med.	Bldgs.	% of GPI Med.	Low	High	$/Sq.Ft. Med.	Low	High	$/Unit Med.	%GPI Med.	$/Sq.Ft. Med.	$/Unit Med.	Bldgs.
Income																
Rents—Apartments	(5)	93.7	7.89	6,150	(44)	96.4	94.7	97.0	8.54	7.29	9.73	7,138	96.7	29.14	33,254	(4)
Rents—Garage/Parking	( )				(5)	.5			.04			39	4.4	1.58	1,586	(2)
Rents—Stores/Offices	( )				(1)	1.2			.12			112				( )
Gross Possible Rents	(5)	93.7	7.89	6,150	(44)	96.5	94.8	97.0	8.59	7.29	9.76	7,138	97.1	29.14	33,515	(4)
Vacancies/Rent Loss	(5)	7.6	.73	444	(42)	11.2	7.5	14.6	.91	.67	1.32	838	16.5	3.70	4,912	(4)
Total Rents Collected	(5)	86.1	6.51	5,394	(44)	85.4	80.9	90.5	7.39	6.42	8.53	6,300	91.1	27.46	27,658	(4)
Other Income	(5)	6.3	.61	370	(42)	3.9	3.1	5.3	.36	.24	.48	274	3.3	1.00	1,152	(4)
Gross Possible Income	(5)	100.0	8.52	6,402	(44)	100.0	100.0	100.0	8.89	7.43	10.31	7,382	100.0	30.14	34,667	(4)
Total Collections	(5)	92.4	7.15	5,821	(44)	88.9	85.7	93.1	7.74	6.66	9.13	6,597	94.4	28.46	28,956	(4)
Expenses																
Management Fee	(5)	3.7	.37	225	(40)	4.0	3.4	4.6	.34	.28	.41	299	3.4	.84	999	(4)
Other Administrative**	(5)	11.4	.80	733	(44)	7.4	4.8	10.0	.64	.43	.85	608	2.5	.88	885	(4)
Subtotal Administrative	(5)	15.0	1.08	962	(44)	10.2	8.6	13.0	.98	.79	1.12	851	6.9	2.04	2,049	(4)
Supplies	(4)	1.9	.18	111	(37)	.3	.2	.4	.02	.01	.04	17	.5	.06	59	(4)
Heating Fuel-CA only*	(5)	.6	.05	44	(31)	.7	.5	.9	.06	.04	.09	58	.0	.00	0	(2)
CA and Apartments*	( )				(4)	1.4			.09			87	4.6	.56	537	(1)
Electricity-CA only*	(3)	1.2	.09	79	(37)	1.4	1.0	1.7	.13	.09	.16	111	2.3	.51	683	(2)
CA and Apartments*	(2)	2.6	.19	165	(6)	1.7			.12			119	2.0	.54	617	(2)

Account	(n)				(n)								(n)			
Water/Sewer—CA only*	(3)	4.1	.40	239	(14)	4.6	3.4	5.0	.43	.36	.50	349	(2)	.8	.30	303
CA and Apartments*	(2)	5.8	.40	372	(30)	5.2	3.5	6.6	.44	.35	.49	340	(2)	1.6	.19	187
Gas—CA only*	(4)	3.1	.24	219	(15)	.3	.2	.4	.03	.02	.04	22	(2)	1.2	.44	442
CA and Apartments*	(1)	.3	.02	18	(9)	.5			.04			35	(1)	.6	.16	189
Building Services	(4)	2.5	.17	160	(35)	1.1	.4	1.8	.10	.05	.15	78	(4)	1.0	.29	295
Other Operating	(3)	1.1	.12	69	(22)	.5	.1	.6	.05	.01	.07	41	(1)	.1	.02	21
Subtotal Operating	(5)	10.0	.86	652	(44)	8.1	6.6	10.5	.73	.66	.81	611	(4)	6.6	1.48	1,486
Security**	(1)	.4	.03	23	(24)	.7	.3	1.1	.06	.04	.09	50	(2)	7.4	.90	868
Grounds Maintenance**	(5)	2.7	.25	177	(42)	1.9	1.2	2.5	.17	.10	.24	148	(4)	.9	.22	276
Maintenance—Repairs	(5)	2.3	.17	149	(44)	3.3	2.4	6.4	.34	.20	.58	248	(4)	2.5	.69	745
Painting/Decorating**	(3)	3.4	.23	214	(42)	2.1	.6	2.7	.17	.04	.25	146	(4)	.8	.16	156
Subtotal Maintenance	(5)	8.2	.58	522	(44)	8.7	7.0	10.1	.77	.59	.95	638	(4)	3.4	1.07	1,071
Real Estate Taxes	(5)	5.9	.41	377	(44)	6.9	5.5	7.8	.57	.43	.80	462	(4)	10.7	2.77	3,298
Other Tax/Fee/Permit	(2)	.1	.00	2	(33)	.1	.0	.1	.00	.00	.01	2	( )			
Insurance	(5)	1.1	.08	69	(44)	1.5	1.1	1.8	.14	.10	.15	111	(4)	.4	.13	152
Subtotal Tax–Insurance	(5)	8.6	.60	550	(44)	8.6	7.3	9.5	.76	.56	.95	642	(4)	11.0	2.90	3,375
Recreational/Amenities**	(1)	.1	.01	8	(29)	.2	.1	.2	.01	.01	.02	11	(3)	.5	.11	141
Other Payroll	(3)	7.0	.50	450	(33)	4.2	2.1	7.8	.44	.22	.58	332	(4)	1.1	.29	291
Total All Expenses	(5)	44.1	4.11	3,090	(44)	41.2	36.6	45.8	3.79	3.29	4.09	3,014	(4)	27.6	8.33	8,946
Net Operating Income	(5)	42.6	3.63	2,827	(44)	47.8	43.6	54.3	4.43	3.35	5.24	3,730	(4)	56.0	19.89	20,009
Payroll Recap**	(4)	13.7	1.32	816	(38)	12.1	9.9	15.0	1.09	.92	1.23	897	(4)	7.9	1.61	1,617

Figure 10.1 Metropolitan area reports. *Note:* For a description of Utility Expenses (*) and Payroll Cost (**) reporting and an explanation of the report layouts and method of data analysis, refer to the sections entitled *Guidelines for the Use of this Data and Interpretation of a Page of Data.* For definitions of the income and expense categories, refer to the Appendix. Copyright © 2002, Institute of Real Estate Management.

Income

1. *Apartment Rentals:* This figure should reflect all apartment rents which could have been collected, including employee apartments, if 100% of your building had been occupied.

2. *Garage and Parking Income:* If there is a separate charge made for use of garage parking areas, report the total amount that could have been collected, if 100% of this area had been occupied. If you include garage or parking area in the apartment rent, reduce the apartment rent total on Line 1 by the portion applicable to garages and parking and report this portion on Line 2.

3. *Stores and Offices:* Show the rental income you could have received from stores and offices if both of these had been 100% occupied.

4. *Gross Possible Rental Income:* This is the total of Lines 1, 2, and 3.

5. *Less Vacancies and Rent Loss:* See Total Rents Collected.

6. *Total Rents Collected:* Show what you actually collected from all sources indicated on Lines 1, 2, and 3 (Apartment Rentals, Garage and Parking Income, Store and Office Income, and including the rental value of apartments given to employees as part of their compensation). Then subtract Line 6 from Line 4 (Gross Possible Rental Income) and enter the difference on Line 5 as Vacancies and Rent Loss.

7. *Miscellaneous Income:* Report here all the income collected from such sources as maid service, gas and electricity sold to tenants, commissions from telephones, laundry and vending machines, signs on the building, and air-conditioning charges. *DO NOT include interest or dividend income.*

Figure 10.2   Income form. *Source:* Institute of Real Estate Management, Income/Expense Analysis.

QUALIFYING FOR THE MAXIMUM TAX WRITE-OFF

The IRS provides up to a $25,000 write-off to individuals who actively participate in the management of a property. Active participation is defined as: "participating in the making of management decisions regarding a rental property (in a significant and bona fide manner), or the arrangement of others to provide services in an ongoing manner."

The property management agreement should incorporate these seven guidelines to assist in qualifying for the Active Participation Status according to IRS Code 469:

- Specifically state that the owner(s) will actively participate.
- Owner(s) to authorize expenditures over a predetermined limit.
- Only directed day-to-day operations to be performed by management company.
- Emergency repairs can be made without approval.

Expenses

Management Fee: This figure should represent the agency fee paid directly by the building owner.

Other Administrative Costs (including wages of administrative personnel only): This figure should represent the salaries of any administrative personnel paid directly by the owner; any leasing, rental or renewal fees paid in addition to the management fee; any alteration supervisory charges paid by the owner; the cost of all advertising, legal and auditing fees; dues in professional organizations; architectural or professional engineer's fees; and all telephone and building office expenses and supplies paid by the owner. Includes on-site manager if an administrative expense, otherwise put in Other Payroll. Do not include rent concessions.

Supplies: On this Line show all janitorial supplies, light bulbs, uniforms for employees and other such supplies which do not belong under painting, decorating, maintenance or repairs.

Heating Expense: This figure should represent the cost of any fuel used for space heating of your building whether you use coal, gas, oil, electricity or any other fuel. DO NOT include the costs of ash removal or cost of gas, electricity, etc. used for cooking or hot water. If you receive a combined gas or electric bill for heating and utilities, take your lowest bill for a summer month and multiply it by 12. Subtract this amount from your total annual cost to arrive at an estimated heating expense.

Electricity (excluding Heating Expense): This includes electricity for tenant and public areas, air conditioning, elevators, hot water, laundry and other related purposes. DO NOT report electricity used for space heating on this line. This figure includes 100% of your electrical (non-heating) expense, even if you bill some of it back to your tenants (electricity income is provided for under the Income category Miscellaneous Income).

Water and Sewer: Show all water costs including, if applicable in your community, sewage charges. If other utility charges are included in the water bill, give an estimate of each charge on the appropriate line.

Gas: (excluding Heating Expense): Show here the cost of gas for utilities, i.e. cooking, air-conditioning, hot water, swimming pools, etc. DO NOT include the cost of gas used for space heating on this line. (This should be reported on the Heating Expense line).

Building Services: This covers such contracted outside services as window washing, lobby directory, exterminating, rubbish removal, TV antenna service, but NOT services chargeable against the painting, decorating, janitorial, or maintenance and repair categories.

Other Operating Expenses: This category is designed to include operating costs which do not fit under any other caption. Among such items might be damage to property of others not covered by insurance, intercom service, directional signs, door lettering, etc. Do NOT use this category if any other caption may be used.

Security (including wages of security personnel): List any in-house or contracted services on a full or part-time basis for securing the premises against crime. Include doormen and security equipment in this category but DO NOT include intercom service.

Grounds Maintenance (including wages of ground maintenance personnel): This category represents gardening, landscaping, sidewalks, and street sweeping, snow removal, water feature maintenance, and outside light maintenance. Include grounds maintenance supplies.

Maintenance and Repairs - Interior & Exterior (excluding M&R Payroll to be reported under Other Payroll): This category is to account for all items of general maintenance and repairs, both interior and exterior. This includes exterior painting or cleaning; elevator maintenance contracts; boiler inspection and repair contracts; air-conditioning service contracts, parts, small hand tools; fire protection services and equipment; plumbing; electrical, plastering masonry, carpentry, heating, roofing or tuck pointing contractor's service unless such bills properly constitute a capital expenditure.

Painting and Decorating - Interior only (including wage): Include on this line the cost of all contracted labor, decorators on building payroll, and all materials and supplies used in the decorating of the interior of the building. Paint, wall-paper, brushes, wall-washing, and similar items belong in this category. Replacement of floor coverings, draperies, furnishings or light fixtures (if not a capital expenditure) also belong in this category. Exterior painting should be included in Maintenance and Repairs.

Real Estate Taxes: This includes all local or state real estate taxes as well as any noncapitalized assessments.

Other Taxes, Fees and Permits: Show on this line any personal property taxes applicable to the building, franchise taxes, sign permit fees or any other tax necessary to the operation of the building.

Insurance: Include all one year charges for fire, liability, theft, boiler explosions, rent fidelity bonds, and all insurance premiums except those paid to FHA for mortgage insurance or employee workman's compensation and benefit plans. If the building policies are paid on a multi-year basis, pro-rate and include only one year's cost.

Recreational Amenities (including wages): Include in this category all operating and maintenance cost of indoor and outdoor recreational facilities and amenities such as sauna, gymnasium, billard room, pool, jacuzzi, tennis courts, etc. This should include payroll, materials and supplies, services, equipment replacement, and contractual costs (including any net expenses from cable TV operations).

Other Payroll (excluding payroll reported in other categories): Amount paid to janitors, maids, elevator operators, telephone switchboard operators, maintenance personnel, including market rental value of apartment, payroll taxes, welfare benefits and workman's compensation. DO NOT INCLUDE wages reported under Other Administrative Costs, Security, Grounds Maintenance, Painting & Decorating, and Recreational Amenities.

Total All Expenses: Total all Expense categories.

Figure 10.3 Expenses form. *Source:* Institute of Real Estate Management, Income/Expense Analysis.

- Capital repairs made under owner(s) directive.
- Owner(s) establish rental terms/rates.
- New tenants approval based on owner(s) established guidelines.

Establishing Active Participation

In addition to enumerating the conditions of active participation in the property management contract, every owner should perform the following functions, not only to qualify as an active participant, but also to adequately control his or her investment:

- Owner(s) should physically inspect the property prior to the close of escrow and at least annually thereafter. Since a picture is worth a thousand words, it's best to take photos for discussions with your consultant. Receive and review three estimates on all major improvements before authorizing the expenditure.
- Plan to meet at least semiannually. Record all meetings. Policy and procedural changes should be based on operating reports and physical inspections.
- Owner(s) should either prepare a periodic independent rental survey or arrange to have it done. Include such items as rental rates, amenities, or promotional specials, for example. They should be used to establish future rents and marketing strategies.
- Before locating a property, interview management companies to determine which one best fulfills your needs. Evaluate each company based on their procedures manual and the other criteria discussed in Chapter 4 on consultants.
- To verify vacancies when doing physical inspections, tenants should provide move-in dates, monthly rent, and a security deposit.
- Obtain a printout of amounts paid to vendors. If one is used frequently, find out why. There could be a conflict of interest.

SUMMARY

The consultant who will affect the outcome of your investment the most is the property manager. If there is a definite plan for your building, you will be able to maintain better control over its outcome.

When looking for apartment buildings, concentrate on projects where obsolescence is minimal. When you do make repairs, make a plan to recover your costs as soon as possible.

Always ask your property manager how he or she is going to increase income and reduce expenses on an item-for-item basis. Continually compare your apartment's performance with others. Be sure the reports provided are adequately explained and use them to control your property.

Be active in managing your investment. Not only do you receive substantial tax benefits, but you also maintain control of your investment.

11

Useful Strategies in Marketing Your Property

THE BEST TIME TO SELL YOUR PROPERTY

How do you know when to sell your property? Presumably, certain parameters or goals were established at the time of purchase. Once they have been achieved, it's time to sell.

A good indicator of when to sell is an increase in residential building permits. This usually occurs when selling prices become equal to or greater than replacement costs. Your apartment building should be put on the market as soon as you anticipate this happening. For example, if you purchased your apartment complex for $20,000 per unit and the cost of replacement is $40,000, consider selling when market values begin to approach the $40,000 mark.

Another indicator is when there are major changes in the vacancy and rental rates.

Never get greedy. Adhere to the established game plan. It's true your apartment building might continue to go up in value, but you should always be looking for opportunities to increase leverage. It's part of the standard operating procedure (SOP). Don't deviate from it by refusing to sell.

GETTING YOUR PROPERTY READY FOR SALE

Renovating income property is an ongoing process. By continually renovating while you own the property, the value of the building will go up. Increasing the rental income is the key to increasing value. What should you be doing to increase the rental income? You should have a plan that includes a market study to determine what the cost of renovations will be and their impact on the rental income and property value. Determining what the rental of new construction is in an area and what the potential rental value of the renovations is will give you a clear indication of how much you should spend and where.

To obtain the higher rentals, the first step is repositioning your property. Rename the complex to reflect a higher type building. Do not do major remodeling, do *cosmetic remodeling*, including constructing a new facade, repair work around the pool, and pool furniture, re-coating the parking structure, and painting the trim. Inside, the units should have new carpeting or flooring. If the appliances are old try to get new appliances, lighting fixtures, blinds, new ceiling fans, and refurbish the cabinets and counters.

Your renovation plan should weigh what the approximate cost will be versus the expected return. The increase in income and value should be much higher than the actual cost.

Overspending will not make an old property competitive with new property. What you're trying to do is reposition your older property somewhere below the new property as to rental income. If you spend too little, repositioning your property will not be achieved. Maintenance of property requires a plan that will increase the value of your property and increase the rents.

Maintaining the property in top-notch condition at all times is a sound management policy. Cosmetic improvements such as painting and landscaping are inexpensive. A good appearance will help to both rent and sell your apartment complex. It should always be maintained in tip-top condition to attract the best tenants and the highest rents. Major renovations should be made when needed, not just to sell the property. The primary responsibility of a good property management company is to see that renovations are carried out in a timely and expeditious manner.

YOUR MARKETING PLAN CAN BE INDIVIDUALLY TAILORED

When a group of investors owns an apartment complex, it is recommended that they have a written agreement defining the conditions of sale.

If the group was formed using the method of ownership introduced in this book, each co-owner has the option to tailor the transaction to meet his or her individual needs. Some owners might want all cash at the time of sale. Others may simply trade or carry back notes. Having this flexibility makes it easier to sell.

CHOOSING THE RIGHT PERSON TO MARKET YOUR PROPERTY

Once the decision has been made to sell, you must establish whether you're going to employ the services of a consultant, such as a real estate licensee or attorney, or market the property yourself. Review Chapter 4 on consultants before making this decision.

How Much You Should Pay a Real Estate Licensee

Licensees can perform many of the services discussed in this chapter. They usually charge a commission based on a sliding scale. The higher the selling price, the lower the commission and vice versa; however, keep in mind that there are no "standard" commission schedules. It's whatever the market will bear. Commissions on lower priced apartment complexes should range between 3 and 6 percent. On the more expensive ones, the range is 2 to 4 percent.

Remember, a consultant's service can also be contracted out on an hourly basis instead of a commission. This arrangement might be less expensive, especially if conflicts of interest arise. However, whatever the fee arrangement is, always get it in writing.

Having the assistance of a third-party when negotiating can be advantageous. I've seen amiable face-to-face discussions between buyers and sellers turn into hostile confrontations. It's easier to talk through a third-party consultant, especially if the atmosphere is filled with volatile emotions.

AT WHAT POINT DO YOU BECOME LIABLE FOR REAL ESTATE COMMISSIONS?

Many real estate listing contracts provide that the procuring real estate licensee is entitled to a commission. The licensees become procuring agents by presenting properties to potential buyers during the listing period and sometimes within a stated period thereafter. If one of these potential buyers attempts to circumvent the licensee to avoid a commission, they are legally barred from doing so. Never get involved with anyone who suggests it. In addition to being unethical, you'll eventually end up paying the commission anyway.

If a real estate licensee is not diligently working on your property, there are remedies governing broker/client relationships. Beating the licensee out of a commission is not one of them. Always try to resolve any problems with the broker before going to any regulatory agencies. It is usually more effective and less time consuming.

DISCOVER AN EFFECTIVE WAY TO SELF-MARKET YOUR PROPERTY

If you decide to market the property yourself, using consultants on an as-needed basis, prepare a set-up sheet with a complete description and operating information. Highlight the main features. It is an effective tool in self-marketing your property. Include in your package interior and exterior photographs that show its best features. Place your advertisement in the newspaper, and return all calls immediately. All offers should be discussed with your consultant before responding.

An essential first step to successfully market your property is to determine current mortgage conditions. Your strategy is based on it. Local lenders and loan brokers can be helpful in this endeavor. If mortgage money is plentiful, the buyer should secure new financing. If not, you may have to finance part of the sale yourself. Be careful, some lenders won't allow it. Make sure you're working with one that will.

MAKING YOUR NOTE MORE VALUABLE

Ideally, when you do sell, plan to have all your equity exchanged into another apartment building. However, if you have to carry back a note, be sure it has real value so it can either be sold or used as a down payment for another property. The following provisions and conditions increase its value:

- A higher rate of interest than current market
- A shorter payback period (five years or less)
- Amortized payment (both principal and interest paid monthly)
- Ample buyer's equity securing the note
- Variable as opposed to fixed interest
- Points for assumption
- Acceleration clause
- Maximum late penalties
- Payee's good credit rating

When using leverage, a good quality note can be equal to or greater than the value of cash for a down payment. It can also provide more flexibility when planning tax strategies.

DETERMINING SELLING PRICE

To determine selling price, consider having a Member Appraisal Institute (MAI) appraisal. It is a comprehensive report of the current value. This report will also assist in your marketing efforts. Other sources discussed in earlier chapters, such as local real estate boards, property management companies, and existing owners, can also be used to establish a selling price.

Conservative Set-Up Sheets Are Important

Use actual numbers only, no projections or estimates, in the set-up sheets. The information supplied should be conservative. Inflated profit projections will make potential buyers leery. If there's any crystal ball gazing to be done, let the prospective buyers do it. You never know, their projections might be more generous than yours. Don't put yourself out on this limb.

Make it absolutely clear on the set-up sheet that the resident manager and the tenants are not to be disturbed. Sellers sometimes let their resident managers know in advance that the building is being sold. These owners feel that it is better to learn about it from them, rather than to hear it from an "overly informative" buyer. Be careful. Resident managers' perception of job security becomes cloudy when they know the building is for sale.

Some owners, however, want to keep the lid on everything until escrow actually closes, because if buyers don't perform, day-to-day operations can be needlessly disrupted. They feel it's better to let well enough alone. What method you choose to handle this situation will depend on your relationship with your resident manager.

Controlling Drive-By Inspections

Prospective buyers like to do drive-by inspections. A drive-by means exactly that. It doesn't mean having afternoon tea with the resident manager. Make this perfectly clear in your set up. Also inform the resident manager that anyone without an appointment should be politely escorted off the property. Dialog between resident managers and prospective buyers at this stage of your marketing program can be counterproductive. If you are not adamant on this point, you'll end up with managerial headaches.

Keep Your Property Management Company Informed

The property management company must be told that the building is being sold. They will be able to assist with all inspections, and they are in the best position to answer questions. As an additional incentive, this gives them the opportunity to make points with the new buyers.

What to Do When Dark Clouds Appear on the Title Report

As an added precaution, have the title report updated. If there are any dark clouds hanging over the title, you should know up front before spending time and money on a marketing program. Make sure that these problems are corrected. Contact the title company or your attorney to help you clear the title.

Looking for Buyers

The first place to look for prospective buyers is in the county records. Apartment owners who own property in the same general area as your building are excellent prospects. Contact them to see if they're interested in buying. You'll be surprised at the response. People tend to gravitate toward similar investments. Stock market investors generally stick with stocks, real estate investors with real estate, bonds with bonds, and so forth.

A Successful Newspaper Advertisement

Have newspaper advertisements run in both the local and nearest big city Sunday editions. Don't waste your advertising dollars on the other days of the week. Serious apartment buyers primarily look at the Sunday newspapers. The advertisement should include the following information:

- Number of units and the unit mix
- Price and down payment
- Special seller financing
- Location—city or section of town
- If it's a new or newer building
- One or two special features
- Phone number
- Selling by owner

If your advertisement is not producing results, change it every other month. Phrases like "flexible terms" and "submit all offers" will generate additional interest.

Don't overexpose the property. Buyers might think something is wrong. Very little or no response could mean discontinuing the advertisement for a few weeks. When you do resume, create a new advertisement. Instead of weekly, try advertising every other week.

Responding to an Offer

When inquiries are received, set-ups are sent, and prospective buyers are contacted. The ball is now in motion. Remember, send set-ups promptly. Follow up within a few days with a telephone call. Make notes of all conversations. These notations will help you to monitor the marketing program. If the selling price and/or down payment are too high, financing is not available, or market conditions have changed, it will readily become apparent when analyzing your notes.

As your marketing activity grows to a crescendo, and you start receiving offers, review Chapter 9 on negotiations. After you've done that, take a deep breath. The battle is beginning.

PROTECTING YOURSELF WHEN YOUR PROPERTY IS TIED UP

Negotiating from the seller's position is just the reverse of the buyer's. Time is not on the side of the seller; therefore, taking your property off the market for any length of time isn't to your advantage. To avoid this, be sure all buyers contingencies have an expiration date. Use a specific date (not number of days) when removing contingencies. Using number of days to remove contingencies can cause uncertainty as to the actual start date, especially if it's dependent on a nebulous event. For example, if the inspection of all books and records is to be made within 10 working days of receipt, who determines if all the books and records have been received? Buyers can stall by continually asking for more and more information and can extend those 10 days ad infinitum. To avoid confusion, always use a specific date rather than number of days to remove contingencies!

DETERMINING IF YOU HAVE A REAL BUYER

Before accepting an offer, gather as much information as you possibly can about the buyer—credit reports, financial statements, track record, and references. The buyer's track record will show if he or she is experienced in similar transactions. It's easier to work with experienced buyers than holding hands with one who's not. They've been through a learning curve so they're able to make decisions quickly, thereby reducing the amount of time your property is off the market.

To be certain you're working with a real buyer, have the buyer release the deposit to you as soon as all contingencies (other than loan approval) have been removed. If a qualified buyer is genuinely serious in closing the transaction, there shouldn't be any objection to this request. If the buyer says, "Suppose you back out of the deal, I have no protection." You should answer, "You can put a cloud on the title and I won't be able to sell it to anyone." This cloud is called a *lis pendens*. It gives constructive notice to anyone interested in your property that legal action is about to be taken. The outcome might have serious implications as to the marketability of the property, as your property can be tied up in legal proceedings for years.

GETTING OUT OF ANY CONTRACT LEGALLY

Always be careful when signing offers and counteroffers. A legally binding contract can be created once your signature goes on the dotted line. Unless you've retained an escape clause, your property is effectively taken off the market. Phrases like "subject to the approval of" my attorney, the co-owners, my property management company, my wife, or my astrologer are all legitimate reasons to beat a path out the back door and out of the contract.

CLOSING THE SALE WITH NO STRINGS ATTACHED

Don't deposit funds into an escrow account for repairs. Funds tied up under this arrangement subject you to further involvement in the property while waiting for the work to be done. Don't tie yourself down. Go on to other deals. If repairs are required, reduce the selling price instead. Be sure the buyer releases you from all claims when you do. Have your attorney prepare the paperwork.

Remember, reducing the selling price will lower both income and property taxes. This is an added benefit to buyer and seller.

Have all documentation routed through the escrow company. It is an effective way to authenticate "received" and "sent" dates. Questions that may arise later as to whether paperwork was received on time can be verified by simply referring to the date stamp.

All walk throughs and physical inspections should be conducted by the property management company. They are knowledgeable about all legal requirements for tenant notices and should have sufficient information as to the condition of the building to answer any and all questions. The management company should properly notify all vendors when the building is sold to avoid further liability. Keep copies of these notifications in your permanent files for protection.

SUMMARY

If you really want to sell your property, be serious in your efforts. Don't waste your time and the time of potential buyers exposing your property just to see what it's worth.

When working with a broker, be sure a marketing plan is submitted that includes advertising recommendations (with budgets), methods of evaluating potential buyers, and cooperative agreements with other real estate licensees. Ask for specific dates as to when each aspect of the marketing plan should unfold. Establish a reporting system and monitor it closely.

If you are marketing the property yourself, prepare conservative, accurate, and professional-looking set-up sheets. Follow up quickly and never stop selling.

Time is on the buyer's side. Don't let unqualified buyers take your property off the market.

Be careful when signing. Remember when you put your signature on the line, you're in all likelihood, activating a legally enforceable contract. Keep your attorney close by and use him or her!

Buyers, like newborns, come anytime, day or night. Always be ready to deliver!

12

The Internal Revenue Service's Best Kept Secret

Income tax liability is derived by multiplying taxable income by the applicable tax bracket rate. The lower the taxable income, the lower the rate, thus the lower the tax liability. Herein lies the secret to significant tax savings. Reduce taxable income, and, in turn, tax liability will be less. According to John T. Reid in his book *Aggressive Tax Avoidance for Real Estate Investors* (Reed Publishing: Danville, CA, 1994), the goal for tax planning is to maximize after-tax income, not minimize taxes. To maximize after-tax income, you have to reduce the income tax liability. That's the primary goal of all tax planning. Let's find out how this is accomplished.

WAYS TO LOWER TAXABLE INCOME

This chapter gives you a basic understanding of the following three simple underlying concepts used to reduce taxable income:

1. Spread income over time
2. Spread income to various entities
3. Group income and expenses

Knowing something about each of these concepts will permit you to intelligently implement a sound tax program. With the assistance of a competent tax advisor, your tax savings will be significant.

Spreading Income over Time

Real estate provides the opportunity to spread income over several years using the installment sales method of reporting. By accepting a relatively low down payment and spreading the principal payments over several years, total taxable income for any one year is reduced.

In the tax-deferred exchange method, income can also be spread over time. Both methods can be structured to give you maximum reporting flexibility.

If you're a real estate licensee purchasing a property and you want to spread taxes on your commissions over time, have them contingent upon some event taking place to avoid constructive receipt, if the situation warrants. For example, your commissions could be conditioned upon the property maintaining certain levels of cash flow and/or profits.

Spreading Income to Various Entities

Spreading income to various entities reduces the income any one entity has to report. By transferring ownership of assets to either corporations, partnerships, relatives, or trusts, an effective transfer of income can be accomplished as well.

Relatives in low-income brackets can be paid for services provided. As long as these services represent legitimate business transactions, spreading income in this manner can save you thousands of tax dollars.

When operating entities have dissimilar tax reporting years and basis (cash or accrual), it's possible to spread income and expenses over different years to take advantage of the tax laws.

Group Income and Expenses

Grouping income and expenses can lower taxable income. Real estate provides the flexibility to implement this kind of tax-planning tactic. More specifically, apartments do, because they fit nicely within the definition of active participation rules (which allow a $25,000 write-off against salaries and other active income). This write-off alone represents a substantial tax savings to many individual investors. See the section on this loophole on p. 167.

When changes in either income or expenses can be projected, the benefits of grouping are phenomenal. For example, refinancing will create a higher interest expense deduction to offset anticipated increases in rental income. Short-term loan contracts with high points will accomplish the same thing.

If expenses are projected to increase, offset them by increasing receipts from installment contracts. Avoid reporting income when notes become due by renegotiating an extension of time. If the senior mortgage matures before your note, subordinate it to new financing to avoid payment.

Investing in midsize apartments gives you the advantage of acquiring properties outside your hometown. As a result, travel and transportation expenses related to your investments can be deducted. These deductions should be timed to give you the maximum tax savings using the "grouping method." By rearranging the selling price and interest rate (within certain limitations), it is possible to create either higher or lower interest and/or depreciation expense deductions.

Capital gains and losses can also be grouped to maximum tax benefits. With restrictions, capital losses may be used to offset capital gains plus additional amounts of ordinary income.

These represent only a few of the many techniques available. Always consult your tax advisor to assist you in making these moves.

INCREASING THE DEPRECIATION DEDUCTION

Maximize the deduction for depreciation:

1. To increase the depreciable basis of the asset, take the higher of either the tax role or an independent appraisers evaluation.
2. To decrease the length of time the asset is depreciated, identify personal property assets. They can be depreciated over shorter lives.

Various methods of depreciation are used for different classifications of personal property. Properties with lives of three, five, seven, and ten years may be depreciated by the 200 percent declining balance method. The greater the depreciation, the higher the expense deduction, and the more the Internal Revenue Service (IRS) helps to pay for your investment.

Converting Real Property into Personal Property

The IRS defines *tangible personal property* as any personal property except land and improvements thereto, such as buildings or other inherently permanent structures (including items that are structural components of such buildings or structures) (Reg. 1.48-1[c]). The courts have concluded that "permanency" is the most pertinent test in the determination of whether an asset is a structural component and not personal property. They have applied six tests to assist:

1. Is the property capable of being moved and has it in fact been moved?
2. Is the property designed or constructed to remain permanently in place?
3. Are there circumstances that tend to show the expected or intended length of affixation?
4. How substantial a job is the removal of the property and how time-consuming is it?
5. How much damage will the property sustain upon removal?
6. How is the property affixed to the land?

Personal Property Items Found in Apartment Buildings

The following represent assets found in apartment complexes that normally qualify as personal property:

- Furniture such as beds, tables, chairs, lamps, and sofas
- Carpets, drapes, blinds
- Security and decorative lighting
- Refrigerators, garbage disposals, washers and dryers
- Pool equipment and furnishings including pumps and filtering apparatus
- Recreational equipment pool table, weights, and exercise equipment

Typically, personal property amounts to less than 3 percent of the building's component costs. The remainder of the apartment is assigned a depreciable life of 27.5 years. The trick is to hire a *cost segregation analyst,* who maximizes the benefits by identifying, classifying, and segregating more than 3 percent of the building's assets for an accelerated depreciation for federal income tax purposes. This may mean 3 to 20 times more savings than the 3 percent found in identifying personal property. Power outlets in the office, decorative paneling in your reception area and conference room, oversized cooling systems, and kitchens are just a few items that a cost segregation specialist looks for when working to identify a tax savings in your apartment building.

The personal property assets are grouped under several IRS classifications. The cost segregation specialist identifies which components of each system, according to federal tax laws, can be assigned accelerated life of 5, 7, or 15 years rather than the straight line of 27.5 years. Cost segregation studies should be initiated as early as possible during the acquisition process to obtain the maximum tax savings.

Remember, by maximizing the deduction for depreciation, you increase your after tax internal rate of return (IRR). That's the money you put in your pocket without the IRS going in after it.

THE LAST REMAINING LOOPHOLE THAT SURVIVED TAX REFORM

Apartment ownership still provides the opportunity to easily qualify as an active participant. In doing so, qualified owners can deduct up to $25,000 per year against salaries and other nonpassive income. You'll notice that I said "qualified owners." That's because there are five basic conditions that must be met to qualify for this write-off:

1. The person seeking the write-off must be an individual taxpayer. Corporations and limited partners do not qualify. The IRS considers a married couple filing jointly to be an individual, so a husband and wife can share the write-off. Tenants-in-common form of ownership meet this requirement.
2. The property must be a real estate rental activity. That is, its primary purpose must be that of a rental. Apartment buildings qualify beautifully.
3. The individual must own a minimum of 10 percent of the rental property at all times. A husband and wife can own 10 percent combined and still qualify because they're considered to be an individual by the IRS. An individual may own more than 10 percent, but not less.
4. The maximum write-off of $25,000 is phased out when adjusted gross income (AGI) exceeds $100,000. The phase-out is $2 for each $1 of AGI over the minimum of $100,000 for married taxpayer filing jointly. This exemption is unavailable once AGI reaches $150,000.
5. The individual must be considered an *active participant.* The active participation standard requires only that the individual participate (in a significant and bona fide manner) in the making of management decisions or arranges for others to provide services. Examples of management decisions would include setting rental rates and terms and approving capital and repair expenditures. A management company can handle the day-to-day operations as long as the owner makes the major decisions.

It is difficult to get this deduction owning real estate other than apartment buildings. The tax codes have specially questioned whether triple-net lease arrangements found in shopping centers, office buildings, and industrial parks meet these requirements. Apartment complexes fully comply because rents are generally on a gross not on a triple-net basis.

DEDUCTING ACCRUED INTEREST WHEN YOU'RE ON THE CASH BASIS

Some consider accrued interest to be the single most important deduction in apartment investing. However, many taxpayers are on the cash basis and can't benefit from it unless they file on the accrual basis. The IRS has to be notified when this change is made, and there are restrictions. This area of real estate tax law is not well known. The requirements necessary to deduct accrued interest when you're on the cash basis include considerations of:

- The all-events test and economic performance
- Accounting method
- Limitations

The All-Events Test and Economic Performance

In general, accrued interest expenses are not deductible for cash-basis taxpayers unless the accrual method of accounting is used and the all-events test is met, but not earlier than when economic performance with respect to when such items occur (Code Sec. 461[h]). The all-events test is met if all events have occurred that determine the fact of liability and the amount with reasonable accuracy.

Economic performance has special rules for tax shelters. Any entity, if more than 35 percent of its losses are allocable or any investment plan, the principal purpose of which is the avoidance or evasion of federal income tax (Code Sec. 461 [i][3]), is considered to be a tax shelter. Also, under the 1986 Tax Reform Act Code Sec. 448, a tax shelter may not compute its taxable income on the cash basis. Once under the tax shelter rules, the recurring item exception under economic performance does not apply. Generally, economic performance occurs within the shorter of a reasonable period after the close of such taxable year or eight and one-half months after the close of such taxable year. Economic performance occurs for a tax shelter at the time the property is provided to the taxpayer by another person (Code Sec. 461 [h][2][ii]).

Accrued interest expense will qualify for the deduction at the time the apartment is purchased from the seller. Because (1) the property is purchased from another party, (2) the fact of the liability has been determined with reasonable accuracy, and (3) economic performance occurs since the seller provides the property to the buyers.

Accounting Method

Can an individual use the accrual method of accounting whose overall method is on the cash basis? The code specifically provides that the IRS commissioner's consent must be obtained before changing the method of accounting (Code Sec. 446 [e]). However, the regulations also provide that the first tax return on which the item involved is reported may incorporate any appropriate method of accounting without the commissioner's consent. A taxpayer may adopt any permissible method of accounting in connection with each separate and distinct trade or business, the income from which is reported for the first time (Reg. 44-1 [e][1]). In addition, where a taxpayer has two or more separate and distinct trades or business, a different method of accounting may be used for each trade or business, provided the method used clearly reflects the income of that particular trade or business.

The method first used in accounting business income and deductions in connection with each trade or business, as evidenced in the taxpayer's income tax return in which such income or deduction is first reported, must be consistently followed thereafter. No trade or business will be considered separate and distinct unless a complete and separate set of books and records are kept for such trade or business. Also, if by reason of maintaining different methods of accounting, there is a creation of shifting of profits or losses between trades or businesses of the taxpayer so that income of the taxpayer is not clearly reflected, the trades or businesses of the taxpayer will not be considered to be separate and distinct (Reg. 1.466.1 [d]). If the above rules are satisfied, the rental activity qualifies as a distinct trade or business; then the "change in method of accounting" rules will not apply since the activity involved will be reported for the first time. Consequently, the overall cash method of accounting for the individual doesn't have to be changed.

It is important that a rental activity qualify within the definition of a trade or business. Neither the law nor the regulations provide a clear definition of what is meant by a "trade or business." This is because no one definition can consistently apply to all situations. There are however various tax cases that support rental property as being a trade or business (*Hazard and Lagreide*). Management activity and ownership along with specific facts will determine this issue.

Limitations

The investment interest deduction is limited to the taxpayer's net investment income for the taxable year (Code Sec. 163 [d][1]). However, under Code Sec. 162 (d)(3)(B), the term *investment interest* does not include any interest taken into account under Code Sec. 469 in computing income or loss from a passive activity. What is considered a passive activity? Any activity that involves the conduct of a trade or business and which the taxpayer does not materially participate (Code Sec. 469 [c][1]) is passive activity. In addition, the definition includes any rental activity, whether or not the taxpayer materially participates (Code Sec. 469 [c][2]).

Rental activity is considered a passive activity. Under these rules, deductions from passive trade or business activities to the extent that they exceed income from all such passive activities generally may not be deducted from other income. However, relief is provided for rental real estate activities in which the taxpayer actively participates. If an individual qualifies under the active participation rules, up to $25,000 of passive losses can be deducted against income from nonpassive sources subject to the phaseout previously mentioned.

YOU SHOULD ALWAYS DEFER PAYING TAXES

As a rule of thumb, it is best to defer payment of taxes to a later date because:

- You'll be paying with inflated dollars. During periods of inflation, obligations paid at a later date are, in effect, paid with inflated dollars. For example, if a $100 tax bill can be deferred for five years, the purchasing power of those dollars, when paid, will only be worth $75 (assuming a 5 percent annual inflation). The IRS's loss can be your gain if you've invested wisely during those five years.
- More investment dollars will be at your disposal. The fewer dollars expended for taxes, the more will be available to investments. "Before tax dollars" investments will net a higher rate of return than those made with "after tax dollars." Simply, you have more money to work with. In a tax-deferred exchange involving "gross equities," more investment dollars are available to work with to substantially increase your net worth.

- The government giveth and taketh away. Take advantage of every-thing and anything the IRS gives you whenever it's given. You'll never know whether or not it'll be taken back. This has always been my philosophy. Make it yours, too.

HOW TO NOT PAY ANY TAXES ON CAPITAL GAINS

Based on a new tax law, you can avoid capital gains if you follow these strategies. Example one: If you have a rental property and you sell it for $3 million and your cost is $1.5 million, your profit will be $1.5 million. Your taxes on the profit will be between $500,000 and $700,000. You and your spouse or significant other can avoid paying those taxes by trading for three single-family rental properties—Property A, Property B, and Property C. You then rent them out. If you try to rent Property A and you can't, live in it for two years and sell it, the $500,000 profit based on the new tax law, is excluded. Then you move to Property B and live in it two years. When you sell it, you do not pay any taxes on the $500,000. Then, live in Property C for two years. Sell it and you don't have to pay any taxes on the $500,000 either.

Example two: Sell your rental property for $3 million to a limited partnership whose partners are *not* blood relatives. Take $1 down and a note for $2,999,999. The tax on that dollar is 33 percent. The limited partnership sells the property for fair market value to an unrelated third party for $3 million. The tax is zero because the basis is $3 million. The partnership can pay you installment principal payments on your note, and you'd be paying percent taxes on that profit. But you'd be spreading income over a number of years. You can gift portions of that note to individuals, thereby spreading the income over entities. Or you can leave it in your estate; it is possible that you will not have to pay taxes on it at all.

CATCH-UP DEPRECIATION

New IRS tax laws allow you to take what's called *catch-up depreciation* deductions that you have not previously taken. This procedure allows you to take the entire deduction in the current year. The election must be made in the first half of the tax year in which the catch-up deduction will be taken. This method benefits anyone who is allowed to take a de-preciation deduction. For example, if you didn't take deductions in the prior years for one reason or another, and you decide, based on your in-come, to offset an anticipated increase in income with catch-up depre-ciation, you may do so. This is called grouping income and deductions.

LANDLORD/LEASEE TAX STRATEGIES

Instead of paying for the lease improvements, have your landlord pay for any lease improvements. The landlord can write these lease improvements off over a 39-year period. If you made the lease improvements and paid the cost of the improvements, you would have to write them off over 39 years. To increase the deduction, pay for the cost of these improvements by increasing the rent. Therefore, you're accelerating the rent expense instead of deducting the lease improvements over 39 years. The landlord is reimbursed for the improvements in the form of rent payments and also enjoys the annual deduction for the appreciation. Instead of spreading the cost of these improvements over 39 years, you're actually spreading them over the life of the lease which could be less than 39 years.

HOW TO MAKE A TAX DEDUCTIBLE GIFT

If you give your children a gift every year for tax purposes, it is not deductible. But you can instead treat your child's home as your second home and make the mortgage payment on it. This only applies if you don't own a second home yourself. The same strategy can be used to make gifts to your parents or certain other family members. Make the home mortgage payments for them and deduct the mortgage interest portion of the payment on your tax return. This will free up cash for your children or parents that they would otherwise have used for mortgage payments. In this way, you're indirectly making a tax-deductible gift to your children. Interest payments must be legally enforceable debt, therefore, you must co-sign the loan. This strategy is called *spreading the income and deductions to entities.* If your family members are in a higher income bracket, it won't work. It doesn't have to be made on the same house each year. For example, if you have five family members and you co-sign on all five loans, you can make loan payments in any one year to any one of the five. Children are not the only ones who qualify. You can also have this arrangement for your parents, grandparents, grandchildren, or your brother or sister.

GIVE THE BOOT TO BOOT

Based on an IRS revenue ruling, it is now possible to offset *boot* (see Glossary) with other transactional expenses. For example, if an investor traded down from a $500,000 property to a $400,000 property, a $100,000 boot would be recognized. When the transaction is reported, he automatically reduced the amount of the $100,000 boot by all transitional cost, such as commissions and other closing costs incurred.

UNLIMITED REAL ESTATE LOSSES FOR REAL ESTATE PROFESSIONALS

The new law now makes individuals eligible to deduct real estate losses if:

1. More than half of all personal services they perform during the year are for real estate trade or businesses in which they materially participate.
2. They perform more than 750 hours of service per year in those real estate activities.

Unlimited loss deductions are adjustment to adjusted gross income (AGI), and they're not subject to the same limitations as deductions from adjusted gross income. Rules in a calculation can be complicated. For a specific advice, it's recommended that you contact your accountant or your tax attorney.

LIKE-KIND EXCHANGES INCLUDE LEASES

General short-term leases (less than 30) do not constitute a like-kind exchange with real property. However, lease hold interest with 30 years or more remaining at the time of transfer may be treated as a like-kind interest for the purpose of the 1031 tax-deferred exchange (see next section). Tax considerations may vary based on who gives and receives the lease as to rents and the nature of the transaction. Arrange the lease to be initially six years with five additional renewal options. The options are exercisable without obtaining consent from the lessor.

TAX-DEFERRED EXCHANGES

A fantastic way to take all of your profits from a sale of real estate and put it into a new property without having to initially pay taxes is done through 1031 tax-deferred exchange. Funds from the sale should be held by a qualified intermediary or an accommodater until the exchange transaction is complete and the requirements have been met. You have 45 days from the date escrow closes to identify an "up property" and 180

days to complete the exchange. The 180 days includes the 45-day identification period. If you receive cash or reduction in the mortgages, it's
considered boot and you have to pay capital gains taxes on it. One of the
advantages of doing a tax-free exchange is that you retain more of the
funds for investment and defer taxes to a later date. Postponing the taxes
is a good tax strategy because, when the taxes are finally paid, they're
generally paid with inflationary dollars. The longer the payment is de-
layed, the lower the present value of the taxes, and the larger the benefit
of the deferment. Also, when the property is transferred at death, the
basis is adjusted to current market values, thus all or mostly all of the
deferred capital gains tax liabilities can be eliminated.

REVERSE EXCHANGES

The IRS allows investors to do a tax-deferred exchange in reverse. Basically the guidelines are the same as a forward exchange. The reverse exchange avoids both time and constraints by closing the purchase of the
replacement property prior to the sale of the existing property. In doing
a forward exchange, the investor cannot take control of the proceeds or
the exchanged property. The accommodater takes control of the property and the proceeds. Basically, the "up property" is purchased prior
to selling the existing property. The forward exchange and the reverse
exchange are complicated and we recommend that you use the services
of a qualified accountant or attorney and a qualified intermediary or an
accommodater.

DEPRECIATING LAND COST

The cost of land cannot be written off for tax purposes until the land is
sold. Yet under certain conditions, some land improvements can be depreciated over 15 years. This depreciation deduction can provide substantial tax savings.

Not all real estate property is real estate under Modified Accelerated
Cost Recovery System (MACRS). For example, single-purpose agricul-
tural structures are in the seven-year class. More importantly, land improvements are not included in the definition of 27.5-year residential
property. Land improvements such as parking lots, sidewalks, roads,
landscaping and fences have a 20-year midpoint, and are 15-year recovery properties under MARCS. Thus land improvements, a major expense of any large project appear to qualify for 150 percent declining
balance recovery over a 15-year period.

PAYING CAPITAL GAINS . . . A GOOD STRATEGY

The capital gains rates at this printing are being reduced from 20 percent to 15 percent. It just might be wise to pay the capital gains and take a greater basis for the depreciation deduction on the "up property." This should be considered in your tax planning. On the other hand, if you happen to be in the 10 percent to 15 percent regular income tax bracket, the rate for capital gains starts at 8 percent. For assets held for at least a five-year period and sold after December 31, 2000, it might behoove you to just pay the capital gains taxes at the lower rate and not be subjected to the time constraints of a 1031 tax-deferred exchange. You might possibly find a much better deal given enough time.

SUMMARY

This chapter is by no means a complete guide to real estate taxation. Its primary purpose is to make you aware of areas in the tax codes that are important to investing in apartment buildings.

Choose a tax consultant knowledgeable in real estate taxation. The explanation of accrued interest is comprehensive because of its significance in tax savings. References to IRS codes will be of assistance to your tax advisor.

Whenever you can get the IRS to underwrite your investment, you'll be money ahead. When you apply this strategy, you'll be working with what is known as "soft dollars." This simply means that the IRS is paying for your investment, and the "hard dollars" (your own money) expended will be fewer. Never forget, however, the IRS has the divine authority to broadly interpret the tax strategies discussed in this chapter and reserves this consecrated right to draw diverse conclusions.

If there's a reasonable basis for a deduction, our philosophy is "When in doubt, DEDUCT." Ask yourself "What is my down side?" The answer is practically nothing. At worst, you'll have to pay the taxes plus interest, which, by the way, has been historically low. Profits from the money invested may more than offset the rate the IRS charges.

The suggestions in this chapter will help you *avoid*—not *evade*—paying taxes. The former can save you money, the latter will cost not only money, but may also cost you your freedom!

13

Introducing Tenants-in-Common Form of Ownership

In this book, I recommend purchasing midsize apartments. Buying them usually requires more money than investing in single-family homes or smaller units. If additional capital is needed, consider forming a small group of active investors.

There are various entities available to group or gather investors. Some of the more familiar ones are limited partnerships, corporations, general partnerships, and real estate investment trusts. A relatively unknown form of ownership to effectively gather active investors is the tenants-in-common (TIC) form of ownership. It's an easy, low-cost method of funding real estate investments while maintaining tax benefits.

OWNERSHIP FEATURES THAT PROVIDE FLEXIBILITY

Tenants-in-common is a form of ownership that may involve two or more people, and it does not require a marital relationship. With a tenants-in-common ownership:

1. There can be two or more co-owners, but their ownership interests need not be equal. For example, if three people are co-owners,
   one could have a share of 25 percent, another 30 percent, and the
   third 45 percent.
2. There is no automatic right of survivorship. Unlike joint tenancy,
   a share in the property held by one owner does not automatically
   pass to the other owners at death. When a tenants-in-common
   owner dies, that owner's interest is transferred to his or her heirs
   and not to the other tenants-in-common, unless there's an agreement giving title to the co-owners.
3. Interest held by tenants-in-common may be sold separately by individual owners. In many cases, when tenants-in-common first
   acquire the property, they agree to give the other co-owners a
   "first right of refusal" to buy out one another.

WAYS TO SAVE WITH A TENANTS-IN-COMMON OWNERSHIP

Here are seven advantages of the tenants-in-common ownership over
other entities:

1. *Low set-up costs:* Compared to other forms of ownership, tenants-
in-common has one of the lowest set-up costs. You don't need an attorney to prepare offering circulars or registration with governmental
agencies. In fact, all that is required is to have the names of the owners
recorded when the transaction closes. A formal document is not necessary, though we would recommend one. Accounting fees for preparing
partnership, trusts, and corporation returns are eliminated as well as
state and federal income taxes.

2. *Low down payment:* In some public offerings, restrictions are imposed on the use of leverage. Using the tenants-in-common form of ownership, there are none. This is an important investment strategy in
purchasing and selling midsize apartment complexes. The lower the
down payment, the more leverage, and the more property you can control.

3. *Active voice in management:* An important investment goal is to reduce taxes. The tenants-in-common form of ownership does this by allowing an active voice in management. Tenants-in-common owners,
with the help of qualified consultants, are extremely effective in making the right decisions. The old adage "two heads are better than one"
hits the bull's-eye, especially when these heads are concentrating on becoming wealthy.

4. *Ease of transferability:* Unlike a certification of ownership in a partnership, the tenants-in-common ownership has a greater degree of transferability. Each owner's name is on the deed and is recorded. An owner's interest can be sold, hypothecated, willed, or transferred without the consent of the other co-owners, and each owner has complete control of his or her interest. In evaluating collateral, lenders generally give more credence to an interest in a recorded tenants-in-common interest than in a limited partnership.

5. *Economy of scale:* Because investment dollars are being accumulated by a group, there are more dollars available to purchase larger properties. Many individual investors don't have the opportunity to use the economies of scale unless they form a group. How does this concept apply to apartment complexes? If one unit is vacant in a four-unit complex, what would the vacancy factor be? If you said 25 percent, you are correct. On the other hand, if one unit is vacant in a 40-unit complex, what would that vacancy factor be? Right, 2.5 percent.

Just think about it! When the carpet layer is called, to whom do you think the better square-foot price will be given, the owner of the 40-unit building or the four-unit building. The same applies to all vendors.

6. *No mortgage or qualifying restrictions:* Unlike most public limited partnerships, tenants-in-common ownership doesn't have any restrictions for financing or investor qualifications. Financing can be structured to give the greatest flexibility to each individual owner either at the time of purchase or sale. The group is formed based on the needs and desires of its members not on standards imposed by governmental agencies. Individual owners don't need a minimum or maximum net worth to invest. They're not required to have someone attest to their capability of making their own investment decisions. Nor are they forced to have experts make these decisions for them.

7. *Tax advantages:* Using the tenants-in-common form of ownership, gives you the opportunity to become an active investor. As such, you can qualify for the $25,000 per year write-off against your salary, dividends, interest, and other income. This form of ownership provides the flexibility needed to implement the tax-saving strategies discussed earlier. Other forms of ownership satisfying only passive investor requirements do not have these capabilities.

8. Neither a real estate nor a securities license is required to form a private tenants-in-common group to invest in real estate. If you do not manage or control the group, it doesn't have to be registered or qualified with any governmental agency as a security.

TAX IMPACT OF TENANTS-IN-COMMON OWNERSHIP

Deferred income on recognition of taxable gain when selling rental property (the Internal Revenue code section 1031) mandates that the tenant-in-common co-ownership must meet these four requirements:

1. To form a tenants-in-common group, each of the co-owners must hold interest as tenants-in-common. No one can previously have held interest in property in any other legal entity (for example partnership).
2. The allocation of income and expenses as well as liability for blanket and encumbrance shall be in accordance with the co-owners percentage interest and ownership interest.
3. All of the co-owners of the entity must have the right to vote on all issues of the ownership. An owner or sponsor or manager may advance funds to cover payments due from another co-owner. This debt is recourse and must be paid within 31 days.
4. There is an exit requirement that each co-owner retains a right to transfer, petition, or encumber their ownership interest.

New Guidelines for Tenants-in-Common Interest

Procedure 2022-22 provides guidelines in the use of fractional interest in the replacement properties in the 1031 exchange. The key criteria are:

1. The number of tenants-in-common cannot exceed 35.
2. The sponsor of interest may own the property or an interest there for only 6 months before 100 percent of the interest can be sold.
3. Any decision has a material impact on the property owners must be approved unanimously by the owners.
4. The management agreement must be renewed annually and must provide for market rate compensation.

THE NUMBER ONE PITFALL OF SECURITY TRANSACTIONS

Simply stated, if you control a group and the outcome of the investment, you, in effect, have created a *security transaction*. This means that you cannot publicly advertise for investors unless it's properly registered. The cost and time involved for most people to register their offering is prohibitive. Not being able to advertise freely can be a severe handicap. So, where do you find investors? Your best source for potential investors is relatives, friends, associates, and clients. Relatives, who know you personally, are more likely to entrust their money with you rather than a stranger. People who know you—those who are familiar with your background and who can count on you to do the best job for them.

Family relationships sometimes get strained in these matters. It is important to evaluate kinships. The last thing you want is a family dispute over investments. However, if relatives insist on becoming part of your group, have each one sign a statement acknowledging the risks. Have your attorney prepare this document.

Ideally, you should have compatible investors in your group who have had previous diversified investment experience and fall within the wealth-building period on the chronological time line.

As an additional precaution, have the investor's qualified representative review all the information pertaining to the investment and complete a Purchaser's Representative Questionnaire (Figure 13.1). This independent third party, in effect, determines the merits of the investment for the investor.

If you don't have any qualified relatives or personal or business contacts, how do you find prospective investors? It's very hard to do because of the restrictions on public advertising. The only way to advertise is to have a registered public offering or a nonsecurity transaction. The registered public offering is terribly expensive. The nonsecurity transaction won't cost you a thing.

CREATING A NONSECURITY TRANSACTION

When putting a group together, it is important to determine whether it's a security or a nonsecurity, as defined by both the Howey Test (see *SEC v. Howey* [1946] 328 U.S. 293) and the Risk Capital Test (see *Silver Hills Country Club v. Sobieski* [1961] 55 Cal. 2d 811). If the transactions satisfy either test, it will be classified as a security (see *People v. Schock* [1984] 152 Cal. App. 3rd 379) and you would not be permitted to publicly advertise for investors.

Howey Test

The Howey court case established the definition of a security. It states, "If the scheme involves an investment of money in a common enterprise with profits to come solely from the efforts of others" a securities exist. Whether the profits are said to come "solely from the efforts of others" has been interpreted to mean, "whether the efforts made by those other

Dear Sir or Madam:

The information contained herein is being furnished to you in order for you to determine whether a sale of an interest in certain real property commonly referred to as _____ may be made to the following prospective Purchaser

_____
(insert name of prospective Purchaser)

in light of the requirements of Section 4 (2) of the Securities Act of 1933, as amended (the "Act"), and Regulation D and state securities laws. The undersigned understands that (a) you will rely upon the information contained herein for purposes of such determination, (b) the interest will not be registered or qualified under the Act in reliance upon the exemption from registration afforded by Section 4 (2) of the Act as explained in Regulation D, (c) the interest will not be registered or qualified under any state securities laws, and (d) this questionnaire is not an offer to sell the interest or any other securities to the undersigned Purchaser Representative.

I note that you have provided the above-named Purchaser with disclosure materials prepared by

_____
(your firm's name)

It should be noted by you that nothing herein shall be construed as a representation by me that I have attempted to verify this information.

RATHER, TO THE CONTRARY, THE SCOPE OF MY ENGAGEMENT BY, AND MY DISCUSSION WITH, THE ABOVE-NAMED PURCHASER HAVE BEEN LIMITED TO A DETERMINATION OF THE SUITABILITY OF AN INVESTMENT BY THE ABOVE-NAMED PURCHASER IN LIGHT OF SUCH PURCHASER'S PRESENT INVESTMENT CIRCUMSTANCES, AS SUCH CIRCUMSTANCES HAVE BEEN PRESENTED TO ME. FOR THIS PURPOSE I HAVE ASSUMED, BUT DO NOT IN ANY WAY REPRESENT OR WARRANT, EITHER TO YOU OR TO THE ABOVE-NAMED PURCHASER, THAT THE INFORMATION IS ACCURATE AND COMPLETE IN ALL MATERIAL ASPECTS. EACH AND EVERY STATEMENT MADE BY ME IN THE FOLLOWING PARAGRAPHS ARE QUALIFIED BY REFERENCE TO THE FOREGOING.

With the above in mind, I herewith furnish you with the following information:
(1) I have discussed the disclosure materials with the above-named Purchaser with a view to determining whether an investment by such a Purchaser is not inappropriate in light of such Purchaser's financial circumstances, as such circumstances have been disclosed to me by such Purchaser.
(2) The undersigned is not an affiliate, director, officer, or other employee of

_____
(your firm's name)

Figure 13.1 Purchaser's representative questionnaire.

or beneficial owner of an equity interest in the property except as follows: (state "No Exceptions" or set forth exceptions and give details).

_____

_____

_____

(3) The undersigned has such knowledge and experience in financial and business matters as to be capable of evaluating the merits and risks of this investment. The undersigned offers as evidence thereof the following additional information (for example, investment experience, business experience, profession, education):

_____

_____

_____

(4) There is no material relationship between me or my affiliates and

_____
(your firm's name)

or its affiliates that now exists, is mutually understood to be contemplated, or which has existed at any time during the previous two years, nor has compensation been received or will be received as a result of any such relationship, except as follows:

_____
(NO EXCEPTIONS PERMITTED)

The undersigned agrees to notify you promptly of any changes to the information described in this questionnaire that may occur prior to the completion of the transaction.

Very truly yours,

Dated: _____

_____
Print or type name of Purchaser's Representative

_____
Purchaser's Representative's Signature

_____
Street Address

_____
City and State

_____
Telephone

Figure 13.1 *Continued*

than the investor(s) are undeniably significant ones, those essential managerial efforts that affect the failure or success of the enterprise."

If it is determined that the profits were made by undeniably significant and essential managerial efforts of everyone in the group (active participation), and not others, then the investment would not be considered a security. Therefore, the restriction on advertising wouldn't apply.

Risk Capital Test

Under the Risk Capital Test, the court will be looking to determine: (1) whether funds are being raised for a business venture or enterprise; (2) whether the transaction is offered indiscriminately to the public at large; (3) whether the investors are substantially powerless to effect the success of the enterprise; and (4) whether the investor's money is substantially at risk because it is inadequately secured.

Establishing suitability requirements of potential co-owners should not be construed as an "indiscriminate" offering. Further, co-owners retain control over the success of their investment. In this, they are not "powerless" as such. Finally, it may be argued that the fair market value of the investment, based on its potential income production, is at least equal to the purchase price as a determinant of whether a co-owner's investment is inadequately secured (*Leyva v. Superior Court* [1985] 164 Cal. App. 3d 462).

The March 1989 issue of *California Business Law Reporter,* Volume X, Number 6, "Terms of Partnership Agreement Determine Whether General Partnership Interest Is a Security," written by David M. Greenberg, provided by the 1989–1990 Regents of the University of California Continuing Education of the Bar's *California Business Law Reporter,* elaborates further on this issue.

Is a general partnership a security for purposes of the federal securities law? Joining a debate that has led to differing views among the circuit courts, the Ninth Circuit Court of Appeals decided that the issue is determined by examination of the general partnership agreement, as opposed to the manner in which the partnership functioned in carrying out its business affairs. (*Matek v. Murat* [9th Cir. 1988] 862 F2d 720.) In reaching this conclusion, the court rejected the "bright-line" rule, which holds that a general partnership interest is not a security because of the broad management and control powers conferred on general partners by partnership law. (*Goodwin v. Elkins & Co.* [3rd Cir. 1984] 730 F2d 99.) The court also rejected the test fashioned in *Williamson v. Tucker* [5th Cir. 1981] F2d 404 (dicta), which required "not solely from the efforts of others." (*SEC v. W. J. Howey Co.* [1946] 328 US

293, 301.) The Ninth Circuit has interpreted the word "solely" in the Howey test as requiring that the efforts of those other than the investor be "the undeniably significant one." (*SEC v. Glen W. Turner Enters., Inc.* [9th Cir. 1973] 474 F2s 476, 482.) In determining whether the efforts of the plaintiffs in the fish-processing venture were the "undeniably significant ones," the court of appeals in *Matek* rejected both the "bright-line" test of *Goodwin* and the postformation factual examination required under *Williamson.* Instead, the court fashioned its own modified *Williamson Test.*

Williamson Test

EXAMINATION OF AGREEMENT   The court held that only the first prong of the Williamson Test should apply, that is, a determination of whether the partnership agreement left "so little power in the hands of the partners or ventures that the arrangement in fact distributes power as would a limited partnership." Applying this test to the partnership agreement at issue in *Matek,* the court found that the agreement was a "standard general partnership contract." The contract placed managerial control and access to partnership information in the hands of the general partners. No partner could withdraw capital from the partnership without the consent of all partners, and no partner could lend money to the partnership without the approval of the majority of partners. Although the document called for the appointment of managing partners with power to control the day-to-day business of the partnership, the managing partners were required to consult "as far as practicable" with the other partners about business decisions. Various acts could be done only with the consent of the majority of partners, including the borrowing of money, the transferring or hypothecating of partnership claims, and the sale of partnership property other than the ordinary course of business. Partnership interests were not freely transferable (admission of new partners required the agreement of a majority of partners), and the agreement could be amended only with the approval of all partners. Finally, the books of the partnership were open for inspection to all partners.

The court added that plaintiffs had "made no showing and are unable to show that they were prevented from exercising their powers under the agreement," and further noted that "there is no evidence that the general partnership agreement was purposely drafted to escape the application of securities laws" (862 F2d at 731). Because of the foregoing features of the partnership agreement, the court concluded that the venture was controlled by the plaintiffs, and not by "others." According to the court, the general partnership agreement provided the partners, including the plaintiffs, with access to information and the ability to protect their investment that the securities laws would otherwise provide. The agreement created powers and duties in the general partners that were not typical of passive investors in a security. Accordingly, the general partnership interests were not investment contracts for purposes of the definition of a security under the federal securities laws.

CONCURRING OPINION   In a concurring opinion, the court agreed with the rejection of the "bright-line rule," but favored adopting the *Williamson Test* and looking beyond the terms of the general partnership agreement in determining whether, as an "economic reality," a general partnership interest is a security. The court acknowledged that an investor claiming that a general partnership interest is a security has a difficult burden. In meeting that burden, a plaintiff should be allowed to introduce facts extrinsic to the partnership agreement. However, the court agreed with the majority opinion because plaintiffs failed to satisfy the Williamson factors.

COMMENTS   The court's decision in *Matek* is a welcome development for attorneys drafting general partnership agreements. The court's reference to a "standard" general partnership that is not a security, is helpful to practitioners. It is significant that the court reached its conclusion in *Matek* despite a provision vesting day-to-day control in managing general partners who were required to consult with the other partners on business decisions only "as far as practicable." As long as general partnerships are not drafted to evade the securities laws, counsel should feel confident that a general partnership interest will not be held to be a security. Establishing a group of investors to attain all the benefits described herein (including tax benefits) constitutes a legitimate reason for drafting a tenants-in-common agreement.

A NOVEL WAY TO MARKET A NONSECURITY

How can a marketing program be implemented to form a group of investors without running afoul of the securities laws? In order to accomplish this, you must demonstrate that you're offering professional consulting services. Offer advice, not control. A marketing plan that is designed to accomplish this objective would include your advertising publicly in the newspaper, on television, through direct mail, or through any other media for a "paid" educational seminar. For the best response, place your advertisements two weeks in advance of the actual date of the seminar—with at least two exposures. If you have books, audio and video tapes on related subjects, or if you are trying to get clients for your consulting services, you might want to make it a free seminar. Remember, never advertise for investors!

Diligently prepare a meaningful, informative, and educational program, and present it in a skillful manner. Having it approved for continuing education credits by the related professional organizations will help in the marketing.

The best time to conduct seminars is either midweek in the evenings or on a Saturday morning. Keep it under three hours, allowing time for questions and answers. Provide refreshments. Use an overhead projector to make visual presentations.

During the meeting distribute a Seminar Evaluation form (Figure 13.2).

How to Tap an Unlimited Supply of Buyers

Using the seminar, you will be able to tap into the pool of people who are interested in being informed of future real estate opportunities. You can send property set-up sheets and make property presentations. Also, you will be able to offer your professional services in locating areas of opportunity and analyzing properties.

If a number of people are interested in a particular property, a tenant-in-common investment group should be formed (not under your control), to make an offer either to you or through you, if properly licensed.

If you are not a real estate licensee and you simply want to sell your position in the property rather than being part of the group, you can legally do so by using the techniques described earlier. In this particular case, not having a real estate license could work to your advantage because of various disclosure laws.

Protect Yourself When Dealing with Nonsecurity Transactions

To strengthen your position that the transaction is not a security, take only a minority interest in the group. Be sure the group maintains control of the outcome of the investment—not you. All decisions must be strictly those of the group. Make the tenants-in-common group aware that, under *no* circumstances, are you allowed to manage its affairs. If you do, you could be considered a promoter, subjecting the entire transaction to security laws, giving each investor a built-in insurance policy against all losses they may incur if the investment goes belly up.

If you enter into a real estate consultant agreement (see sample form in Chapter 4, Figure 4.3), limit your activities to those performed by a real estate licensee, not a managing general partner.

Seminar Evaluation

WELCOME . . . Please take a few minutes to fill out the information requested on this card. We will collect the cards as you are leaving the seminar. Thank you for your help!

Name _____   Date _____

Address _____   Daytime Phone _____

City _____   Evening Phone _____

State _____   Zip _____

How did you hear about us?

1. ____ Major Newspaper   8. ____ Realtor
2. ____ Local Newspaper   9. ____ CPA
3. ____ T.V.   10. ____ Attorney
4. ____ Radio   11. ____ Financial Planner
5. ____ Mailing   12. ____ Insurance Agent
6. ____ Friend or Relative   13. ____ Other _____
7. ____ Stock Broker

(circle)

I'd like to receive information on future Real Estate Opportunities YES NO
Please circle one for each question:

The speaker was informative.
Strongly Agree   Agree   Strongly Disagree

The material was presented in an interesting way.
Strongly Agree   Agree   Strongly Disagree

What information could be made more clear? _____
_____
_____
_____

How can we improve this seminar? _____
_____
_____
_____

Thanks again for your help!

Figure 13.2 Seminar evaluation. *Source:* The Center for Real Estate Studies.

PARTICIPATING IN PROFITS WITHOUT OWNERSHIP

If ownership is not in your plans but you still want to participate in potential profits, sell the property to the tenants-in-common group, and take back a participating note and deed of trust on the property. As an offset, offer a below-market interest rate and/or accruals. By taking this approach, not only will you save significantly on taxes, but you will also be making a statement to the buyers of your faith in the property.

With the help of one of the nation's largest accounting firms, we developed a tenants-in-common agreement to protect the individual co-owner's interest as well as their tax benefits. It is designed to meet the requirements of active participation. It can be used for both security and nonsecurity type transactions. This agreement is made available by The Center for Real Estate Studies (see page 226).

SUMMARY

There are definite advantages to group ownership. Probably the most prevalent is economy of scale. The tenants-in-common form of ownership provides a simple, low-cost way for investors to form groups, while maintaining many tax benefits.

Depending on your preference, the tenants-in-common group can be formed as a security or a nonsecurity. If classified as a security, no public advertising is permitted unless it is registered as a public offering. Conducting nonsecurity transactions is relatively easy and inexpensive.

If a co-ownership group is being formed as a nonsecurity, don't jeopardize your position by acting as a promoter or general partner. By doing so, you'll be indemnifying its members against all losses.

14

Gain Freedom from Lawsuits

PAINTING A TRUE PICTURE OF LITIGATION

In my attorney's office hangs a picture depicting a farm scene entitled "Litigation." In the middle of the picture is a drawing of a cow. At one end of the cow is a very angry man gripping the cow's horns and trying to pull the cow toward him. His caption reads, "The Plaintiff." At the other end is another very angry man tugging on the cow's tail trying to move the cow in his direction. His caption reads, "The Defendant." In the middle, sitting on a stool, is a well-dressed man with a big smile on his face, milking the cow. His caption reads, "The Attorney." And so it goes!

Unfortunately, litigation has become a way of life in this country. Both time and money are lost because of this national pastime. There are over 16 million lawsuits filed each year in this country. More than 70 percent of the attorneys in the world live in the United States. It's no wonder that our legal system is in such a mess.

There are two unique aspects of the U.S. system that are alleged to encourage frivolous lawsuits and out-of-court settlements. First is the contingency fee arrangement with attorneys. This is when attorneys are compensated only if they win. In other words, a person can sue without having to pay any attorney fees up front. Defendants, of course, have no such privilege.

Then there is the "one-way" fee system, which means the plaintiff collects costs and fees from the defendant if the plaintiff wins. A successful defendant receives nothing. Defending a case can cost thousands of dollars. Regardless of its merits, defendants will usually end up making a business decision and will settle the suit out of court.

A movement requiring disputing parties to arbitrate their disputes is winding its way through the legal system. I hope it takes hold and is soon adopted by the entire legal profession. Arbitration generally costs less, is quicker, and it is not as likely to cause the major disturbances brought by lengthy court trials. An experienced judge hears the facts and, based on a legal interpretation of the law, makes a decision. The judge doesn't get involved emotionally, and the decision is based on the judge's comprehensive knowledge of the law. Because arbitration tends to reduce attorney fees, the movement is slow in coming. In the interim, you must take measures to protect yourself and your assets.

PROTECTING YOURSELF FROM LAWSUITS

The best safeguard is not to have any attachable assets. This can be accomplished by creating an estate plan that transfers all your assets into a family-limited partnership. It's best to make the transfer before the threat of a lawsuit and/or actual judgment is rendered against you. If you wait, the transfer might be considered a fraudulent conveyance of property. However, transfers made after can also afford a powerful degree of safety.

Warning Signs of a Fraudulent Conveyance

Fraudulent conveyance is determined on a case-by-case basis by the courts. The following represents some of the warning signs when making that judgment:

1. Consideration paid
2. Solvency of a debtor before and after transfer
3. Pending claims at the time of transfer
4. Intent of the debtor

If a judgment creditor proves that the transfer was fraudulent, a levy can be placed on the property transferred and the creditor can proceed against the debtor as if the transfer had never been made.

Avoiding Fraudulent Conveyance

Debtors who transfer assets without receiving reasonable value in exchange subject the transaction to either the Uniform Fraudulent Conveyance Act (UFCA) or the Uniform Fraudulent Transfers Act (UFTA). If you transfer assets into a family-limited partnership (FLP) as part of an estate plan, and you receive limited partnership interest of equal value, then you've, in effect, complied with the "fair value" section of this act.

The transfers of assets into the FLP does not create insolvency because, as a limited partner, you retain an interest in the partnership. This interest has value because the partnership has value. Both you and the partnership are solvent, before and after the transfer; thereby, conforming with the "solvency" test of both UFCA and UFTA.

If a transfer is made because of probable liability as a result of pending lawsuits, a court could find the transfer fraudulent. However, if it can be proven that the claim was merely possible and not probable, the transfer would not be considered fraudulent. Generalized complaints from clients about the quality of goods or services should not be considered probable causes for liability.

Making Yourself Judgment Proof

Can future creditors challenge transfers of property when the transfer occurred prior to the date of the creditor's claim? As to future creditors, the courts have consistently held that future creditor's rights are limited. Representative cases are as follows:

> *Hurlbert vs. Shackleton*, 560 S. 2d. 176, June 1, 1990. The court drew a distinction between "probable" and "possible" future creditors. The court said it found no cases holding a transfer of assets to be fraudulent as to "possible" future creditors. At the time of the conveyance, there must be evidence establishing actual fraudulent intent by one who seeks to have the transaction set aside. A transfer of property by a debtor is not fraudulent unless the act is directed against creditors who have just, lawful, and existing claims. Even if the debtor intends to deceive the public, if the act in transferring the property does not hinder or delay the creditors, no legal fraud exists.
>
> Transfers of assets (or liabilities incurred) with the actual intent to hinder, delay, or defraud a present or future creditor can be set aside as a fraudulent conveyance. If the intent is to create both an estate and a tax plan, then it would not run the risk of being a fraudulent transfer. Whether a transfer was in contemplation of a creditor's claim is an important point in a fraudulent conveyance claim. The

transfer of assets for legitimate estate tax planning, business, or investment purposes complies with the "intent" portion of both the UFCA and UFTA.

Re Oberst, 91 Bankr. 97, C.D. Cal. 1988. The court regarding the question of denial of discharge stated that Congress has decided that the key is the intent of the debtor. If the debtor has a particular creditor(s) in mind and is trying to remove assets from the creditor(s) reach, there are grounds to deny discharge. But, if the debtor is merely looking for his or her future well being, the discharge will be granted.

Horbach vs. Hill, 112 U.S. 144. The U.S. Supreme Court stated that the one who was not a creditor of the grantor at the time a deed was executed cannot complain of its fraudulent execution.

Never get involved in any conspiracy to conceal assets from creditors. Fraudulent conveyances fall under civil codes, and intentional concealment is criminal. There is a fine line between legitimate asset protection and asset concealment. In creating business and estate planning, negate inference of fraudulent intent by properly documenting all transfers. Always time the transfers to correspond to justifiable reasons.

THE UNIFORM FRAUDULENT CONVEYANCE ACT

SECTION 1. DEFINITION OF TERMS   In this act "assets" of a debtor means property not exempt from liability for debts. To the extent that any property is liable for any debts of the debtor, such property shall be included in the debtor's assets. "Conveyance" includes every payment of money, assignment, release, transfer, lease, mortgage, or pledge of tangible or intangible property, and also the creation of any lien or encumbrance.

"Creditor" is a person having any claim, whether matured or unmatured, liquidated or unliquidated, absolute, fixed, or contingent.

"Debt" includes any legal liability, whether matured or unmatured, liquidated or unliquidated, absolute, fixed, or contingent.

SECTION 2. INSOLVENCY

1. A person is insolvent when the present fair salable value of assets is less than the amount that will be required to pay probable liability on existing debts as they become absolute and matured.
2. In determining whether a partnership is insolvent, there shall be added to the partnership property the present fair salable value of the separate assets of each general partner in excess of the

amount probably sufficient to meet the claims of separate creditors, and also the amount of any unpaid subscription to the partnership of each limited partner, provided the present fair salable value of the assets of such limited partner is probably sufficient to pay the debts, including such unpaid subscription.

SECTION 3. FAIR CONSIDERATION   Fair consideration is given for property, or obligation.

1. When, in exchange for such property, or obligation, as fair equivalent therefor, and in good faith, property is conveyed or previous debt is satisfied, or,
2. When such property, or obligation is received in good faith to secure a present advance or antecedent debt in an amount not disproportionately small as compared with the value of the property, or obligation obtained.

SECTION 4. CONVEYANCES BY INSOLVENT   Every conveyance made and every obligation incurred by a person who is or will be thereby rendered insolvent is fraudulent as to creditors without regard to the person's actual intent, if the conveyance is made or the obligation is incurred without a fair consideration.

SECTION 5. CONVEYANCES BY PERSONS IN BUSINESS   Every conveyance made without fair consideration when the person making it is engaged or is about to engage in a business or transaction for which the property remaining in the person's hands after the conveyance is an unreasonable small capital, is fraudulent as to creditors and as to other persons who become creditors during the continuance of such business or transaction without regard to the person's actual intent.

SECTION 6. CONVEYANCE BY A PERSON ABOUT TO INCUR DEBTS Every conveyance made and every obligation incurred with actual intent, as distinguished from intent presumed in law, to hinder, delay, or defraud either present or future creditors, is fraudulent as to both present and future creditors.

SECTION 8. CONVEYANCE OF PARTNERSHIP PROPERTY Every conveyance of partnership property and every partnership obligation incurred when the partnership is or will be thereby rendered insolvent, is fraudulent as to partnership creditors, if the conveyance is made or obligation is incurred

1. To a partner, whether with or without a promise to pay partnership debts,

   or

2. To a person (not a partner) without fair consideration to the partnership as distinguished from consideration to the individual partners.

SECTION 9. RIGHTS OF CREDITORS WHOSE CLAIMS HAVE MATURED

1. Where a conveyance or obligation is fraudulent as to a creditor, such creditor, when the claim has matured, may, as against any person except a purchaser for fair consideration without knowledge of the fraud at the time of the purchase, or one who has derived title immediately from such a purchaser,
   a. Have the conveyance set aside or obligation annulled to the extent necessary to satisfy the claim,

      or

   b. Disregard the conveyance and attach or levy execution upon the property conveyed.
2. A purchaser who without actual fraudulent intent has given less than a fair consideration for the conveyance or obligation, may retain the property or obligation as security for repayment.

SECTION 10. RIGHTS OF CREDITORS WHOSE CLAIMS HAVE NOT MATURED Where a conveyance made or obligation incurred is fraudulent as to a creditor whose claim has not matured, the creditor may proceed in a court of competent jurisdiction against any person against whom he or she could have proceeded had the claim matured, and the court may,

1. Restrain the defendant from disposing of the property,
2. Appoint a receiver to take charge of the property,
3. Set aside the conveyance or annul the obligation, or,
4. Make any order that the circumstances of the case may require.

SECTION 11. CASES NOT PROVIDED FOR IN ACT In any case not provided for in the act, the rule of law and equity, including the law merchant, and in particular the rules relating to the law of principal and agent, and the effect of fraud, misrepresentation, duress or coercion, mistake, bankruptcy, or other invalidating cause, shall govern.

SECTION 12. CONSTRUCTION OF ACT   This act shall be so interpreted and construed as to effectuate its general purpose to make uniform the law of those states that enact it.

SECTION 13. NAME OF ACT   This act may be cited as the Uniform Fraudulent Conveyance Act.

SECTION 14. INCONSISTENT LEGISLATION REPEALED   Sections _____ are hereby repealed, and all acts or parts of acts inconsistent with this act are hereby repealed.

LIMITED LIABILITY COMPANIES

Limited liability companies (LLCs) are entities formed to protect the owners personal assets from the risks of owning real estate. These combine the liability protection of a corporation and the flexibility and tax benefits of a partnership. LLCs are the answer to the legal goals of real estate investing today because they provide the basic advantages of corporations and limited partnerships with few requirements and very little paperwork.

LLCs can be used for estate planning and to clarify management structure. When you form an LLC, you take advantage of anonymity. The documents in a public LLC require very little personal information. LLCs can be used for 1031 exchanges also. For example, if five investors own property under a TIC form of ownership and want to exchange it, they can form five separate LLCs and still meet the requirements for 1031 exchange.

Estate planning using an LLC can save a great deal of money. Based on evaluation, no one can argue that $50,000 in cash is worth $50,000. But what is the value of $50,000 interest or a 10 percent interest in an LLC? Because the value of an LLC is less marketable than $50,000 in cash, the IRS tends to allow discounts on the evaluation in an interest on an LLC thereby reducing the estate taxes.

THE LEGAL BASIS FOR THE FAMILY-LIMITED PARTNERSHIP

How will the transfer of assets into a FLP protect those assets? The answer lies in the California court ruling in *Centurion Corp. v. Crocker Nat'l Bank* (1989) 208 Cal. 3d 1, 255 CR 794. The 1989/1990 The Regents of the University of California Continuing Education of the Bar's *California Business Law Reporter* printed this article in Volume X,

Number 8 (June 1989) publication, written by David M. Greenberg. A synopsis of the case is as follows:

In an apparent case of first impression, the First District Court of Appeals has held that a limited partnership interest may be sold at an execution sale at the request of a limited partner's judgment creditor. In *Centurion Corp. v. Crocker Nat'l Bank* (1989) 208 Cal. 3d 1, 255 CR 794, Crocker National Bank obtained a judgment for more than $1 million against the defendant, the only limited partner in a partnership known as Turn-Key Storage. The defendant's mother was the sole general partner in Turn-Key. The bank received no funds as a result of its charging order, and moved for an order to sell the defendant's limited partnership interest. The defendant received notice at a federal prison, where he was a prisoner. His mother filed a statement of nonopposition to the sale, stating that the partnership had no objections, provided that, in compliance with the partnership agreement, the purchaser would have the right to receive profits and losses only, but not to become as substituted limited partner. The trial court issued an order permitting the sale. The court of appeals affirmed. The court reviewed long-standing California statutory law that prevents a partner's judgment creditor from executing on partnership assets or directly on a partner's interest in the partnership. Rather, a judgment creditor is first required to seek a charging order to reach the debtor partner's interest in the partnership. The California Uniform Partnership Act, the Uniform Limited Partnership Act, and the Revised Limited Partnership Act each provide for this charging order procedure. (See Corp C 15028, 15522, 15673.) Thus, for example, Corp C 15673 provides as follows:

> On application to a court of competent jurisdiction by any judgment creditor of a partner, the court may charge the limited partnership interest of the partner with payment of the unsatisfied amount of the judgment with interest. To the extent so charged, the judgment creditor has only the rights of an assignee of the limited partnership interest. This chapter does not deprive the partner of the benefit of any exemption laws applicable to the partner's limited partnership interest.

The defendant did not appeal the validity of the charging order. He argued that the trial could not order his limited partnership interest sold at an execution sale. The court looked to the relevant statutory language, as well as to statements in previous cases, and held for the first time that a court may authorize the sale of a judgment debtor's partnership interest, when three conditions have been met: (1) the judgment creditor has obtained a charging order; (2) the judgment remains unsatisfied; and (3) all partners other than the debtor have consented to the sale of the interest. According to the court, allowing an execution sale under these conditions will prevent the sale from disrupting partnership business, but will also prevent a debtor's use of partnership law to foil judgment creditors when no legitimate interest of the partnership or the remaining partners would be served.

The defendant argued that the execution sale order was improper because it was not consistent with Turn-Key's limited partnership agreement. Under the agreement, the defendant had a 50-percent interest in profits and losses, but not direct interest in partnership real or personal property. Also, as a limited partner, the defendant could not be active in management and could not sell his interest in the partnership. The court acknowledged both that a charging order cannot grant a creditor a greater interest in the partnership than the debtor had at the time of the order, and that an order for sale cannot allow the purchases to acquire more rights in the partnership than the debtor partner possessed. The court held that the execution sale of the defendant's interest did not constitute an order to sell property owned by the partnership. Rather, the execution sale order required the sale of whatever interest the defendant held in the limited partnership by reason of his being a limited partner. The purchaser at the execution sale could not become a substituted limited partner without the further consent of the general partners. All of this was consistent with the limited partnership agreement.

COMMENT: PARTNER'S CONSENT   The court did not discuss why it believed the consent of all partners other than the judgment debtor was required to allow an execution sale. In *Centurion,* the defendant was the sole limited partner and the sole general partner consented to the sale. Thus, there was no problem in satisfying the unanimity requirement. However, in many partnerships, it is difficult to achieve unanimity on such matters. Any of the other partners will be able to prevent a judgment creditor from executing on the debtor's limited partnership interest.

Most limited partnership agreements provide that the purchaser of a limited partnership interest has only the rights of an assignee until the purchaser becomes a substituted limited partner with the consent of the general partner. Because of these limitations, the assignee cannot interfere with the operation of the partnership. Generally, the consent of the other limited partners is not required for an assignment. Consequently, there is no apparent reason for requiring approval of all limited partners when a creditor seeks an execution sale of a limited partnership interest.

Many limited partnership agreements drafted under the California Revised Limited Partnership Act limit the voting rights of limited partners in order to avoid the default voting provisions of that act otherwise available under Corp C 1536 (f) and 15632 (b) (5). If the partnership agreement does not provide specifically for limited partners to vote on an execution sale, it may be necessary to obtain a court order or to amend the partnership agreement in order to authorize the vote.

Most limited partnership agreements require the consent of the general partner to the admission of a substituted limited partner. If the general partner consented to the execution sale, but refused further to consent to the purchaser's admission as a substituted limited partner, the judgment creditor would have no voting rights and would not be entitled to the other rights given to limited partners under partnership law and most partnership agreements.

In any event, from a creditor's standpoint, an execution sale may provide limited assistance, especially when the creditor is the purchaser at the sale.

RESTRICTION IN PARTNERSHIP AGREEMENT   One issue raised but not decided by Centurion is the validity of a provision in a partnership agreement stating that a limited partnership interest cannot be transferred pursuant to an execution sale order. The court indicated that such a provision probably would not be enforceable, citing *Tupper v. Kroc* (Nev 1972) 491 P2d 1275, 1280, which held that a partnership agreement could not divest a court of its powers to charge and sell a partnership interest. A right of first refusal in a partnership agreement, however, might still be effective and would, at least, complicate the execution sale of a partnership interest.

HAMPERING CREDITORS

The key to hampering creditor's action is the vote. If the family limited partnership is created whereby the judgment creditors, who become assignees of the debtor's interest, cannot vote, the capacity to direct the activities of the partnership is curtailed. Without this ability, they cannot disburse partnership assets to satisfy their claims.

Paying Yourself without Paying the Creditors

Judgment creditors can attach a limited partner's interest in the partnership and receive any disbursement made to that particular limited partner. However, if the partners decide not to make any disbursements, creditors receive absolutely nothing.

The partnership may make loans to individual limited partners without making distributions or withdrawals. These loans are very difficult to attach. The partnership may decide to pay wages to the limited partner. If judgment creditors attach the limited partner's wages, there are severe limitations on the amounts they can take.

Eliminating or Reducing the Cost of Personal Liability Insurance

By properly protecting your assets from creditors claims, you can effectively reduce the cost of personal liability insurance. Only carry the minimum required by law. If not required by law, seriously consider why you're carrying it in the first place. You can reduce expenses for personal liability insurance substantially or eliminate them entirely when your assets are adequately protected.

Stumbling Blocks of Creditors

The net effect of having your assets protected is to eliminate or reduce your exposure. This is a valuable bargaining chip if you do decide to negotiate claims. In most cases, you'll find the plaintiff and his or her attorney most cooperative when the uphill battle becomes apparent, as they try to reach your assets with absolutely no assurances of success.

A creditor attempting to go after a limited partner is in a dilemma. The creditor will have to decide whether or not to expend additional time and money overcoming the following formidable obstacles:

- Obtain judgment against the debtor
- Prove that the creditor has an interest in the limited partnership
- Have the court issue a charging order
- Obtain appointment of a receiver
- Apply for foreclosure
- Attempt a forced sale (without the right of an accounting)
- Secure judicial dissolution of the limited partnership
- Upon dissolution, receive what is left after priority-paying claims

More often than not, the creditor ends up with a charging order against the interest of the limited partner that can generally be discharged or settled for an inconsequential sum.

The charging order entitles the creditor to income or assets only when they are distributed. Even if income is not distributed out of the partnership, the creditor is still taxed on it because the creditor is named on the K-1 (partnership tax return). Since the creditor cannot force the distribution of assets or income, the creditor may suffer negative cash flow for several years from paying taxes on his or her share of partnership income that hasn't been received.

Negotiating a Settlement

Once the creditors know the position they're in, they will probably want to settle their claims as soon as possible. Your goal is the opposite. If you decide to settle, use the following strategies:

- Start off with paying 10 percent of the amount due, and go up in increments of 5 percent, if you feel it's appropriate.
- Extend the payments out as far as possible.
- Don't offer any collateral or cosigners.
- If they want to charge interest, prime rate is okay.
- Have them erase any negative marks on your credit rating.

Never forget to let your creditors know that, if you go into bankruptcy, they may wait several years for a very small part of the proceeds without interest.

Protection from Creditors of a Family-Limited Partnership

The most significant advantage an FLP has over a revocable living trust is that assets are protected from creditor claims. This is not the case in a revocable living trust. Anyone who has a legal claim against you can effectively satisfy that claim by penetrating the revocable trust and removing its assets. In an FLP, this cannot be done because you control the vote. In addition to the asset protection, the FLP can be used as part of your estate plan to avoid probate and estate taxes in the same manner as a revocable living trust.

Estate Planning

The FLP is an excellent mechanism for estate planning. It will give you the asset protection you need to reduce liability exposure and stop lawsuits. The Center for Continuing Real Estate Studies has developed a comprehensive program to implement your own FLP (see page 197).

If your attorney reviews the agreement, please keep in mind that new ideas which adversely affect anyone's ability to generate income, tend to be discarded. The FLP is designed to curtail litigation. Select an expert who has the expertise to properly counsel you in this area.

Protecting Yourself from Existing Claims

For additional protection from existing creditors, transfer domestic FLP assets into a foreign asset protection trust (APT). You'll be allowed to maintain control of your assets in the United States and still shield them from existing lawsuits and creditors.

This is how it works. Foreign trust laws provide several advantages over domestic trust laws, even though you have the right to revoke or amend the trust, dispose of its assets, appoint or remove trustees, or to retain a beneficial interest. If a debtor with existing creditors is not rendered insolvent with the transfer of assets to the trust, the debtor is protected even if he or she subsequently becomes insolvent. If the creditor wishes to challenge the transfer, the creditor must do it in the appropriate foreign jurisdiction within a definite limited time period, typically two years, or the claim will lapse.

Because of the two-year statute of limitations it is advisable to domicile the APT in the Cook Islands (a self-governing territory under the protection of New Zealand) (see Figure 14.1).

In 1989, they amended their International Trusts Act (ITA) to provide additional protection for APTs. The Cook Islands offers flexible, commercially-oriented legislation; the ITA is at the same time soundly based on legal concepts hundreds of years in the making. The amendment addressed the issues of protecting trusts in the event of alleged fraudulent conveyance and matters relating to the establishment of a trust.

The value and effectiveness of this legislation has been confirmed by the fact that to date no action in a Cook Islands court has set aside an international trust or a transfer to an international trust, or resulted in any injunction being issued against an international trust or a settler or trustee of an international trust.

In addition, no action or judgment of a foreign court, in respect to bankruptcy or debt, has recognized or enforced against any international trust or persons and property associated with such trust.

In fact, the secure shielding of international trust under Cook Islands law has been widely acknowledged. Legal recognition of this protection has actually led to advantageous settlements with creditors.

Asset Protection Plan Using a Foreign Trust

STEP 1   Select a portion of your assets you want to isolate and protect from lawsuits and creditors. (See Figure 14.2.)

STEP 2   The partnership consists of yourself as the managing general partner and you and/or your family as the limited partners. As the

Advantages of Foreign Jurisdiction Trust
Cook Islands

The Cook Islands are one example of a foreign jurisdiction with more favorable asset-protection trust statutes. Highlights of the statutes are:

Cook Islands International Trust Act:

13A. *Bankruptcy:* International Trust ("IT") not to be void or voidable in the event of the settlor's bankruptcy, notwithstanding any provisions of a settlor's domicile and notwithstanding that an IT is voluntary.

13B. *Fraud:* Where creditor proves an IT was settled with principal intent to defraud that creditor and that such settlement rendered the settlor insolvent or without property then such settlement is not void or voidable, but the IT is liable to satisfy claims out of property which but for settlement would have been available. In determining whether settlement rendered settlor insolvent, regard should be given to the fair market value of the property (not the subject of the trust) immediately after settlement took place.

  3. IT not fraudulent as against a creditor where:

    (a) settlement or disposition takes place after expiration of two years from the time the creditor cause of action accrued and

    (b) then creditor fails to bring an action before the expiration of one year from the date the assets are placed into the trust.

  4. IT not fraudulent as against a creditor where the settlement took place before the cause of action accrued or arose.

  5. Settlor does not have intent to defraud creditor imputed solely by reason that he or she:

    (a) settles an IT within two years from the date of cause of action accruing or

    (b) the settlor retained, possess or acquires power or benefits if specified at (a)–(f) of 13 C (see infra.).

  7. The onus of proof of a settlor's intent to defraud creditor under this section lies with the creditor.

13C. *Retention of Control:* An IT is not invalid by reason of the settlor(s) retaining possessing or acquiring:

    (a) power of revocation of trust;

    (b) power of disposition of property;

    (c) power to amend trust;

    (d) any benefit from time of disposition;

    (e) power to remove or appoint a trustee or protector;

    (f) power to direct a trustee or protector;

    (g) a beneficial interest.

13D. *Enforcement of Foreign Judgments:* This section prohibits the enforcement of a foreign judgment to respect to an IT and forces a litigant to commence action de novo in a Cook Island Court. This section provides that notwithstanding the provisions of any rule of law or equity, no proceedings for the enforcement of recognition of a foreign judgment against an IT, a settlor, a trustee, a protector, a beneficiary or any person appointed by an instrument in connection with an IT or against the property of an IT shall be entertained by any court in the Cook Islands if that judgment is based upon any law inconsistent with the provisions of the IT or if that judgment related to a matter governed by the law of the Cook Islands.

13G. *Governing Law:* This section provides that regard shall be given to the terms of the settlement. A term expressly selecting the law of the Cook Islands is conclusive.

Figure 14.1 Advantages of foreign jurisdiction trust—Cook Islands.

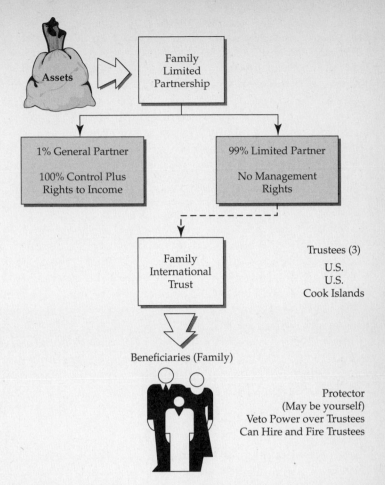

Figure 14.2 Four-step asset protection plan using a foreign trust.

managing general partner, you own 1 percent, and you and/or your family, as limited partners, own 99 percent of the partnership. You, as managing general partner have 100 percent management control of the partnership, including the right to buy and sell assets and the power to determine whether or not the partnership distributes income to the limited partners. The limited partners have no say in the day-to-day management of the assets.

STEP 3 A gift of the 99 percent limited partnership interest is made to a family international trust. Generally, the trust's only asset will be the interest in the family limited partnership. The trust will have no say in the management of the partnership. There are no gift tax consequences incurred by this transfer.

English law defines the *protector* as one who acts on behalf of the beneficiaries. The protector, who can be yourself, has veto power over the trustee's activities regarding investments and distribution, and the protector has the authority to replace any or all of the trustees at any time and the authority to appoint the replacement trustees.

The *family international trust* is a grantor trust with: two U.S. trustees (personal friends, lawyer, CPA, not yourself or beneficiaries) and one foreign trustee, such as a trust company located on Cook Islands.

Beneficiaries are spouse, children, relatives, or others including charities.

STEP 4   If a lawsuit or serious creditor problem occurs, depending on the timing and seriousness of the claim, we recommend the dissolution of the partnership to allow the trustee to control the assets. After the lawsuit or creditor problem is settled or otherwise reconciled, the client can reestablish rights of direct control over the assets by merely reestablishing the family limited partnership.

If you should wish to remove assets from the plan, there are several methods of doing so. Among the simplest is to merely appoint assets to your spouse. There are other methods available to remove assets from the plan if you are single.

SUMMARY

In any asset protection plan, the primary goal is to create an environment where assets can be utilized to their fullest extent while at the same time receiving the maximum protection from frivolous and immoral lawsuits. By legally removing assets from the reach of creditors, you will be able to settle or discharge existing or potential liabilities on terms advantageous to you.

The family limited partnership gives you the vehicle to legally transfer assets. Other entitles, such as corporations and trusts are costly and time consuming. A wrong move can expose your estate to the whims of creditors. Professional fees could add up to more than the value of the assets. Putting aside all these headaches, these other entities still don't come close to offering the protection a family limited partnership does.

Glossary

acceleration clause   A stipulation in a mortgage that provides for the entire principal and interest to become immediately due and payable if ownership is transferred or some other stipulated event takes place.

acceptance   The seller agrees to enter into a contract and to be bound by its terms. The buyer must receive notice of acceptance before it becomes legal.

accrued depriciation   Depreciation that has been incurred since the acquisition of an asset. The difference between the cost of replacement new as of the date of the appraisal and the present appraised value of the property.

accrued interest   Interest that is earned but not yet received.

acknowledgment   A declaration that is part of a document made before an authorized person (usually a Notary Public).

active income   Income earned by one's labor compensated for in salary, wages, commissions, fees, or bonuses. Also called earned income.

add-on interest   The amount of interest calculated on the original principal that is added on.

adjustable rate mortgage (ARM)   A mortgage note that allows a lender to adjust the interest rate at periodic intervals. The rate change is most commonly limited to the movement of a regular approved index.

after-tax cash flow   Before-tax cash flows less income taxes paid as a result of owning the property in question or plus income taxes saved (tax shelter) as a result of owning it.

agent   One who is legally authorized to act on behalf of another person.

agreement for sale   A written instrument in which the parties agree to sell under certain terms and conditions.

alienation clause   A condition in the note that requires payment of the entire loan balance upon sale or other transfer of interest in property.

all-inclusive deed of trust (AITD)   Purchase money trust deed that is subordinate to but wraps the original indebtedness or trust deeds on the property.

American Land Title Association (ALTA)   A national association of title insurance companies, and related real estate professionals.

amortization   Periodic reduction of the principal debt. The systematic and continuous payment of an obligation through installments until such time as the debt has been paid off in full.

amortized loan   Payment of both the interest and principal by series of level payments that are equal or nearly equal, without any special *balloon payment* prior to maturity.

appraisal   A report from a qualified professional as to the value of an asset using the cost, income, and market approach.

appraised value   A determination of the value of an asset by an appraiser based upon a study of pertinent data.

appraiser   One qualified by education, training, and experience to estimate the value of real and personal property.

arbitration   The determination of a dispute by a qualified disinterested third party usually a judge.

arbitration clause   Clause in a contract that provides a procedure for settling disputes between parties to be decided by an independent arbitrator rather than by a court of law.

asking price   The price the seller is offering his property to the public.

assessment   The value placed on property by the government for taxation purposes. It could also mean a levy against property for a special purpose, such as a school assessment.

assignee   The entity to whom an agreement or contract is assigned.

assignment   The transfer of rights in a contract to another.

assumption fee The fee paid to a lender to assume a mortgage.

assumption of mortgage The buyer assumes the existing mortgage and primary liability for the payments.

at-risk rule IRS rule that limits the amount of losses that may be deducted based on your actual liability.

authorization to sell A contract in which a principal employs an agent to perform certain acts.

Usually it authorizes the agent to secure a buyer that is "ready, willing, and able" to purchase the property at the price and terms that it is offered for sale rather than to sell the property.

backup offer An offer made to purchase or lease a property that is submitted to the owner with the understanding that the owner already accepted an offer on the property. The seller may accept the backup offer with the *condition precedent* that the first sales transaction fails to be completed. (See *tender.*)

balloon mortgage A mortgage that has a lump-sum payment at the maturity date.

balloon payment A lump-sum payment usually paying off the debt.

bill of sale A written document used to transfer title to personal property.

binder, insurance A written evidence of liability or title coverage that's for a limited time.

boot Money received and/or a reduction of loan liability or value received in an *IRC § 1031 Exchange.*

capital gain The profit realized from the disposition of an asset to be reported to the IRS.

capitalization A computation that gives the present value of an asset based on the desired rate of return of a series of anticipated future installments of income.

cash basis taxpayer Reporting to the IRS on income when received and deductions and expenses when paid.

cash flow Money received from your investment(s) after paying all expenses and loans.

certificate of title A proclamation furnished by title company that states the title to property is legally vested in the present owner.

chattel Personal property.

closing costs   Fees and costs incurred in the transfer of or refinancing property, such as escrow fees, title insurance premiums, conveyance taxes, loan prepayment penalties, termite inspection charges, attorney's fees, and so on.

cloud on title   An unsatisfactory recorded impediment on the property shown by a title search that may affect the transfer of title.

co-insurance   A sharing of insurance risk between insurer and insured.

collateral   Assets pledged as security. Example, as the real estate securing a mortgage.

commission   An agent's compensation (fee) for acting on behalf of his principal.

contract of sale   Agreement between the buyer and seller in which the buyer agrees to buy under certain terms and conditions and seller agrees to sell. To be enforceable, it must be in writing and properly executed by both parties.

cost approach   A valuation method used to determine the replacement cost of an asset.

debt coverage ratio   The ratio of effective annual net income to annual debt service.

declining balance method   A method of depreciation whereby an asset is written off more rapidly in the early years.

deed   A written instrument to convey ownership of real property.

deed of trust   A security instrument used to convey title to a trustee as collateral for the payment of a debt. The trustee has the power to sell the property in the event of default and to reconvey title when debt is paid in full.

deposit receipt   An acknowledgement that earnest money has been received to purchase real property.

depreciation   Generally, it means a loss of value in real property due to age, physical deterioration, or functional or economic obsolescence.

discount   The value of a note for less than its face amount.

double escrow   A situation where buyer sells the property while it is still in escrow.

downpayment   The difference between the sale price of real estate and the mortgage amount(s).

due diligence   Basically, it means that you find out all about the property before you purchase it, which includes physical inspection and inspections of books and records.

earnest money   Money paid as evidence of good faith or actual intent to complete a transaction, usually forfeited by willful failure to complete the transaction.

economic life   The estimated period of time during which a property can be utilized profitably.

eminent domain   The right of a government to take private property for public use.

encroachment   Wrongful extension of an improvement that intrudes illegally on another's property.

equity participation   A loan in which the lender not only receives payment on the loan but also acquires an interest in the property.

escrow   A third party, acting as the agent for the buyer and the seller carries out instructions for both.

escrow instructions   In real estate it is a contract between both buyer and seller that instructs the escrow agent.

estoppel   A legal term in which a person is barred from denying a fact because of his previous acts because the denial would be inconsistent his representation.

exclusive right to sell listing   Agreement employing a real estate broker to act as agent for the seller. It doesn't matter who sells the property. The listing broker is entitled to a commission if the property is sold during the duration of the listing period.

fair market value   The price at which the seller is willing to sell and the buyer us willing to buy, each of whom has a reasonable knowledge of all pertinent facts and neither being under any compulsion to buy or sell.

fee simple   The greatest possible interest a person can have in real estate.

first right of refusal   A right given by the seller to a potential buyer to purchase property before he offers it to other buyers.

foreclosure   A legal procedure taken by a lender to take back the property.

gift deed   Deed for which consideration is love and affection.

grantee   A person to whom a grant is made. The purchaser.

grantor   The person conveying an interest in real property. The seller.

gross income   Total income from a property before any expenses are deducted.

gross rent multiplier   An index used to compare rental properties. It is the relationship between the gross rental income and the sales price.

highest and best use   The use that will produce the highest property value.

holdback   That portion of a loan that will be held back until some additional requirement, such as rental or completion, is attained.

income approach to value   An appraisal technique used determine real property value by capitalizing net income.

installment sale   The sale in which the payments for the property are made over a period of time.

insurable title   A condition whereby the title insurance company is willing to issue a policy of insurance.

interest   The cost for using money.

internal rate of return (IRR)   Method of calculating the present value of the return on an investment based on the discounted rate of future cash flows.

involuntary lien   A lien put on real estate without the consent of an owner. Examples include taxes, special assessments, federal income tax liens, judgment liens, mechanics liens, and materials liens.

joint and several note   A note signed by two or more persons, each of whom is liable for the full amount of the debt.

joint tenancy   An equal undivided ownership of property by two or more persons, the survivors to take the interest upon the death of any one of them.

judgment proof   An entity that has no assets that can be sought to satisfy a court judgment.

late charge   A penalty charge imposed on the borrower for failure to pay a regular installment when due.

lease option   A lease that provides that the tenant has the right to purchase the property under certain conditions.

letter of credit   A letter authorizing a financial institution to honor the issues credit.

leverage   Using borrowed money to purchase real estate.

like kind property Property qualifying for an *IRC § 1031 Exchange*. Like kind property is any real property exchange for real property.

limited partnership An entity that has one or more general partners who are fully liable and one or more limited partners who are liable only for the amount of their investment.

lis pendens A notice recorded in the official records to indicate there is a pending suit affecting the real estate.

loan-to-value The relationship between the mortgage and the appraised value of the security.

market data approach to value The value of real estate is based on actual prices paid in market transactions.

market value Highest price at which a property will bring in a competitive and open market, with knowledgeable buyers and sellers.

mechanics lien A recorded judgement against the property put on by building contractors, laborers, and suppliers who have not been paid.

member appraisal institute (MAI) The highest professional designation awarded by the American Institute of Real Estate Appraisers.

mortgage broker An individual who brings the borrower and lender together.

mortgagee An entity to whom property is conveyed as security for a loan.

multiple listing An exclusive agreement to sell, taken by a member of an organization of real estate brokers.

negative cash flow Paying more cash expenditures of an income producing property than cash receipts.

net income The difference between effective gross income and the expenses, excluding debt service and depreciation.

net rentable area The rentable square footage of a building, excluding halls, lobbies, stairways, elevator shafts, maintenance areas, and so on.

non-recourse note A debt instrument that restricts the lender to rely solely on the property for repayment.

obsolescence The loss of value of a property because of going out of style or becoming less suitable for use, or by other economic influences.

operating expenses Usually refers to all expenses of running a property, except depreciation and mortgage payments.

option   A right to purchase, sell, or use property at a stated price during a stated period of time.

passive activity income   A tax term that refers to the amount of time spent in operating a trade or business. If a taxpayer does not materially participate, the income is considered passive.

point   A loan fee of one percent of the principal amount of the loan charged by the lender.

possession   The act of constructively occupying a property that gives notice to others that the party in possession may have certain rights to that property.

potential gross income   The highest amount of revenue a property would produce if fully rented at market rates.

preliminary title report   A title search by a title company prior to issuance of a title binder or commitment to insure.

prepayment fee   An amount paid to the lender for the privilege of prepaying the loan.

principal   One of the parties to a transaction of one who hires an agent.

proforma statement   A projection of performance of real estate within a period of time based on estimates and assumptions.

promissory note   A promise to pay a specified sum at a specific date.

property management   The act of operating property on a day-to-day basis.

quit claim deed   A transfer of rights to property that contains no representation or warranty as to the quality of the title being conveyed.

real estate owned (REO)   Ownership of real property of lending institutions acquired for investments or as a result of foreclosure.

real property   Usually, land and appurtenances (that which by law is immovable).

Realtor®   Registered trademark of the National Association of Realtors. A broker who is an active member in a local real estate board affiliated with the National Association of Realtors.

recognized gain   The gain made in a property exchange that is subject to taxation.

refinancing   The repayment of a loan using the proceeds of a new loan with same property as security.

rental concession   A marketing strategy to give up part of the advertised rent in an effort to attract tenants.

replacement cost   An evaluation of real property based on cost of construction using modern materials and according to current standards, design, and layout.

reproduction cost   Replacements using the exact replica, having the same quality of workmanship, design, and layout.

rescission   The cancellation of a contract by the operation of law.

restrictive covenant   A provision in the deed limiting use of the property.

right of survivorship   A joint tenant has the right to acquire the interest of deceased joint tenant(s).

secondary mortgage market   A market place where existing mortgages are bought and sold.

short-rate   A method of calculating a lower premium on an insurance policy for a short period of time.

standby commitment   An agreement from the lender to loan with specified terms for a specified amount of time.

subject to mortgage   Purchasing property subject to the existing mortgage. The seller still is held for any deficiency.

subordination   Allowing your note to become inferior to the interest of others. Subordination also applies to leases, real estate rights, and other debt instruments.

supply and demand   The basis of determining valuation of a property. The net effect of either too many inventories or to many people wanting the product.

tax lien   A recorded demand against property for the amount of unpaid taxes.

tax shelter   Refers to advantages of taking certain deduction to reduce tax liability.

tenancy by entirety   The joint ownership of property that is viewed as one person under common law that provides for the rights of survivorship.

tenants-in-common   A type of ownership created when real or personal property is granted to two or more persons without the right of survivorship.

title   The evidence of ownership in property in whom the legal estate is vested and the history of ownership and transfers.

title insurance policy   An insurance policy usually issued by a title insurance company in which they agree to pay certain claims made against legal ownership.

trust deed   Legal document by which real property is used as a guarantee for the repayment of a loan. The trustee, not the borrower, is granted title to the property and has the power of sale, which the trustee can exercise upon default by the trustor (borrower).

usury   Charging a greater rate of interest than is permitted by state law.

vacancy and rent loss   Unrented rent-ready rental units. Rent loss refers to units that can't be rented because they are not physically ready to rent or because of the tenant's inability to pay.

vacancy factor   The percentage of unrented income over the gross possible rental income.

warranty deed   An instrument in which the grantor or seller warrants or guarantees that good title is being conveyed.

will   A person's written declaration expressing how assets are to be distributed upon their death.

without recourse   A loan that protects the endorser from liability in which the lender can only look to the property for repayment.

wrap-around   See *all-inclusive deed of trust.*

Apartment Periodicals

Apartment Age Magazine
621 S. Westmoreland Ave.
Los Angeles, CA 90005-3981

Apartment Finance Today
220 Sansome, Floor 11
San Francisco, CA 94104

Apartment Management
  Magazine
15502 Graham St.
Huntington Beach, CA 92649

Apartment News
12822 Garden Grove Blvd., Ste. D
Garden Grove, CA 92843-2010

Apartment Owner
15025 Oxnard St.
Van Nuys, CA 91411

Apartment Report
P.O. Box 1150
Novato, CA 94948

Commercial Investment
  Real Estate Expense Analysis:
  Conventional Apartments/
  Expense Analysis: Federally
  Assisted Apartments/Journal
  of Property Management
430 N. Michigan Ave., Ste. 800
Chicago, IL 60611-4092

Journal of Real Estate Finance and
  Economics
101 Philip Dr., Assinippi Pk
Norwell, MA 02061-1615

Multi-Unit Report
5253 Yonge St., Ste., 1000
Toronto, ON M2N 6P4 Canada

National Real Estate Investor
  National Real Estate Investor
  Source Book
4200 S. Shepherd Dr. #200
Houston, TX 77098

217

*National Register of Commercial
Real Estate*
1055 Washington Blvd.
Stamford, CT 06901-2216

*Professional Apartment
Management*
149 5th Ave., 16th Fl.
New York, NY 10010-6801

*Property Tax Service/
Real Estate Review*
610 Opperman Dr.
Eagan, MN 55123

Real Estate Economics
350 Main St.
Malden, MA 02148

Real Estate Finance & Investment
488 Madison Ave. 12th Fl.
New York, NY 10022

Real Estate Finance Today
1919 Pennsylvania Ave. NW
Washington, DC 20006

Real Estate Forum
111 8th Ave., Ste. 1511
New York, NY 10011-5215

Real Estate News
3550 W. Peterson Ave., #100
Chicago, IL 60659-3320

Real Estate Tax Digest
201 Mission St., 26th Fl.
San Francisco, CA 94105

Units
201 N. Union St., Ste. 200
Alexandria, VA 22314-5603

Urban Land
1025 Thomas Jefferson St. NW,
Ste. 500 West
Washington DC 20007-5201

Index

Seller's remorse, handling, 141
Seller's warrant, 89
Selling price, determining, 157–159
Settlement, negotiating, 202
Set-up sheet, 70–77
  conservative, 157–158
  financial analysis, 72–75
  opening statements, 70, 72
  other income, 76–77
  reading, 70
  rental income, 75–76
Sleep growth, 98
Sole investing, step to locating
  apartment buildings, 35–36
"Solvency" test, 193
Statements:
  financial, 81, 93, 160
  operating, 146–147
Strategies, financing, 131–132
  all-inclusive trust deed, 131–132
  lease option, 132
  price, 135–136
  "subject to" loan, 131
  tax, 172
Strong buyers market, 93
"Subject to" loan, 131, 133
Supply and demand, 14

Taxable income, ways to lower,
  163–164
  group income and expenses,
    164–165
  spreading income over time, 164
  spreading income over various
    entities, 164
Tax advisors, 132, 134, 136, 164, 165,
  175
Tax-deferred plans, 2
Taxes:
  on capital gains, 171
  defer paying, 170–171
  reducing, 10
Tax-free bonds, 6
Tax impact, tenants-in-common, 180
Tax planning, goal, 163
Tax reform loophole, 167–168
Tax strategies for landlord/leasee, 172
Tax write-off, qualifying for, 150–152
Team approach, advantages of, 39
Tenants:
  profiles, 123
  relations, 145

Tenants-in-common (TIC), 167
  agreement, 189
  ownership:
    advantages of, 178–179
    creating nonsecurity transaction,
      181, 184–186
    features, 177–178
    marketing nonsecurity, 186–187
    pitfall of security transactions,
      180–181
    profits, 189
    tax impact of, 180
Title companies, 49
Title insurance, 90, 140
Title report, 74, 85, 89, 158
Track record, 81
Transfer title, 89
Trust deed, 137

Uniform Fraudulent Conveyance Act
  (UFCA), 193, 194–197
Uniform Fraudulent Transfers Act
  (UFTA), 193
Uniform Limited Partnership Act, 198
Unit mix, 26
"Up property," 173, 175

Vacancy:
  in apartments, 24
  delinquencies, 147
  factors, 64
  rate movements, 25
Valuation, assessed, 74
Value:
  market, 52, 76, 91, 93, 99
  present, 133
  provisions and conditions, 156–157
Variable interest rate, 157

Walk through, 161
Warranties, 89
Weak buyers market, 93
Weak market, 55, 56
Wealth building, 1, 7
Wealthy, becoming, 4–6
Williamson test, 185–186
Wrap-around loan, 131
Write-off, 10, 131, 150–152, 165, 167, 179
Written cost estimates, 43
Written plan, 143

Yield, 23, 132

For More Information on
The Center for Real Estate Studies

Contact

The Center for Real Estate Studies
P.O. Box 3315
Palos Verdes, California 90274
(800) 955-3135